Praise for Marshall Goldsmith:

'The number seven greatest business thinker in the world'
Harvard Business Review

'One of the most credible thought leaders in the new era of business' *The Economist*

'An influential practitioner in the history of leadership development' *Businessweek*

'A top executive educator' *Wall Street Journal*

'One of the five most-respected executive coaches in the world'
Forbes

'A great communicator' *O (Oprah Magazine)*

MARSHALL GOLDSMITH is corporate America's preeminent executive coach. He is one of a select few consultants who have been asked to work with more than eighty CEOs in the world's top corporations. He has helped implement leadership development processes that have impacted more than one million people. His PhD is from UCLA and he is on the faculty of the executive education programs at Dartmouth College's Tuck School of Business. The American Management Association recently named Marshall one of fifty great thinkers and business leaders who have impacted the field of management, and *Businessweek* listed him as one of the most influential practitioners in the history of leadership development. In 2006, Alliant International University renamed their schools of business and organisational psychology The Marshall Goldsmith School of Management.

MARK REITER has collaborated on thirteen previous books. He is also a literary agent in Bronxville, New York.

'I love Marshall Goldsmith for lots of reasons: his generous soul, his capacity to bring out the best in people, his zen-like ability to create an evocative community – the mark of a great teacher, and his way of getting people, just about everybody, to laugh their way into deep and penetrating insights. He is the very model of a professional – reliable, trustworthy, always "on" – and always has your heart at heart.'

Warren Bennis, Distinguished Professor of Business, University of Southern California, and bestselling author

'We were a very successful team who took our performance to the next level. With Marshall's help we identified our two areas and went to work. We used everyone's help and support, exceeded our improvement expectations, and had fun! A team's dedication to continuous improvement combined with Marshall's proven improvement process ROCKS!'

Alan Mulally, CEO, Ford Motor Company, former President and CEO, Boeing Commercial Airlines

'Helping high achievers recognise their sharper edges, become self-aware, and increase their personal effectiveness is at the heart of leadership development. Many years of patient practice have made him the best "diamond cutter" in the business – he can take a rough diamond and polish it rapidly to reveal its brilliance. He is one of a kind.'

C. K. Prahalad, bestselling author and Paul and Ruth McCracken Distinguished University Professor of Corporate Strategy and International Business, University of Michigan

'Marshall Goldsmith has helped me become a more effective leader, as judged by the people who are most important at Getty Images – our employees. Marshall has helped me and my executive team members to be much better positive role models for living our Leadership Principles.'

Jonathan Klein, CEO, Getty Images

'Marshall is a great coach and teacher. He has done a lot to help both me and our high-potential leaders. His approach is practical, useful, helpful, and fun!'

J. P. Garnier, CEO, GlaxoSmithKline

'Marshall's valuable insights on leadership development and the related responsibilities of coaching and mentoring are critical to our general officers and spouses. These are turbulent times, and the tools and techniques that Marshall shared with them are therefore vitally important as they return to their various commands and leadership responsibilities.'

General Eric K. Shinseki, former Chief of Staff, U. S. Army

'Perhaps the greatest teacher of leadership on the planet. I have personally watched him help thousands of executives in three companies improve their leadership in measurable ways. As a result, their performance improved, their relationships improved, and they lived happier lives.'

Jim Moore, served as the Chief Learning Officer of BellSouth, Nortel, and Sun Microsystems

'There is simply no better coach for your most important leaders than Marshall Goldsmith. He excels on the only metric that matters – he achieves positive, measurable change.'

Marc Effron, Chief Learning Officer, Avon, and co-author of *Leading the Way* and *Human Resources in the 20th Century*

'Marshall helped GE human resources professionals customise his coaching process for use with our high-potential leaders. Our internal HR coaches have achieved outstanding results with hundreds of our leaders. Marshall's model has been a real win for us!'

Linda Sharkey, vice president, Organizational Development and Staffing, GE Capital Solutions

'Marshall Goldsmith easily ranks among the very best teachers and coaches of executives anywhere – bar none. His years of experience and his proven methods have helped hundreds of leaders achieve positive, lasting behavioural change.'

John Alexander, president, Center for Creative Leadership

'Marshall helped us determine that the role of a leader is about inspiring others. He showed us how to inspire and build lasting relationships. He challenged our team and they loved working with him.'

Cass Wheeler, CEO, American Heart Association

'Marshall has that rare combination that makes a great teacher – thought leadership, classroom management, and presence. He is a tremendous asset to Tuck School at Dartmouth.'

Vijay Govindarajan, Professor and Director, Center for Global Leadership, Tuck School of Dartmouth

'With great energy and excellent content, Marshall engaged, excited, and even enthralled his audience of several hundred participants at the Wharton Leadership Conference. Marshall was a star!'

Dr Michael Useem, William and Jacalyn Egan Professor of Management and Director of the Center for Leadership and Change Management, Wharton Business School, University of Pennsylvania

'I consider Marshall to be the number one thought leader and coach in the field of leadership and executive development to-day. I sincerely appreciate his honest, straightforward, positive, and purposeful approach to executive coaching – it is second to none.'

Louis Carter, President and CEO, Best Practice Institute, a global leader in creating and sustaining communities of practice

'As the CEO of the Girl Scouts, I was working to help a great organization be "the best that we could be." The first person Marshall volunteered to work with was me – this sent an important message. I was exuberant about the experience, I improved, and we moved this process across the organisation. Twenty-four years later, I am chairman of the Leader to the Leader Institute – and we are still working together to serve leaders.'

Frances Hesselbein, winner of the Presidential Medal of Freedom

'Marshall is a dynamo. He helps highly successful people get better and better and better. His advice helps me enormously at work, but it makes an even bigger impact at home. My wife and kids stand up and applaud Marshall for helping me become a better husband and dad. What could be better than that?'

Mark Tercek, Managing Director, Goldman Sachs & Co.

'At McKesson, we are on a mission – together with our customers – to fundamentally change the cost and quality of how health care is delivered. To fully realise the potential that lies in this transformation, our leaders must be able to demonstrate values-based leadership practices to maximize employee engagement each and every day. Marshall's teachings remind us of how personal growth and change are a never-ending journey.'

John Hammergren, CEO McKesson

'Marshall is the coach's coach. No one is more of a listener, who learns from us (his students), from what we say or do not say. Taking from what he has heard, he moulds for all of us a program to make us and our people better for having been in his presence.'

Alan Hassenfeld, Chairman, Hasbro

'Marshall Goldsmith has a simple, yet powerful approach for helping leaders excel. Its power lies not only in its simplicity, but in his unique ability to deliver practical insights that leaders can act upon. I seldom leave a session with Marshall without feeling a bit wiser than before.'

Jon Katzenbach, founder, Katzenbach Partners, former Director, McKinsey and Company, and author of many books, including *The Wisdom of Teams*

'Marshall is the rock star of coaching. His adoration is well deserved. He cares about the people he work with. He focuses on their issues. He connects great people with other great people so that they can continue to learn. He is honest, helpful, bold, and sensitive. He focuses on what can be, not what has been, and creates a future unbound by the past.'

David Ulrich, leading HR Consultant and author of many books, including *Why the Bottom Line Isn't*

'In his charming, rascal-like manner, Marshall is able to address uncomfortable issues in a non-threatening way. As a result, not only does the leader get better – the whole team gets better!'

George Borst, CEO, Toyota Financial Services

'Marshall has helped me personally to improve as a leader and has provided the tools and dynamics to turn a well-functioning management team into a high-performance team where all the members have improved individually and considerably added to team performance.'

David Pyott, CEO, Allergan

'Marshall Goldsmith has extraordinary life skills, the ability to connect deeply with others while remaining objective, and a passion for sharing everything he knows. He focuses – and helps others to focus – on what matters most in life.'

Sally Helgesen, global expert on developing women leaders and author of *The Female Advantage* and *The Web of Inclusion*

What Got You Here Won't Get You There

How Successful People Become
EVEN MORE SUCCESSFUL!

Marshall Goldsmith

with Mark Reiter

PROFILE BOOKS

This edition published in 2013

First published in Great Britain in 2008 by
PROFILE BOOKS LTD
3A Exmouth House
Pine Street
London EC1R 0JH
www.profilebooks.com

First published in the United States of America in 2007
by Hyperion

53

Printed and bound in India by
Manipal Technologies Limited, Manipal

MIX
Paper from
responsible sources
FSC
www.fsc.org   FSC® C043100

A CIP catalogue record for this book is available from
the British Library.

ISBN 978 1 78125 156 0
eISBN 978 1 84765 131 0

To all successful leaders
who want to
"take it to the next level"
and get even better

"Happy are they that can hear their detractions and put them to mending."

—WILLIAM SHAKESPEARE,
Much Ado About Nothing

Contents

Acknowledgments

This book is a collaborative effort that has been built upon the contributions of many great people:

My mentors and teachers: Peter Drucker and Richard Beckhard, who will never cease being my heroes; Paul Hersey, who gave me the opportunity to be an executive educator; Frances Hesselbein, my permanent role model; Bob Tannenbaum, John Ying, and Fred Case, who were great teachers and made sure that I graduated.

My collaborator and agent: Mark Reiter, who has helped me "find my voice" and communicate in print the way that I communicate in person.

My publisher: Will Schwalbe, Ellen Archer, Bob Miller, Zareen Jaffery, and all of the folks at Hyperion who have supported our book.

My family: Lyda, Kelly, and Bryan, whom I love and who love me (in spite of my annoying habits); they keep everything in perspective and make it all fun.

Alliant International University: President Geoff Cox and his staff, who have had the faith required to name a college after me, the Marshall Goldsmith School of Management; and their faculty and students; working with them has been a joy.

My professional partners over the past thirty years: from

Keilty, Goldsmith and Company, to A4SL, and now Marshall Goldsmith Partners, who have helped me spread the word; Linkage, IMS, the Conference Board, the AMA, HR.com, ChartHouse, Talent Management, and Targeted Learning, who have helped me to reach over a million leaders; Sarah McArthur, John Wheaton, and Andrew Thorn, who provided specific contributions to this book (they know where, what, and why).

My writing friends: John Byrne at *BusinessWeek*, who has always encouraged me to express myself; Larissa MacFarquhar at *The New Yorker*, who wrote a wonderful profile about my work; Gardiner Morse at the *Harvard Business Review*, Bob Lenzner at *Forbes*, Ken Shelton at *Leadership Excellence*, and, closest to home, Michael Kinsman at the *San Diego Union Tribune*. All have written stories about me that were both fun and fair. Mark Vamos at *Fast Company* as well as Wiley, Amacom, FT, and Davies Black, who have published my work in the past and who have given me permission to build upon that work in this book.

And, most importantly, my clients, who are already unbelievably successful, yet strive to get even better. They have taught me far more than I have ever taught them.

Despite the help of all of the people named above, I am sure these pages contain at least a few errant statements. For these I ask your forgiveness and take full responsibility. To paraphrase another hero of mine, Buddha: *Please just use what works for you and let go of the rest.*

What Got You Here
Won't Get You There

The Trouble with Success

In which we learn how our previous success often prevents us from achieving more success

CHAPTER 1

You Are Here

YOU KNOW THOSE MAPS in shopping malls that say, "You Are Here"? They exist to orient you in unfamiliar territory, to tell you where you are, where you want to go, and how to get there.

A few people never need these maps. They're blessed with an internal compass that orients them automatically. They always make the correct turn and end up where they intended via the most economical route.

Some people actually go through life with this unerring sense of direction. It guides them not only in shopping malls but in their school years, careers, marriages, and friendships. When we meet people like this, we say they're grounded. They know who they are and where they're going. We feel secure around them. We feel that any surprises will only be pleasant surprises. They are our role models and heroes.

We all know people like this. For some of us, it's our moms or dads—people who served as moral anchors in our stormy childhoods. For others it's a spouse (the proverbial "better half"). For others (like me) it's a college professor who was the first person to puncture our pretensions (more on that later). It could be a mentor at work, a coach in high school, a hero from the history books such as Lincoln or Churchill, a religious leader such as Buddha, Mohammed, or Jesus. It could even be a celebrity. (I know one man who solves every dilemma by asking himself, "What would Paul Newman do?")

What all of these role models have in common is an exquisite sense of who they are, which translates into perfect pitch about how they come across to others.

A few people never seem to need any help in getting to where they want to go. They have a built-in GPS mechanism.

These people do not need my help.

The people I meet during the course of my working day as an executive coach are great people who may have lost their internal "You Are Here" map. For example:

Case 1. Carlos is the CEO of a successful food company. He is brilliant, hard-working, and an expert in his field. He started out on the factory floor and rose through sales and marketing to the top spot. There is nothing in his business that he hasn't seen firsthand. Like many creative people, he is also hyperactive, with the metabolism and attention span of a hummingbird. He loves to buzz around his company's facilities, dropping in on employees to see what they're working on and shoot the breeze. Carlos loves people and he loves to talk. All in all, Carlos presents a very charming package, except when his mouth runs ahead of his brain.

One month ago his design team presented him with their ideas for the packaging of a new line of snacks. Carlos was delighted with the designs. He only had one suggestion.

"What do you think about changing the color to baby blue?" he said. "Blue says expensive and upmarket."

Today the designers are back with the finished packaging. Carlos is pleased with the results. But he muses aloud, "I think it might be better in red."

The design team in unison roll their eyes. They are confused. A month ago their CEO said he preferred blue. They've busted their humps to deliver a finished product to his liking, and now he's changed his mind. They leave the meeting dispirited and less than enthralled with Carlos.

Carlos is a very confident CEO. But he has a bad habit of verbalizing any and every internal monologue in his head. And he doesn't fully appreciate that this habit becomes a make-or-break issue as people ascend the chain of command. A lowly clerk expressing an opinion doesn't get people's notice at a company. But when the CEO expresses that opinion, everyone jumps to attention. The higher up you go, the more your suggestions become orders.

Carlos thinks he's merely tossing an idea against the wall to see if it sticks. His employees think he's giving them a direct command.

Carlos thinks he's running a democracy, with everyone allowed to voice their opinion. His employees think it's a monarchy, with Carlos as king.

Carlos thinks he's giving people the benefit of his years of experience. His employees see it as micromanaging and excessive meddling.

Carlos has no idea how he's coming across to his employees.

He is guilty of Habit #2: Adding too much value.

Case 2. Sharon is the editor of a major magazine. She is highly motivated, energetic, articulate, and loaded with charisma. For someone who has spent much of her adult life working with words and pictures, she has developed impressive people skills. She can coax delinquent writers into meeting their deadlines. She can inspire her staff to stay at their desks late into the night when she decides to tear up the next issue at the last minute. She believes she can persuade anyone if she really puts her mind to it. Her publisher often invites her on sales calls to advertisers because of her charm and her ability to sell the magazine.

Sharon is particularly proud of her ability to spot and nurture young editorial talent. The proof is in the bright energetic editorial team she has assembled. Editors at competitive magazines call them the Sharonistas, because of their almost militant allegiance to Sharon. They've been working with her for years. Their loyalty is unwavering. And Sharon returns their affection with equally fierce loyalty. That loyalty may seem excessive, especially if you work for Sharon but don't quite qualify as a Sharonista.

In today's editorial meeting, where future assignments are meted out to the staff, Sharon offered up an observation that might make a good cover story. One of the Sharonistas immediately seconded the idea, saying it was "brilliant." Sharon assigned the story to her. And so the meeting proceeded, with Sharon handing out plum assignments to her staff favorites—all of whom returned the favor by fawning over Sharon and agreeing with everything she said.

If you happened to be one of Sharon's favored staffers, the lovefest at the editorial meeting would be the highlight of your month. On the other hand, if you were not one of Sharon's favored staffers or happened to disagree with her, the sycophancy level in the room would have been transparent and sickening. After a few months of this treatment, you would have been emailing your résumé to other magazines.

None of this was apparent to Sharon, who was otherwise extremely shrewd about people and their motives. She believed she was being an effective leader. She was developing people who shared her vision for the magazine. She was building a solid team that could operate seamlessly.

Sharon thought she was encouraging the staff to grow and eventually emulate her success. The staffers outside her inner circle thought she was encouraging sucking up.

Sharon is guilty of Habit #14: Playing favorites.

Case 3. Martin is a financial consultant for a prominent New York City firm. He manages money for high-net-worth individuals.

The minimum starting account is $5 million. Martin is very good at what he does. He takes home a seven-figure salary. That's a lot less than most of his clients make in a year. But Martin doesn't envy or resent his clients. He lives and breathes investments. And he loves providing a valued service for his well-heeled clients, many of them CEOs, some of them self-made entrepreneurs, some of them entertainment stars, and the rest of them beneficiaries of inherited wealth. Martin enjoys rubbing shoulders with his clients. He likes talking to them on the phone and giving them the benefit of his expertise over lunch or dinner—almost as much as he likes beating the market by four points each year. Martin is not a manager of other people. He operates as a lone wolf at his firm. His only obligation is to his clients and seeing that they're happy with the state of their portfolios from year to year.

Today is one of the biggest days of Martin's life. He's been invited to manage a portion of the investment portfolio of one of America's most admired business titans. People with enormous net worth often do that, parceling out their millions to several money managers as a protective hedge. Martin has a chance to join an elite group in the titan's stable. If he's successful, there's no telling how many more clients will spring from this relationship.

He's calling on the titan in his office perched high atop Rockefeller Center. Martin knows that this will be his only chance to make a good impression on the titan. He has one hour to gain his confidence and trust—and the millions in his account.

Martin has done this many times. He has a veteran's poise and confidence when he sells himself to a prospect—and he also has a superlative track record of market-beating returns. So it's a little surprising that he doesn't rise to the occasion in his meeting with the titan.

Immediately upon entering the titan's office, when the titan says, "Tell me a little about yourself," Martin starts selling his expertise. He tries to dazzle the titan with a rundown of his more prescient trades, explaining in great detail his investment rationale and how he ended up miles ahead of the competition. He talks about some of his more prominent clients. He outlines some ideas he has for the titan's portfolio and where he sees various markets heading in the near and long terms.

Martin is on such a roll that he doesn't notice that the scheduled hour has gone by in a flash. That's when the titan stands up and thanks Martin for taking the time to see him. Martin's a little surprised by the abrupt ending to the meeting. He never got the chance to ask the titan about his goals, his attitude to risk, and what he was looking for in a portfolio manager. But as he rewinds the meeting in his mind, Martin is satisfied that he presented a strong case for himself, hitting all the high notes in his pitch.

The next day Martin receives a handwritten note from the titan thanking him again but informing him that he will be going in another direction. Martin has lost the account and he has no idea why.

Martin thought he was winning over the titan with overwhelming evidence of his financial acumen.

The titan was thinking, "What an egotistical jackass. When's he going to ask what's on <u>my</u> mind? I'm never letting this fellow near my money."

Martin is guilty of Habit #20: An excessive need to be "me."

It's not that these people don't know who they are or where they're going or what they want to achieve. Nor is it that they don't have an adequate sense of self-worth. In fact, they tend to be very successful (and their self-esteem can often be excessive). What's wrong is that they have no idea how their behavior is coming across to the people who matter—their bosses, colleagues, subordinates, customers, and clients. (And that's not just true at work; the same goes for their home life.)

They think they have all the answers, but others see it as arrogance.

They think they're contributing to a situation with helpful comments, but others see it as butting in.

They think they're delegating effectively, but others see it as shirking responsibilities.

They think they're holding their tongue, but others see it as unresponsiveness.

They think they're letting people think for themselves, but others see it as ignoring them.

Over time these "minor" workplace foibles begin to chip away at the goodwill we've all accumulated in life and that other people normally extend to colleagues and friends. That's when the minor irritation blows up into a major crisis.

Why does this happen? More often than not, it's because people's inner compass of correct behavior has gone out of whack—and they become clueless about their position among their coworkers.

In an article that ran in *The New Yorker*, film director Harold Ramis commented on the reasons behind the fading career of Chevy Chase, one of the stars of Ramis's *Caddyshack*. Ramis said, "Do you know the concept of proprioception, of how you know where you are and where you're oriented? Chevy lost his sense of proprioception, lost touch with what he was projecting to people. It's strange because you couldn't write Chevy as a character in a novel, because his whole attitude is just superiority: 'I'm Chevy Chase and you're not.'"

Well, I work as an executive coach with successful people who have a slightly dented sense of proprioception. They look at the map of their life and career. It tells them, "You Are Here." But they don't accept it. They may resist the truth. They may think (like Chevy Chase's famous line), "I'm successful and you're not." Which is their license to think, "Why change if it's working?"

I wish I had the power to snap my fingers and make these people immediately see the need to change. I wish I could beam them into *Groundhog Day* (another Ramis film and one of my all-time favorites because it's about how people can change for the better), and make them relive the same day—perhaps their worst day—over and over again until they mend their ways. I wish I had the temperament to shake them by the shoulders and make them face reality. I wish I could turn their flaws into life-threatening diseases—because it would compel them to change, on pain of death.

But I can't and I don't. Instead, I show these people what their colleagues at work *really* think of them. It's called feedback. It's the only tool I need to show people, "You Are Here." And in this book, I will show you how to wield that weapon on yourself and others.

It doesn't take much to get people reoriented—out of the maze and back on the right path. The problems we'll be looking at in this book are not life-threatening diseases (although ignored for too long they can destroy a career). They're not deep-seated neuroses that require years of therapy or tons of medication to erase. More often than not, they are simple behavioral tics—bad habits that we repeat dozens of times a day in the workplace—which can be cured by (a) pointing them out, (b) showing the havoc they cause among the people surrounding us, and (c) demonstrating that with a slight behavioral tweak we can achieve a much more appealing effect.

It's a little like a stage actor who keeps stepping on a pivotal line in a comedy, thus ruining any chance of securing a big laugh from the audience. It's the director's job to notice this and alter the actor's delivery so that the line elicits the essential roar of laughter from the audience. No laugh, no play. If the actor can't adjust his delivery successfully, the producer will find someone who can.

Well, think of me as a caring director who helps you deliver your lines for maximum effect.

A journalist once told me that the most important thing he's learned in his career is this: "Put a comma in the wrong place and the whole sentence is screwed up." You may have an admirable skill set for a journalist. You can investigate the facts like the CSI team. You can interview people as if you've known them all your life. You can empathize with victims and excoriate the bad guys. You can spin words together beautifully on deadline and create rich meaningful metaphors that leave readers gasping with admiration. And yet, if you put a comma in the wrong place, that tiny sin of commission can wipe out the rest of your contributions.

Think of me as a friendly grammarian who can shield you from bad punctuation.

A chef at one of my favorite restaurants in San Diego told me that his signature dish succeeds or fails on one secret ingredient (which, like Coca-Cola's heavily guarded recipe, he refuses to reveal). Leave it out and the patrons' plates come back to the kitchen only half eaten. Sprinkle it in the proper amount and the plates come back clean.

Think of me as the honest diner who sends back the meal untouched to let you know that something is missing.

Actors stepping on a line. Writers misusing commas. Chefs leaving out a key ingredient. That's what we're talking about here in the workplace: People who do one annoying thing repeatedly on the job—and don't realize that this small flaw may sabotage their otherwise golden career. And, worse, they do not realize that (a) it's happening and (b) they can fix it.

This book is your map—a map that can turn the maze of wrong turns in the workplace into a straight line to the top.

In the arc of what can be a long successful career, you will always be in transit from "here" to "there."

Here can be a great place. If you're successful, here is exactly the kind of place you want to be. Here is a place where you can be the CEO of a thriving company. Here is a place where you can be the editor of one of America's top magazines. Here is a place where you can be an in-demand financial manager.

But here is also a place where you can be a success in spite of some gaps in your behavior or personal makeup.

That's why you want to go "there." There can be a better place. There is a place where you can be a CEO who is viewed as a great leader because he doesn't get in the way of his people. There is a place where you can be a great editor who builds a strong team and treats all of her direct reports with respect. There is a place where you can be a financial pro who listens well and delivers the message that he cares more about his clients' goals than his own needs.

You don't have to be a CEO or leading editor or financial wizard to benefit from this book. Look at your own personal map. Trace the distance between your vision of here and there.

You are here.

You can get there.

But you have to understand that what got you here won't get you there.

Let the journey begin.

CHAPTER 2

Enough About You

LET'S TALK ABOUT ME. Who am I to tell you how to change?

My career as an executive coach began with a phone call from the CEO of a Fortune 100 company. I had just given a leadership clinic to the CEO's human resources department. That's what I was doing back then in the late 1980s: Advising HR departments about identifying future leaders in their companies and creating programs to form them into better leaders. The CEO attended the session and must have heard something that struck a nerve. That's why he was using his very valuable time to call me. Something was on his mind.

"Marshall, I've got this guy running a big division who delivers his numbers and more every quarter," said the CEO. "He's a young, smart, dedicated, ethical, motivated, hard-working, entrepreneurial, creative, charismatic, arrogant, stubborn, know-it-all jerk.

"Trouble is, we're a company built on team values, and no one thinks he's a team player. I'm giving him a year to change, or he's out. But you know something, it would be worth a fortune to us if we could turn this guy around."

My ears perked up at the word "fortune." Up until then I had been teaching large groups of leaders how to change behavior—their own and that of their peers and direct reports.

I had never worked one-on-one with an executive before, and certainly not with someone who was one click away from the CEO's chair at a multi-billion-dollar company. I didn't know this fellow, but from the CEO's terse description I had a good picture in my mind. He was a success junkie, the kind of guy who had triumphed at each successive rung of the achievement ladder. He liked to win whether it was at work, at touch football, in a poker game, or in an argument with a stranger. He could charm a customer, turn everyone around to his position in a meeting, and get his bosses to want to help him advance through the organization. He had "high potential" stamped on his forehead since the day he entered the company. He was also financially independent—rich enough that he didn't *have* to work, he *wanted* to.

All of these ingredients—the talent, charm, and brains, the unbroken track record of success, the screw-you money in the bank that let him think he could flip off the world—made this fellow a potent mix of stubbornness and pride and defensiveness. How could I help someone like this change, someone whose entire life—from his paycheck to his title to the hundreds of direct reports who did his daily bidding—was an affirmation that he was doing everything right? More important, even if I had an inkling how to do it, why would I want to beat my head against this particular wall?

I was intrigued by the challenge—and the word "fortune." I had coached plenty of mid-level managers in groups before. These were people on the verge of success, but not quite there yet. Could my methods work on a more elite flight of executive material? Could I take someone who was demonstrably successful and make him or her more successful? It would be an interesting test.

I told the CEO, "I might be able to help."

The CEO sighed, "I doubt it."

"Tell you what," I said. "I'll work with him for a year. If he gets better, pay me. If not, it's all free."

The next day I caught a return flight to New York City to meet the CEO and his division chief.

That was twenty years ago. Since then I've personally worked with more than one hundred executives of similar status, brainpower, wealth, and achievement, who have at least one incredible career-damaging interpersonal challenge.

That's what I do now. I have a Ph.D. in organizational behavior from UCLA and 29 years of experience measuring and analyzing behavior in organizations. Now I apply it one-on-one with very successful people who want to be more successful. My job is not to make them smarter or richer. My job is to help them—to identify a personal habit that's annoying their coworkers and to help them eliminate it—so that they retain their value to the organization. My job is to make them see that the skills and habits that have taken them this far might not be the right skills and habits to take them further.

What got them here won't get them there.

But I don't work only with the super-successful. That's a critical part of my business, but I spend most of my time teaching people who reside somewhere below the absolute top rungs of the organizational ladder. They need help too. There is no correlation between an individual's standing in the corporate pyramid and what his coworkers think of his interpersonal skills. Middle managers are no less immune than CEOs to being perceived as arrogant, inattentive, rude, and unfoundedly omniscient. My target audience is the huge cohort of people who are successful in their own minds but want to be even more successful.

I train people to behave effectively in the workplace—by enrolling them in a simple but brutal regimen.

First, I solicit "360-degree feedback" from their colleagues

—as many as I can talk to up, down, and sideways in the chain of command, often including family members—for a comprehensive assessment of their strengths and weaknesses.

Then I confront them with what everybody really thinks about them. Assuming that they accept this information, agree that they have room to improve, and commit to changing that behavior, then I show them how to do it.

I help them *apologize* to everyone affected by their flawed behavior (because it's the only way to erase the negative baggage associated with our prior actions) and ask the same people for help in getting better.

I help them *advertise* their efforts to get better because you have to tell people that you're trying to change; they won't notice it on their own.

Then I help them *follow up* religiously every month or so with their colleagues because it's the only honest way to find out how you're doing and it also reminds people that you're still trying.

As an integral part of this follow-up process, I teach people to *listen without prejudice* to what their colleagues, family members, and friends are saying—that is, listen without interrupting or arguing.

I also show them that the only proper response to whatever they hear is *gratitude*. That is, I teach them how to say "Thank you" without ruining the gesture or embellishing it. I am a huge apostle for thanking.

Finally, I teach them the miracle of *feedforward*, which is my "special sauce" methodology for eliciting advice from people on what they can do to get better in the future.

It's often humbling for these overachievers, but after 12 to 18 months they get better—not only in their own minds but, more important, in the opinions of their coworkers.

As I say, it's a simple process but how I got here could fill a book—this book. And I hasten to add that it is a book that can help a lot more people than just the super-successful among us. That would be like writing a golf instructional just for PGA Tour players. An interesting exercise, perhaps, but useful to only .000001 percent of the golf playing universe. It's not worth the effort.

I don't use a golf analogy lightly. I live next to a golf course, where I can observe golfers, and I am convinced that in the context of helping successful people get better, nothing is more relevant than golf instruction. Golfers suffer all the symptoms of successful people, perhaps even more acutely.

For one thing, they're delusional about their success. They claim (and even believe) they're doing better than they really are. If they break 90 one time out of a hundred rounds, that exceptional round will quickly become their "usual game."

Golfers are also delusional about how they achieved success. That's why they award themselves second shots (called mulligans) when the first ones go in the wrong direction, move the ball from an awkward lie, conveniently neglect to count the occasional errant stroke, and otherwise fiddle with the rules and scorecard, all in an effort to buff up their handicaps and take credit for a better game than they actually possess.

Golfers, like business people, also tend to be delusional about their weaknesses, which they deny. This explains why they spend much of their time practicing what they're already good at and little time on areas of their game that need work.

How are these traits any different than bosses who claim more credit for a success than they're entitled to, who stretch the truth to gain an advantage, and who think they're strong in areas where others know they are weak?

Golfers, like the leaders I coach, have one singularly noble quality: No matter how good they are, whether they sport a 30 handicap or play to scratch, *they all want to get better*. That's why they're always practicing, scheduling lessons, trying out new equipment, fiddling with their swing, and poring over instructional advice in magazines and books.

That's the spirit underlying this book. It's aimed at anyone *who wants to get better*—at work, at home, or any other venue.

If I can help you consider the possibility that, despite your demonstrable success and laudable self-esteem, you might not be as good as you think you are; that all of us have corners in our behavioral makeup that are messy; and that these messy corners can be pinpointed and tidied up, then I can leave the world—and your world—a slightly better place than I found it.

Okay. Enough about me. Let's get back to you.

CHAPTER 3

The Success Delusion, or Why We Resist Change

UNUM, THE INSURANCE COMPANY, ran an ad some years ago showing a powerful grizzly bear in the middle of a roaring stream, with his neck extended to the limit, jaws wide open, teeth flaring. The bear was about to clamp on to an unsuspecting airborne salmon jumping upstream. The headline read: YOU PROBABLY FEEL LIKE THE *BEAR*. WE'D LIKE TO SUGGEST YOU'RE THE SALMON.

The ad was designed to sell disability insurance, but it struck me as a powerful statement about how all of us in the workplace delude ourselves about our achievements, our status, and our contributions. We

- Overestimate our contribution to a project
- Take credit, partial or complete, for successes that truly belong to others
- Have an elevated opinion of our professional skills and our standing among our peers
- Conveniently ignore the costly failures and time-consuming dead-ends we have created
- Exaggerate our projects' impact on net profits because we discount the real and hidden costs built into them (the costs are someone else's problems; the success is ours)

All of these delusions are a direct result of success, not failure. That's because we get positive reinforcement from our past successes, and, in a mental leap that's easy to justify, we think that our past success is predictive of great things in our future.

This is not necessarily a bad thing. This wacky delusional belief in our godlike omniscience instills us with confidence, however unearned it may be. It erases doubt. It blinds us to the risks and challenges in our work. If we had a complete grip on reality, seeing every situation for exactly what it is, we wouldn't get out of bed in the morning. After all, the most realistic people in our society are the chronically depressed.

But our delusions become a serious liability when we need to change. We sit there with the same godlike feelings, and when someone tries to make us change our ways we regard them with unadulterated bafflement.

It's an interesting three-part response.

First, we think the other party is confused. They're misinformed and don't know what they're talking about. They have us mixed up with someone who truly does need to change, but we are not that person.

Second, as it dawns on us that maybe the other party is not confused—maybe their information about our perceived shortcomings is accurate—we go into denial mode. The criticism does not apply to us, or else we wouldn't be so successful.

Finally, when all else fails, we attack the other party. We discredit the messenger. "Why is a smart guy like me," we think, "listening to a loser like you?"

Those are just the initial surface responses—the denial mechanisms. Couple them with the very positive interpretations that successful people assign to (a) their past performance, (b) their ability to influence their success (rather than just being lucky), (c) their optimistic belief that their success will continue in the future, and (d) their sense of control over their own destiny (as opposed to being controlled by external forces), and you have a volatile cocktail of resistance to change.

Four key beliefs help us become successful. Each can make it tough for us to change. And that's the paradox of success: These beliefs that carried us *here* may be holding us back in our quest to go *there*. Let's look more closely at each of these beliefs that can prevent us from changing our "proven" ways.

Belief 1: I Have Succeeded

Successful people believe in their *skills and talent*.

Successful people have one idea coursing silently through their veins and brains all day. It's a mantra that goes like this: "I have succeeded. I have succeeded. I have succeeded." It's their way of telling themselves that they have the skills and talent to win and keep winning. Whether or not they actually voice it inside their heads, this is what successful people are telling themselves.

You may not believe it applies to you. You may think this is egos run amok. But look at yourself. How do you have the confidence to wake up in the morning and charge into work, filled with optimism and desire and the eagerness to compete? It's not because you're reminding yourself of all the screw-ups you created and failures you've endured in recent days. On the contrary, it's because you edit out the failures and choose instead to run the highlight reel of your successes. If you're like most people I know, you're constantly focusing on the positive, calling up images of performances where you were the star, where you dazzled everyone and came out on top. It might be those five minutes in a meeting where you had the floor and nailed the argument you wanted to make. (Who wouldn't run that highlight in their head as if it were the Sports Center Play of the

Day?) It might be your skillfully crafted memo that the boss praised and routed to everyone in the company. (Who wouldn't want to re-read that memo in a spare moment?) Whatever the evidence, if it has a happy ending that makes us look good, we'll replay it for ourselves and retell it to anyone who'll listen.

You'll see this confident mindset in your successful friends, simply by the stories you hear them repeat. Are they recountings of their blunders? Or are they tales of triumphs? If they're successful friends, it's the latter.

When it comes to the thoughts we hold inside our heads, we are not self-deprecating. We are self-aggrandizing. And that's a good thing. Without it, we might not get up in the morning.

I once got into a conversation about this with a major league baseball player. Every hitter has certain pitchers whom he historically hits better than others. He told me, "When I face a pitcher whom I've hit well in the past, I always go up to the plate thinking I 'own' this guy. That gives me confidence."

That's not surprising. To successful people, past is always prologue—and the past is always rose-colored. But he took that thinking one step further.

"What about pitchers whom you don't hit well?" I asked. "How do you deal with a pitcher who 'owns' you?"

"Same thing," he said. "I go up to the plate thinking I can hit this guy. I've done it before against pitchers a lot better than he is."

In other words, not only did he lean on his past success to maintain his successful attitude, but he relied on it even when his past performance was *not* so rosy—i.e., when the evidence contradicted his self-confidence. Successful people never drink from a glass that's half empty.

They do the same even when it's a team effort. No matter how much they respect their teammates, when the team achieves great results, they tend to believe that *their contribution* was more significant than facts suggest.

I once polled three business partners to estimate the percentage that each of them contributed to their partnership's profits. Since I knew the senior partner in this particular enterprise, I knew the true numbers. And yet the three partners' combined estimate came to over 150 percent! Each man thought he was contributing more than half of the firm's profits.

This is not merely true of the people I work with, it's true in any workplace. If you asked your colleagues to estimate their percentage contribution to your enterprise, the total will always exceed 100 percent. There's nothing wrong with this. You want to surround yourself with confident people. (If your total ever comes to less than 100 percent, I suggest you find new colleagues.)

This "I have succeeded" belief, positive as it is most times, only becomes an obstacle when behavioral change is needed.

Successful people consistently compare themselves favorably to their peers. If you ask successful professionals to rate themselves against their peers (as I have done with more than 50,000 people in my training programs), 80 to 85 percent of them will rate themselves in the top 20 percent of their peer group—and 70 percent will rate themselves in the top 10 percent. This number goes even higher among professionals with higher perceived social status, such as physicians, pilots, and investment bankers, 90 percent of whom place themselves in the top 10 percent.

Doctors may be the most delusional. I once told a group of MDs that my extensive research proved that exactly half of all MDs graduated in the bottom half of their medical school class. Two doctors in the room insisted this was impossible!

Imagine trying to tell people like this that they're doing something wrong and need to change.

Belief 2: I Can Succeed

This is another way of saying, "I am *confident* that I can succeed."

Successful people believe that they have the capability within themselves to make desirable things happen. It's not quite like a carnival magic act where the mentalist moves objects on a table with his mind or bends steel. But it's close. Successful people literally believe that through sheer force of personality or talent or brainpower, they can steer a situation in their direction.

It's the reason why some people raise their hand and say, "Put me in, coach" when the boss asks for volunteers to solve a problem—and others cower in the corner, praying they won't be noticed.

This is the classic definition of self-efficacy, and it may be the most central belief driving individual success. People who believe they can succeed see opportunities where others see threats. They're not afraid of uncertainty or ambiguity. They embrace it. They want to take greater risks and achieve greater returns. Given the choice, they will always bet on themselves.

Successful people tend to have a high "internal locus of control." In other words, they do not feel like victims of fate. They see success for themselves and others as largely a function of people's motivation and ability—not luck, random chance, or external factors.

They carry this belief even when luck does play a critical role. Several years ago six of my partners wanted to get involved in a very large deal. Since I was a senior partner, they needed my approval. I was against it, telling them it was idiotic. I finally agreed, but kicking and screaming. Seven years later the return on my "idiotic" investment was the biggest lump sum check I'd ever received—seven digits to the left of the decimal point. There's no other way to describe it except dumb luck. But some of my more successful friends didn't see it this way. They insisted that my good fortune had little to do with luck and was really a payoff for years of hard work. This is the classic response from successful people. We tend to believe that success is "earned" through an individual's motivation and ability (even when it is not).

Of course, this belief makes about as much sense as inheriting money and thinking you're a self-made man. If you're born on third base, you shouldn't think you hit a triple. Successful people, however, believe there is always a link between what they have done and how far they have come—even when no link exists. It's delusional, but it is also empowering.

This belief is certainly better than the alternative. Take the example of people who buy state lottery tickets. It is a statistical fact that state-run lotteries are "regressive taxes" on people who are not the highest income earners. Serious lottery players tend to believe that any success is a function of luck, external factors, or random chance. (This is the opposite belief of most successful people, and why you rarely see millionaires scratching tickets.) These serious scratchers see the lottery as a manifestation of the randomness of success. They feel that they might get lucky and win millions of dollars if they buy enough lottery tickets. Studies show that people with these beliefs tend not to be high achievers or high wage earners.

To make matters worse, many people who win high payouts in the lottery often do a poor job of investing their winnings. The same beliefs that led them to buy hundreds of lottery tickets are reinforced when they win the lottery. That is, they make irrational investment decisions, hoping again that luck—rather than their skill and intelligence—will make them richer. That's why they plunge into questionable schemes. They don't have the base belief that they can succeed on their own, so they rely on luck.

Successful people trade in this lottery mentality for an unshakable belief in themselves. And that presents another obstacle for helping them change their behavior. One of the greatest mistakes of successful people is the assumption, "I am successful. I behave this way. Therefore, I must be successful *because* I behave this way!" The challenge is to make them see that sometimes they are successful *in spite of* this behavior.

Belief 3: I Will Succeed

This is another way of saying, "I have the *motivation* to succeed."

If "I have succeeded" refers to the *past*, and "I can succeed" to the *present*, then "I will succeed" refers to the *future*. Successful people have an unflappable optimism. They not only believe that they can manufacture success, they believe it's practically their due.

As a result, successful people tend to pursue opportunities with an enthusiasm that others may find mystifying. If they set a goal and publicly announce it, they tend to do "whatever it takes" to achieve the goal. That's a good thing. But it can easily mutate into excessive optimism. It explains why successful people tend to be extremely busy and face the danger of overcommitment.

It can be difficult for an ambitious person, with an "I will succeed" attitude, to say "no" to desirable opportunities. The huge majority of executives that I work with feel as busy (or busier) today than they have ever felt in their lives. I have never heard one of my clients say, "I don't have enough on my plate." And this busy-ness is not because they have so many problems to deal with. When I surveyed executives about why they felt overcommitted, none of them said they were trying to "save a sinking ship." They were overcommitted because they were "drowning in a sea of opportunity."

Perhaps this has happened to you. You do something wonderful at work. Suddenly, lots of people want to rub up against you and associate themselves with your success. They think, quite logically, that since you pulled off a miracle once, you can pull it off again for them. So, opportunities are thrust at you at a pace that you have never seen before. You are not experienced or disciplined enough to say no to some of them. If you're not careful, you'll be overwhelmed in due course—and that which made you rise will bring about your fall.

In my volunteer work, my favorite European client was the executive director of one of the world's leading human services organizations. His mission was to help the world's most vulnerable people. Unfortunately (for all of us), his business was booming. When people came to him for help, he didn't have the heart or the inclination to say no. Everything was driven by this belief that "we will succeed." As a result, he promised even more than the most dedicated staff could deliver.

The danger with this, of course, is that, unchecked, this "we will succeed" attitude leads to staff burnout, high turnover, and a weaker team than the one you started with. His biggest challenge as a leader was avoiding overcommitment.

This "I will succeed" belief can sabotage our chances for success when it's time for us to change behavior. I make no apology for the fact that I'm obsessed about following up with my clients to see if they actually get better by using my methods. Almost every participant who attends my leadership development programs *intends to* apply what he or she has learned back on the job. Most do, and get better! And, as our research (to be discussed later) shows, many do absolutely nothing; they may as well have spent the time watching sitcoms instead of attending my training program.

When the "do-nothings" are asked, "Why didn't you implement the behavioral change that you said you would?" by far the most common response is, "I meant to, but I just didn't have time to get to it." In other words, they were overcommitted. It's not that they didn't want to change, or didn't agree with the value of changing. They just ran out of hours in the day. They thought that they would "get to it later"—and "later" never arrived. Overcommitment can be as serious an obstacle to change as believing that you don't need fixing or that your flaws are part of the reason you're successful.

Belief 4: I Choose to Succeed

Successful people believe that they are doing what they choose to do, because they choose to do it. They have a high need for self-determination. The more successful a person is, the more likely this is to be true. When we do what we *choose* to do, we are *committed*. When we do what we *have* to do, we are *compliant*.

You see the difference in any job, even where money is not related to performance. When I attended high school back in Kentucky, even a skeptical wise-cracking jokester like me could see that some teachers had a calling for the profession and some teachers did it to make a living—and the best teachers were the former. They were committed to us rather than being controlled by external forces (such as a paycheck).

Successful people have a unique distaste for feeling controlled or manipulated. I see this in my work every day. Even when I've gotten the greatest advance build-up as someone who can help people change for the better—in other words, I'm effective at helping—I still meet resistance. I have now made peace with the fact that I cannot *make* people change. I can only help them get better at what they *choose* to change.

The basketball coach Rick Pitino wrote a book called *Success Is a Choice*. I agree. "I choose to succeed" correlates perfectly with achievement in virtually any field. People don't stumble on success; they choose it.

Unfortunately, getting people who think "I have chosen to succeed" to say "and I choose to change" is not an easy transition. It means turning that muscular commitment on its head. Easy to say, hard to do. The more we believe that our behavior is a result of our own choices and commitments, the less likely we are to want to change our behavior.

There's a reason for this, and it's one of the best-researched principles in psychology. It's called *cognitive dissonance*. It refers to the disconnect between what we believe in our minds and what we experience or see in reality. The underlying theory is simple. The more we are committed to believing that something is true, the less likely we are to believe that its opposite is true, even in the face of clear evidence that shows we are wrong. For example, if you believe your colleague Bill is a jerk, you will filter Bill's actions through that belief. No matter what Bill does, you'll see it through a prism that confirms he's a jerk. Even the times when he's not a jerk, you'll interpret it as the exception to the rule that Bill's a jerk. It may take years of saintly behavior for Bill to overcome your perception. That's cognitive dissonance applied to others. It can be a disruptive and unfair force in the workplace.

Yet cognitive dissonance actually works in favor of successful people when they apply it to themselves. The more we are committed to believing that something is true, the less likely we are to believe that its opposite is true, even in the face of evidence that shows we may have chosen the wrong path. It's the reason successful people don't buckle and waver when times get tough. Their commitment to their goals and beliefs allows them to view reality through rose-tinted glasses. That's a good thing in many situations. Their personal commitment encourages people to "stay the course" and to not give up when the going gets tough.

Of course, this same steadfastness can work against successful people when they should change course.

How Our Success Makes Us Superstitious

These four success beliefs—that we have the skills, the confidence, the motivation, and the free choice to succeed—make us superstitious.

"Who, me?" you say. "No way. I don't believe in that stuff. I'm successful because I earned it."

That may be true for "childish" superstitions such as bad luck ensuing from walking under a ladder, or breaking a mirror, or letting a black cat cross our path. Most of us scorn superstitions as silly beliefs of the primitive and uneducated. Deep down inside, we assure ourselves that we're above these silly notions.

Not so fast. To a degree, we're all superstitious. In many cases, the higher we climb the organizational totem pole, the more superstitious we become.

Psychologically speaking, superstitious behavior comes from the mistaken belief that a specific activity that is followed by positive reinforcement is actually the cause of that positive reinforcement. The activity may be functional or not—that is, it may affect someone or something else, or it may be self-contained and pointless—but if something good happens after we do it, then we make a connection and seek to repeat the activity. Psychologist B. F. Skinner was one of the first to highlight this inanity by showing how hungry pigeons would repeat their twitches because doing so was randomly followed by small pellets of grain. After twitching in a certain way and then immediately getting fed, the pigeons learned to repeat the twitches. They mistakenly believed that twitching led to food. Twitch, they hoped, and you get fed. Twitch again, and you eat more.

Sounds silly, doesn't it? We would never behave this way. We assure ourselves that we are more highly evolved than Skinner's pigeons. But from my experience, hungry business people repeat certain behavior all the time, day in and day out, when they believe large pellets of money and recognition will come their way because of it.

Superstition is merely the confusion of correlation and causality. Any human, like any animal, tends to repeat behavior that is followed by positive reinforcement. The more we achieve, the more reinforcement we get.

One of the greatest mistakes of successful people is the assumption, "I behave this way, and I achieve results. Therefore, I must be achieving results because I behave this way."

This belief is sometimes true, but not across the board. That's where superstition kicks in. It creates the core fallacy necessitating this book, the reason that "what got us here won't get us there." I'm talking about the difference between success that happens *because of* our behavior and the success that comes *in spite of* our behavior.

Almost everyone I meet is successful *because of* doing a lot of things right, and almost everyone I meet is successful *in spite of* some behavior that defies common sense.

One of my greatest challenges is helping leaders see the difference, see that they are confusing "because of" and "in spite of" behaviors, and avoid this "superstition trap."

This was my biggest hurdle when I worked with an executive I'll call Harry. He was a brilliant, dedicated executive who consistently made his numbers. He wasn't just smart. Harry saw things no one else at the company could see. Everybody high and low conceded this. His creative ideas led to groundbreaking new processes and procedures, for which everyone credited him profusely. There was no doubt that Harry had been instrumental in turning around his organization. Plus, Harry had other positives going for him. He sincerely cared about the company, employees, and shareholders. He had a great wife, two kids enrolled in top colleges, a beautiful home in a great neighborhood. The works. Life was very good for Harry.

The flaw in this perfect picture—and there's always a flaw when superstition comes into play—was that Harry was a poor listener. Even though his direct reports and coworkers respected him, they felt that he didn't listen to them. Even when you factor in that they were somewhat intimidated by his quick mind and creativity, and thus more willing to accept that Harry *didn't have to listen to them all the time*, Harry was still a world-class aggressive non-listener, not just a distracted genius who sometimes didn't pay attention. His colleagues consistently felt that if Harry had made up his mind on a subject, it was useless to express another opinion. This was confirmed up and down the company by feedback I conducted. And it was confirmed at home too, where his wife and kids felt that Harry often did not hear a word they said. If Harry's dog could speak, I suspect he would have barked out the same conclusion.

I suggested to Harry that he was probably successful because of his talent, hard work, and some good luck. I also said that he was probably successful in spite of being an appalling listener.

Harry acknowledged that other people thought he should become a better listener, but he wasn't sure that he should change. He had convinced himself that his poor listening actually was a great source of his success. Like many high achievers, he wanted to defend his superstitious beliefs. He pointed out that some people present awful ideas and that he hated cluttering his fertile brain with bad ideas. Bad ideas were like brain pollution. He needed to filter them out, and he wouldn't pretend to hear out bad ideas simply because it made other people feel better. "I don't suffer fools gladly," he said, with a little more pride than patience.

This was defensive reaction number one. It always happens with people caught in the superstition trap. They cling to the notion that their success is causally linked to specific behavior, good or bad, responsible or risky, legitimate or inappropriate. They refuse to accept that not all good things flow to them because of the less-than-good things they do. Sometimes there's no causal connection at all.

It was my job to make Harry see his flawed logic.

When I asked if he really believed that his coworkers and family members were fools, he shamefacedly conceded that his comment may have been over the top. These were people he respected, people he needed to get things done, people on whose backs his entire success rested.

"Upon further reflection," he said, "perhaps sometimes I am the fool."

That was a big step for Harry—both *conceding* the legitimacy of other people's feelings and *recognizing* that "perhaps sometimes" he was acting like a fool.

But then Harry went into defensive reaction number two: fear of overcorrection. He was concerned that he might start listening too much and that doing so would diminish his creative impulses. He would become too unwilling to share his opinions and eventually dry up creatively. I pointed out that the danger that a 55-year-old man who had been a bad listener for his entire life would overcorrect and suddenly become excessively interested in other people's opinions was extremely remote. I assured him that he could remove this concern from his things-to-worry-about list. We were fixing one bad behavior, not manufacturing a religious conversion. Ultimately Harry decided it was more productive to hear people out than waste time justifying his own dysfunctional behavior.

Harry's case isn't an isolated event. Virtually all of us are superstitious, attaching too much value to bad behavior that we confusedly associate with our success.

I've worked with people who insist their cruel comments to colleagues are absolutely necessary because their pithy memorable zingers are where their great ideas begin. (I ask them if they've ever met a nice person as creative as they are? Hmmm . . . it gets them thinking.)

I've worked with salespeople who think their pushy, belligerent sales tactics with customers are the reason they close more deals than their peers. (If that were true, I point out, how do your nicer colleagues sell anything at all? Could it be that you're selling a great product or making more sales calls?)

I've worked with executives who insist their remoteness, their inscrutable silences, their non-accessibility to their direct reports is a controlled, calculated tactic to get people to think for themselves. (Fostering initiative among the troops is a leader's job, I point out, but are you doing this intentionally for a legitimate purpose? Or are you justifying it after the fact because that is who you are and you refuse to change? Couldn't your people think *better* for themselves if you were steering them in the right direction and showed them how you think? Is it possible that they're thinking for themselves in spite of the fact that you ignore them?)

Now let's turn the spotlight on you, because few of us are immune to superstition. Pick a quirky or unattractive behavior that you habitually do, something that you know is annoying to friends or family or coworkers. Now ask yourself: Do you continue to do it because you think it is somehow associated with the good things that have happened to you? Examine it more closely. Does this behavior help you achieve results? Or is it one of those irrational superstitious beliefs that have been controlling your life for years? The former is "because of" behavior, the latter "in spite of."

Getting out of this superstition trap requires vigilance. You must constantly ask yourself, Is this behavior a legitimate reason for my success, or am I kidding myself?

If you tote up your "because of" and "in spite of" activities, you might be shocked at how superstitious you really are.

We All Obey Natural Law

Barry Diller, the chairman of IAC/Interactive Corp., was at Harvard Business School explaining the rationale behind the mosaic of interactive commerce companies he had assembled at IAC, such as Ticketmaster, Hotels.com., Match.com, and LendingTree.com. One of the students pointed out that these various businesses seemed to be operating independently, not in a coordinated synergistic fashion.

Diller erupted in mock anger. "Don't ever use that word synergy. It's a hideous word," he said. "The only thing that works is natural law. Given enough time, natural relationships will develop between our businesses."

I agree. What applies to disparate parts of a giant company also applies to disparate people in an organization. You can't force people to work together. You can't mandate synergy. You can't manufacture harmony, whether it's between two people or two divisions. You also can't order people to change their thinking or behavior. The only law that applies is natural law.

The only natural law I've witnessed in three decades of observing successful people's efforts to become more successful is this: *People will do something—including changing their behavior—only if it can be demonstrated that doing so is in their own best interests as defined by their own values.*

I'm not being cynical here, or implying that the only motive in life is selfishness. Plenty of people perform selfless acts of goodness *of their own volition* every day with no obvious tit-for-tat payback to themselves.

What I am saying, though, is that when you take self-volition out of the equation and forces beyond your control are involved, natural law applies. In order for me to get you to do what I want, I have to prove that doing so will benefit you in some way, immediately or somewhere down the road. This is natural law. Every choice, big or small, is a risk-reward decision where your bottom-line thinking is, "What's in it for me?"

None of us has to apologize for this. It's the way of the world.

It's the force that gets squabbling rivals to begin cooperating. If you drill down deep enough, you'll find that they're not doing it out of altruism or newfound saintliness. It's the only way each of them can get what they want. You see this all the time in politics when bitter rivals from across the aisle agree to support the same legislation because different parts of the bill will benefit their different constituencies.

It's the force at work when people swallow their pride and admit they were wrong. Hard as it is for many folks to do, they'll do it if it's the only way to put the trouble behind them—and move on.

It's the reason people will turn down a better-paying job because they sense the new situation will not make them happier. They're asking what's in it for them, and concluding that they'd rather be happier than richer.

For my purposes, thank heaven for natural law! Without it, getting successful people to mend their ways would be impossible.

As I mentioned, successful people have very few reasons to change their behavior—and lots of reasons to stick with the status quo, to dance with what brung 'em.

Their success has showered them with positive reinforcement, so they feel it's smart to continue doing what they've always done.

Their past behavior confirms that the future is equally bright. (I did it this way before. Look how far it's gotten me.)

Then there's the arrogance, the feeling that "I can do anything" which develops and bulges like a well-exercised muscle in successful people, especially after an impressive string of successes.

Then there's the protective shell that successful people develop over time which whispers to them, "You are right. Everyone else is wrong."

These are heady defense mechanisms to overcome.

For some people, telling them that everyone hates the way they act doesn't make a dent; they don't care what others think. They assume that everyone else is confused.

For others, warning that their behavior is ruining their chances for promotion fails to scare them; they assume they can snap their fingers and get a better job elsewhere. (Forget whether it's true; they believe it!)

Persuading people to change by invoking an endgame that doesn't matter to them is very hard work. I was once asked to work with a software wizard. He was the technical guts of the company—virtually indispensable. The CEO wanted him to be more of a team player—to mix more with others in the hope that maybe he could spread some of his "genius" around to the rest of the company.

Only problem—which was evident after five minutes with him—was that this man was basically antisocial. His ideal world was a room, a desk, a computer screen, and (oh yes) a state-of-the-art sound system providing round-the-clock back-ground music (opera, as I recall). He didn't want to play well with the other children. He wanted to be left alone.

I suppose we could have threatened to take his toys away if he didn't change. But what would that have accomplished? He wouldn't be better or happier, and the company would have "lost" its most valuable asset. Changing him wasn't worth it, which is what I recommended to the CEO.

"Your plan is nice in theory. But what you are asking is not connected to what he values," I said. "Let him be. He's happy. He's not going anywhere. Why scare him away by turning him into someone that is just not him?"

This fellow was the exception—an aberration.

Most people's resistance to change can be overcome by in-voking natural law. Everyone, even the biggest ego in the room, has a hot button that can be pushed—and that button is self-interest. All we have to do is find it. It's not the same thing in all people.

If there's any art to what I do (and believe me, there isn't much), maybe it happens here—at the decisive moment when I discover someone's hot button.

Fortunately, successful people make it easy to find the but-ton. If you press people to identify the motives behind their self-interest it usually boils down to four items: money, power, status, and popularity. These are the standard payoffs for suc-cess. It's why we will claw and scratch for a raise (money), for a promotion (power), for a bigger title and office (status). It's why so many of us have a burning need to be liked by everyone (popularity).

The hot button is different for each person. And it changes over time, but it's still guided by self-interest. My personal coaching clients have money, power, and status—and most are popular. Having achieved these goals, they turn to higher-level goals, such as "leaving a legacy" or "being an inspiring role model" or "creating a great company." If you look for the hot button of self-interest, it's there.

One of my more notable successes occurred with a sales executive named John, who was consumed by his rivalry with another executive at the firm. The two men had been dueling for years (although it's not clear whether the "other guy" shared this obsession). No matter what John did—playing golf at a company retreat or posting quarterly profits—he didn't "win" unless the other guy finished behind him.

The CEO had called me in because John was a top candidate for the COO spot. Some of his rough edges needed to be smoothed out. John's issue, said the feedback, was an obsessive need to win (surprise!), which manifested itself in a constant one-upsmanship with his direct reports. He always corrected their ideas or improved them by insisting that his suggestions were better.

Getting John to change required a subtle appreciation of what motivated him. Making more money didn't stir the guy; he had enough. Power and status didn't appeal to him either; he was already higher in the organization than he had ever dreamed. Popularity wasn't an issue; with his salesman's touch for getting people to like him, he was already popular. What made him commit to change was the abhorrent thought that failing to do so meant ceding ground to his arch rival. Not the noblest of motives, but I don't pass judgment on why people change. I only care that they do.

Another time when I worked with an executive who was notoriously nasty and sarcastic, he agreed to change because he could see that his two sons were imitating his behavior at home. He didn't want his legacy to be two sarcastic jerks. (More on him in Chapter 6.)

Take a look around you at work. Why are you there? What

keeps you coming back day after day? Is it any of the big four—money, power, status, popularity—or is it something deeper and more subtle that has developed over time? If you know what matters to you, it's easier to commit to change. If you can't identify what matters to you, you won't know when it's being threatened. And in my experience, people only change their ways when what they truly value is threatened.

It's in our nature. It's the law.

The Twenty Habits That Hold You Back from the Top

In which we identify the most annoying interpersonal issues in the workplace and help you figure out which ones apply to you

CHAPTER 4

The Twenty Habits

Knowing What to Stop

As a 10-year board member of the Peter Drucker Foundation, I had many opportunities to listen to this great man. Among the myriad wise things I have heard Peter Drucker say, the wisest was, "We spend a lot of time teaching leaders what to do. We don't spend enough time teaching leaders what to stop. Half the leaders I have met don't need to learn what to do. They need to learn what to stop."

How true. Think about your organization. When was the last retreat or training session you attended that was titled, *Stupid Things Our Top People Do That We Need to Stop Doing Now?* When was the last time your CEO delivered an internal talk, designed to motivate employees, that focused on his negative traits and his efforts to stop this destructive behavior? Can you even imagine your CEO (or immediate supervisor) admitting a personal failing in public and outlining his efforts to stop doing it?

Probably not.

There are good reasons for this, largely allied to the positive tone and fast-forward momentum organizations try to maintain. Everything in an organization is designed to demonstrate a commitment to positive action—and couched in terms of doing something. We will start paying attention to our customers (rather than stop talking about ourselves). We must begin to listen more attentively (rather than stop playing with our Black-Berries while others are talking).

Likewise, the recognition and reward systems in most organizations are totally geared to acknowledge the *doing* of *something*. We get credit for doing something good. We rarely get credit for ceasing to do something bad. Yet they are flip sides of the same coin.

Think of the times you've seen colleagues go on a sales call and return with a huge order. If they're like the salespeople I know, they'll come back to the office brandishing the lucrative sales order and regaling anyone who'll listen with a blow-by-blow account of how they turned the prospect around. They will recount their triumph for months. But turn it around. What if during the sales call these salespeople added up the numbers and realized that they were about to close a deal that actually costs the company money with every unit sold? What if they decided on the spot to stop negotiating and say no to the sale? Do they rush back to the office and boast about the bad deal they've just avoided? Hardly—because avoiding mistakes is one of those unseen, unheralded achievements that are not allowed to take up our time and thought. And yet . . . many times avoiding a bad deal can affect the bottom line more significantly than scoring a big sale.

Think of Gerald Levin when he was the much-admired chairman of Time Warner in the 1990s. Levin was hailed as a visionary CEO, the man who foresaw the future of cable TV and helped invent HBO, transforming Time Warner from just a combo of magazines, movies, and music into a broadcasting powerhouse.

But then in 2000 Levin made a mistake. He merged the

venerable Time Warner with the upstart online service AOL. It was the biggest corporate merger in U.S. history at the time—promising to create a company that would dominate for decades. Of course, it didn't work out that way. The merger nearly destroyed Time Warner. The stock lost 80 percent of its value. Thousands of employees lost the bulk of their retirement savings. As for Levin, he lost his job, a big chunk of his net worth, and all of his reputation. He went from being chairman of Time Warner to being the architect of the worst corporate merger in U.S. history.

Now, imagine if Levin at any point in the negotiation with AOL had applied the brakes and walked away from the deal? Chances are, we'd never know about it. Levin would not hold a press conference to announce, "We are not merging!" He'd keep it to himself, as just one more example of a bad decision avoided. And yet . . . if he had done this—if he had simply *stopped* what he was doing—his reputation and net worth might have remained intact.

That's the funny thing about stopping some behavior. It gets no attention, but it can be as crucial as everything else we do *combined*.

For some reason, we are less likely to poison our thinking this way in normal everyday life. When it comes to stopping behavior or avoiding bad decisions outside the workplace, we congratulate ourselves all the time.

A few years ago my wife and I decided not to invest in a real estate venture. Too risky, we thought. Fortunately for us (though not for some of our friends), it went bust. Not a month goes by when Lyda and I, sitting around the kitchen table paying our bills, don't say to each other, "Thank God we didn't plunk our money into that scheme." We're quiet for a moment, think sadly of our friends' losses, and then resume paying our bills. This is our way of honoring the bad decision we avoided.

Likewise with stopping a bad habit in our personal life. If we successfully stop smoking, we regard it as a big achievement—and congratulate ourselves all the time for it. Others do too (as well they should when you consider that the average smoker tries to quit nine times).

But we lose this common sense in the can-do environment of an organization—where there is no system for honoring the avoidance of a bad decision or the cessation of bad behavior. Our performance reviews are solely based on what we've done, what numbers we've delivered, what increases we have posted against last year's results. Even the seemingly minor personal goals are couched in terms of actions we've initiated, not behavior we have stopped. We get credit for being punctual, not for stopping our lateness.

We can change this. All that's required is a slight tweak in our mindset, in how we look at our behavior.

Get out your notepad. Instead of your usual "To Do" list, start your "To Stop" list. By the end of this book, your list may grow.

Shifting into Neutral

We have to stop couching all our behavior in terms of positive or negative. Not all behavior is good or bad. Some of it is simply *neutral*. Neither good nor bad.

For example, let's say you're not regarded as a nice person. You want to change that perception. You decide, "I need to be nicer."

What do you do?

For many people, that's a daunting assignment, requiring a long list of positive actions. You have to start complimenting people, saying "please" and "thank you," listening to people more patiently, treating them with verbal respect, etc., etc., etc. In effect, you have to convert all of the negative things you do at work into positive actions. That's asking a lot of most people, requiring a complete personality makeover that is closer to religious conversion than on-the-job improvement. In my experience very few if any people can institute that many positive changes in their interpersonal actions all at once. They can handle one at a time. But a half dozen or more changes? I don't think so.

Fortunately, there's a simpler way to achieve the goal of "being nicer." All you have to do is "stop being a jerk." It doesn't require much. You don't have to think of new ways to be nicer to people. You don't have to design daily tasks to make over your personality. You don't have to remember to say nice things and hand out compliments and tell the little white lies that lubricate the gears of the workplace. All you have to do is . . . nothing.

When someone offers a less-than-brilliant idea in a meeting, don't criticize it. Say nothing.

When someone challenges one of your decisions, don't argue with them or make excuses. Quietly consider it and say nothing.

When someone makes a helpful suggestion, don't remind them that you already knew that. Thank them and say nothing.

This is not a semantic game. The beauty of knowing what to stop—of achieving this state of inspired neutrality—is that *it is so easy to do.*

Given the choice between becoming a nicer person and ceasing to be a jerk, which do you think is easier to do? The former requires a concerted series of positive acts of commission. The latter is nothing more than an act of omission.

Think of it in terms of a box. Being a nicer person requires

you to fill up the box with all the small positive acts you perform every day to establish the new you. It takes a long time to
fill up the box, and even longer for people to pay attention and
notice that your box is full.

On the other hand, ceasing to be a jerk does not require
learning new behavior. You don't have to fill up the box with all
your positive achievements; you simply have to leave it empty of
any negatives.

Keep that in mind as you go through the list of interpersonal issues in this section and determine if any apply to you.
Correcting the behavior, you'll discover, does not require pol-
ished skills, elaborate training, arduous practice, or supernatural
creativity. All that's required is the faint imagination to stop doing what you've done in the past—in effect, to do nothing at all.

What's Wrong with Us?

Before we can talk about fixing faulty behavior, we must
identify the most common faults.

I hasten to add that these are a very specific breed of flaws.

They are not flaws of *skill*. I can't fix that. If this were a
baseball team and I was a coach, I'm not the guy to teach you
how to hit a hanging curve ball. That's the hitting instructor's
job. I'm the coach who teaches you how to get along with your
teammates—how to play nice rather than how to play baseball.

Nor are they flaws in *intelligence*. It's too late for me to
make you smarter. If that's the issue, the causative events probably occurred somewhere between birth and the time you left
college. I wasn't around. And I couldn't have helped anyway.

Nor are they flaws of unchangeable *personality*. We're not
attempting psychiatry here, and we can't deliver vital pharmaco-
logical medication via a book. Consult an M.D.

What we're dealing with here are challenges in interpersonal behavior, often leadership behavior. They are the egregious everyday annoyances that make your workplace substantially more noxious than it needs to be. They don't happen in a vacuum. They are transactional flaws performed by one person against others. They are:

1. **Winning too much:** The need to win at all costs and in all situations—when it matters, when it doesn't, and when it's totally beside the point.
2. **Adding too much value:** The overwhelming desire to add our two cents to every discussion.
3. **Passing judgment:** The need to rate others and impose our standards on them.
4. **Making destructive comments:** The needless sarcasms and cutting remarks that we think make us sound sharp and witty.
5. **Starting with "No," "But," or "However":** The overuse of these negative qualifiers which secretly say to everyone, "I'm right. You're wrong."
6. **Telling the world how smart we are:** The need to show people we're smarter than they think we are.
7. **Speaking when angry:** Using emotional volatility as a management tool.
8. **Negativity, or "Let me explain why that won't work":** The need to share our negative thoughts even when we weren't asked.
9. **Withholding information:** The refusal to share information in order to maintain an advantage over others.
10. **Failing to give proper recognition:** The inability to praise and reward.
11. **Claiming credit that we don't deserve:** The most

annoying way to overestimate our contribution to any success.

12. **Making excuses:** The need to reposition our annoying behavior as a permanent fixture so people excuse us for it.

13. **Clinging to the past:** The need to deflect blame away from ourselves and onto events and people from our past; a subset of blaming everyone else.

14. **Playing favorites:** Failing to see that we are treating someone unfairly.

15. **Refusing to express regret:** The inability to take responsibility for our actions, admit we're wrong, or recognize how our actions affect others.

16. **Not listening:** The most passive-aggressive form of disrespect for colleagues.

17. **Failing to express gratitude:** The most basic form of bad manners.

18. **Punishing the messenger:** The misguided need to attack the innocent who are usually only trying to help us.

19. **Passing the buck:** The need to blame everyone but ourselves.

20. **An excessive need to be "me":** Exalting our faults as virtues simply because they're who we are.

Perhaps Machiavelli could paint these flaws as virtues and demonstrate how they function as clever counterintuitive tactics for getting a leg up on our rivals. But in the course of examining each of these irritants, I will demonstrate that correcting them is the best way to enlist people as our allies—which in the long run is a much more promising success strategy than defending behavior that alienates people.

Admittedly, this is a scary pantheon of bad behavior, and when they're collected in one place they sound more like a chamber of horrors. Who would want to work in an environment where colleagues are guilty of these sins? And yet we do every day. The good news is that these failings rarely show up in bunches. You may know one person guilty of one or two of them. You may know another with one or two different issues. But it's hard to find successful people who embody too many of these failings. That's good—because it simplifies our task of achieving long-term positive change.

There's more good news. These faults are simple to correct. The fix is in the skill set of every human being. For example, the cure for not thanking enough is remembering to say, "Thank you." (How tough is that?) For not apologizing, it's learning to say, "I'm sorry. I'll do better in the future." For punishing the messenger, it's imagining how we'd like to be treated under similar circumstances. For not listening, it's keeping your mouth shut and ears open. And so on. Although this stuff is simple, it's not easy (there's a difference). You already know what to do. It's as basic as tying your shoelaces or riding a bike, or any other skill that lasts a lifetime. We just lose sight of the many daily opportunities to employ them, and thus get rusty.

Check yourself against the list. It's unlikely (I pray) that you're guilty of all of these annoying habits. It's not even likely that you can claim six to eight of them as your own. And of those six to eight, it's also unlikely that *all of them* are sufficiently significant problems that we have to worry about. Some are going to be more serious issues than others. If only one out of twenty people says that you have an anger management issue, let it go. On the other hand, if sixteen out of twenty say it, let's get to work.

Whittle the list down to the one or two vital issues, and you'll know where to start.

In that sense, my job is to show you how to do it. It's little more than teaching people to use their positive skills rather than expose their negative flaws. What could be simpler than that?

The Higher You Go, the More Your Problems Are Behavioral

There's a reason I devote so much energy to identifying interpersonal challenges in successful people. It's because the higher you go, the more your problems are behavioral.

At the higher levels of organizational life, all the leading players are technically skilled. They're all smart. They're all up to date on the technical aspects of their job. You don't get to be, say, your company's chief financial officer without knowing how to count, how to read a balance sheet, and how to handle money prudently.

That's why behavioral issues become so important at the upper rungs of the corporate ladder. All other things being equal, your people skills (or lack of them) become more pronounced the higher up you go. In fact, even when all other things are *not* equal, your people skills often make the difference in how high you go.

Who would you rather have as a CFO? A moderately good accountant who is great with people outside the firm and skilled at managing very smart people? Or a brilliant accountant who's inept with outsiders and alienates all the smart people under him?

Not a tough choice, really. The candidate with superb people skills will win out every time, in large part because he will be able to hire people smarter than he is about money and he will be able to lead them. There's no guarantee the brilliant accountant can do that in the future.

Think about how we perceive other successful people. We rarely associate their success with technical skill or even brainpower. Maybe we say, "They're smart," but that's not the sole factor we attribute to their success. We believe they're smart and something else. At some point we give them the benefit of the doubt on skill issues. For example, we assume our doctor knows medicine, so we judge him on "bedside manner" issues—how he tolerates our questions, how he delivers bad news, even how he apologizes for keeping us cooling our heels too long in his waiting room. None of this is taught in medical school.

We apply these behavioral criteria to almost any successful person—whether it's a CEO or a plumbing contractor.

We all have certain attributes that help us land our first job. These are the kind of achievements that go on our résumé. But as we become more successful, those attributes recede into the background—and more subtle attributes come to the fore.

Jack Welch has a Ph.D. in chemical engineering, but I doubt if any problems he encountered in his last 30 years at General Electric were in any way related to his skill at chemical titration or formulating plastics. When he was vying for the CEO job, the issues holding him back were strictly behavioral— his brashness, his blunt language, his unwillingness to suffer fools. He did not pick up these issues back at the University of Illinois chemical engineering labs. General Electric's board of directors didn't worry about his ability to generate profits. They wanted to know if he could behave as a CEO.

When people ask me if the leaders I coach can really change their behavior, my answer is this: As we advance in our careers, behavioral changes are often the only significant changes we *can* make.

Two Caveats

First Caveat: In this book, as we go through the pantheon of personal flaws that none of us is immune to, I don't want readers to think that the people I work with are bad people. To the contrary, they're not. They are outstanding people, invariably in the top two percent of their organization. But they may be held back by a personal failing or two that they either (a) do not recognize, (b) have not been told about, or (c) are aware of but refuse to change.

Keep this in mind, because at times it will seem like I spend my days working in corporate purgatories populated exclusively by psychopaths, misfits, and jerks. Look around you at work. My clients are no different from the most outstanding people in your organization. Actually, they are no different from you except perhaps in one sense: Unlike many people, they accept their flaws and have made a commitment to getting better. That's a significant difference.

Second Caveat: In the course of going through the following list of common flaws, you may recognize yourself. "That's me," you'll say to yourself. "I do that all the time. I had no idea I was coming across that way."

The chances that you'll get a little nudge of self-recognition here are fairly high.

The chances that you'll admit it's a *problem* are less high.

The chances that you'll take corrective action to mend your ways are even slimmer.

But even if you were that extraordinarily enlightened open-minded individual who could cop to all this, I'd still say we're getting ahead of ourselves. You're not ready to change yet.

For one thing, I'm a little skeptical of self-diagnosis. Just as people tend to overestimate their strengths, they also tend to overrate their weaknesses. They think they're really bad at something at which they're only mediocre or *slightly* poor—an F when they're really a C minus. In other words, they see cancer where a professional would see a muscle pull. So let's hold off on self-diagnosis for a moment.

More important, even if the diagnosis were correct—say, you are a chronic interrupter—you cannot be sure that it's a serious problem to other people. It might be a personality tic to your colleagues, a foible they tolerate. But if it doesn't bother them or affect their opinions of you or isn't holding you back at work, you can ease up on yourself—at least on this issue.

We'll get to picking the right thing to fix soon enough in Chapter 6. But first, let's be clear about what the interpersonal challenges really are.

Habit #1 Winning too much

Winning too much is easily the most common behavioral problem that I observe in successful people. There's a fine line between being competitive and overcompetitive, between winning when it counts and when no one's counting—and successful people cross that line with alarming frequency.

Let's be clear: I'm not disparaging competitiveness. I'm pointing out that it's a problem when we deploy it at the service of objectives that simply are not worth the effort.

Winning too much is the #1 challenge because it underlies nearly every other behavioral problem.

If we argue too much, it's because we want our view to prevail over everyone else (i.e., it's all about winning).

If we're guilty of putting down other people, it's our stealthy way of positioning them beneath us (again, winning).

If we ignore people, again it's about winning—by making them fade away.

If we withhold information, it's to give ourselves an edge over others.

If we play favorites, it's to win over allies and give "our side" an advantage. And so on. So many things we do to annoy people stem from needlessly trying to be the alpha male (or female) in any situation—i.e., the winner.

Our obsession with winning rears its noisome head across the spectrum of human endeavor, not just among senior executives. When the issue is important, we want to win. When the issue is trivial, not worth our time and energy, we want to win. Even when the issue is clearly to our disadvantage, we want to win.

If you've achieved any modicum of success, you're guilty of this every day. When you're in a meeting at work, you want your position to prevail. When you're arguing with your significant other, you'll pull out all the stops to come out on top (whatever that means!) Even when you're in the checkout line at the supermarket, you're scouting the other lines to see which is moving faster.

I was at a backyard party once watching a one-on-one basketball game between a father and his 9-year-old son. The father had a two-foot height advantage over the son, plus 120 pounds, and 30 years of experience. He was also the dad, trying to have a good time and maybe impart some court smarts to the young spawn of his loins. The game started off merrily and nonchalantly—with the dad giving the young kid gimmes and do-overs to keep him enthused. But about ten minutes into this alleged fun, the father's "gotta win" genes kicked in, and he started playing as if the score mattered. He guarded his son closely, engaged in trash talk, and actually took pleasure in beating him 11 baskets to 2. That's how pervasive this urge to win is. Even when it's beyond trivial—when it actually can scar someone we love—we still want to win.

It's easy to disapprove of this father's behavior from a distance. We assure ourselves that we would never behave so insensitively.

Is that so?

Let's say that you want to go to dinner at restaurant X. Your spouse, partner, or friend wants to go to restaurant Y. You have a heated debate about the choice. You point out the bad reviews Y has received. But you grudgingly yield and end up going to restaurant Y. The experience confirms your misgivings. Your reservation is lost and you have to wait 30 minutes. The service is slow, the drinks weak, and the food tastes like ripe garbage. You have two options during this painful experience. Option A: Critique the restaurant and smugly point out to your partner how wrong he or she was and how this debacle could have been avoided if only *you* had been listened to. Option B: Shut up and eat the food. Mentally write it off and enjoy the evening.

I have polled my clients on these two options for years. The results are consistent: 75 percent of clients say they would critique the restaurant. What do they all agree that they *should* do? Shut up and have a good time. If we do a "cost-benefit analysis" we generally conclude that our relationship with our partner is far more important than winning a trivial argument about where to eat. And yet . . . the urge to win trumps our common sense. We do the wrong thing even when we know what we should do.

It gets worse.

A few years ago, I offered my coaching services free to one of the U.S. Army's top generals. He asked, "Who would be your ideal client?"

I told him, "Your generals are busy people, with even less free time than I have, so let's make it count. I'd like to work with someone who is a smart, dedicated, hard-working, driven-to-achieve, patriotic, wants-to-do-what's-right, technically gifted, hard to replace, brilliant, competent, arrogant, stubborn, opinionated know-it-all. Do you think you could find me one?"

"Find you one?" he laughed. "We have a target-rich environment."

So, I had the opportunity to train many Army generals that first year.

In one group training session with the generals, their wives attended too. It was fun to watch how the generals handled the dinner quiz. About 25 percent of the generals said they would do the right thing—i.e., they'd shut up and enjoy dinner. That's when their wives stood up, gave their husbands a non-approved salute, and ripped into them. The wives said that their husbands would do no such thing. That's how strong the urge to win is. Even with a material witness in the room (i.e., their spouse) who they know will dispute them, many generals still tried to give the answer that made them appear in the most attractive light.

If the need to win is the dominant gene in our success DNA—the overwhelming reason we're successful—then winning too much is a perverse genetic mutation that can limit our success.

What I'm going to suggest repeatedly in this book is the heretical notion that we can become more successful if we appreciate this "flaw" and work to suppress it in our interpersonal relations.

Habit #2 Adding too much value

The two men at dinner were clearly on the same wavelength. One of them was Jon Katzenbach, the ex-McKinsey director who now heads his own elite consulting boutique. The other fellow was Niko Canner, his brilliant protégé and partner. They were plotting out a new venture. But something about their conversation was slightly off. Every time Niko floated an idea, Katzenbach interrupted him. "That's a great idea," he would say, "but it would work better if you . . ." and then he would trail off into a story about how it worked for him several years earlier in another context. When Jon finished, Niko would pick up where he left off only to be interrupted within seconds by Jon again. This went on back and forth like a long rally at Wimbledon.

As the third party at the table, I watched and listened. As an executive coach, I'm used to monitoring people's dialogues, listening with forensic intensity for clues that reveal why these otherwise accomplished people annoy their bosses, peers, and subordinates.

Ordinarily I keep quiet in these situations. But Jon was a friend exhibiting classic destructive smart-person behavior. I said, "Jon, will you please be quiet and let Niko talk. Stop trying to add value to the discussion."

What Jon Katzenbach was displaying in full flower was a variation on the need to win—the need to add value. It's common among leaders used to running the show. They still retain remnants of the top-down management style where their job was to tell everyone what to do. These leaders are smart enough to realize that the world has changed, that most of their subordinates know more in specific areas than they ever will. But old habits die hard. It is extremely difficult for successful people to listen to other people tell them something that they already know without communicating somehow that (a) "we already knew that" and (b) "we know a better way."

That's the problem with adding too much value. Imagine you're the CEO. I come to you with an idea that you think is very good. Rather than just pat me on the back and say, "Great idea!" your inclination (because you have to add value) is to say, "Good idea, but it'd be better if you tried it this way."

The problem is, you may have improved the content of my idea by 5 percent, but you've reduced my commitment to executing it by 50 percent, because you've taken away my ownership of the idea. *My* idea is now *your* idea—and I walk out of your office less enthused about it than when I walked in. That's the fallacy of added value. Whatever we gain in the form of a better idea is lost many times over in our employees' diminished commitment to the concept.

Katzenbach and I had a laugh over this dinner incident later on. As one of the world's leading authorities on team building, Jon should have known better. But that's how pernicious the need to win can be. Even when we know better, we fall into its clutches.

Don't get me wrong. I'm not saying that bosses have to zip their lips to keep their staff's spirits from sagging. But the higher up you go in the organization, the more you need to make other people winners and not make it about winning yourself.

For bosses this means closely monitoring how you hand out encouragement. If you find yourself saying, "Great idea," and then dropping the other shoe with a tempering "but" or "however," try cutting your response off at "idea." Even better, before you speak, take a breath and ask yourself if what you're about to say is worth it. One of my clients, who's now the CEO of a major pharmaceutical, said that once he got into the habit of taking a breath before he talked, he realized that at least half of what he was going to say wasn't worth saying. Even though he believed he could add value, he realized he had more to gain by not winning.

As for employees who have to bear the brunt of their boss's need to add value, be confident about your expertise, and, short of being insubordinate, stick to your position.

Years ago a chocolate maker I know in San Francisco agreed to make a sampler box of twelve chocolates for the late designer Bill Blass. They designed a dozen different chocolates for Blass's approval, which he insisted upon since the chocolates would bear his name. But sensing that he would resent not having a choice, they seeded the selection with a dozen other types which they regarded as clearly inferior. To the chocolatier's horror, when Blass entered the room for the tasting, he liked all the inferior chocolates. The chocolatiers hadn't expected Blass to be so firm in his opinion. But Blass was a man of great taste, used to getting his way, and he knew what he liked. He needed to add value to the process. After Blass left the room, the chocolate makers looked at each other, all thinking the same thing: *What are we going to do? He picked all the wrong ones.*

Finally, the head of the company, which was a family business that had thrived for seven generations, said, "We know chocolate. He doesn't. Let's make the ones we like and he'll never know the difference."

Sweet.

Habit #3 Passing judgment

There's a cute scene between Jack Nicholson and Diane Keaton in the movie *Something's Gotta Give*. Keaton plays a successful fiftyish divorced playwright, while Nicholson is a sixtyish tycoon with a lothario reputation who happens to be dating her daughter. Nicholson is forced to spend a few nights at Keaton's lavish weekend home, recovering from a mild cardiac episode. He and Keaton start off loathing each other but cool off sufficiently to have a flirtatious discussion late one evening in Keaton's kitchen while she prepares a midnight snack.

Keaton says, "I can't imagine what you think of me."

Nicholson asks, "Do you ever miss being married?"

"Sometimes," she says. "Yeah, at night. But not that much anymore."

The subject shifts momentarily to what they want to eat, but Keaton, in a not-so-subtle attempt to elicit feedback, brings the conversation back on point.

"Did one of us just say something interesting?" she muses.

"You said you can't imagine what I think of you."

"You don't have to answer that," she says.

"Okay," he says agreeably.

"But if you have an opinion I'd be curious," says Keaton.

"Will you tell me first why you only miss being married at night?" says Nicholson.

"Well, the phone doesn't ring that much at night. The whole alone thing happens at night. Sleeping by myself took some getting used to. But I got the hang of it. You gotta sleep in the middle of the bed. It's absolutely not healthy to have a side when no one has the other side," she says.

Encouraged by her explanation, Nicholson says, "Now I'm convinced that what I think of you is right. You're a tower of strength."

"Ugh!" says Keaton.

"Try not to rate my answer," says Nicholson.

I know it's only a romantic comedy, but the scene rings true. Even in the most gentle, intimate moments, when people are offering us their most acute (and helpful) snapshots of ourselves, we can't help passing judgment. We can't help ranking what they tell us—lining it up as more pleasing or insightful than what we expected them to say, or what we think ourselves, or what we have heard from others on the same subject.

There's nothing wrong with offering an opinion in the normal give and take of business discussions. You want people to agree or disagree freely.

But it's not appropriate to pass judgment when we specifically ask people to voice their opinions about us. In those moments when other people have passed judgment on advice they have solicited from me, my first thought is, "Who died and made you the Critic in Chief?"

This is true even if you ask a question and agree with the answer. Consciously or not, the other person will register your agreement. And he or she will remember it with great specificity when you *don't* agree the next time. The contrast is telling. The person thinks, "What was wrong with what I said? Why did I bother?"

It's no different than a CEO in a meeting asking for suggestions about a problem and telling one subordinate, "That's a great idea." Then telling another subordinate, "That's a good idea." And saying nothing at all to a third subordinate's suggestion. The first individual is probably pleased and encouraged to have the CEO's approval. The second individual is slightly less pleased. The third individual is neither encouraged nor pleased. But you can be sure of two things. First, everyone in the room has made a note of the CEO's rankings. Second, no matter how well-intentioned the CEO's comments are, the net result is that grading people's answers—rather than just accepting them without comment—makes people hesitant and defensive.

People don't like to be critiqued, however obliquely. That's why passing judgment is one of the more insidious ways we push people away and hold ourselves back from greater success. The only sure thing that comes out of passing judgment on people's efforts to help is that they won't help us again.

How do we stop passing judgment, especially when people are honestly trying to help us?

One of the awkward situations in my line of work is clients being concerned about whether I approve or disapprove of their behavior—and by extension how I feel about the change they're trying to make.

I try to disabuse them of this thinking immediately.

I tell them that in any campaign for effecting long-term

positive change, we have a choice. We can view the campaign in an approving light, a disapproving light, or with complete neutrality. Mission Positive. Mission Negative. Or Mission Neutral.

I assure them that I am mission neutral. I don't deal in approval or disapproval. I don't judge. It's not my job to weigh in on whether you're a good person or bad because you've decided to change A rather than B.

It's the same as a medical doctor dealing with patients. If you walk into the examining room with a broken leg, the doctor doesn't pass judgment on how you broke your leg. He doesn't care if you broke your leg committing a crime or kicking the dog or tripping down the stairs or getting hit by a car. He only cares about fixing your leg.

You need to extend that same attitude—the doctor's mission-neutral purpose—to dealing with people trying to help you. And here I am not referring only to the people who are trying to help you change. You are not allowed to judge any helpful comment offered by a colleague or friend or family member. No matter what you privately think of the suggestion, you must keep your thoughts to yourself, hear the person out, and say, "Thank you."

Try this: For one week treat every idea that comes your way from another person with complete neutrality. Think of yourself as a human Switzerland. Don't take sides. Don't express an opinion. Don't judge the comment. If you find yourself constitutionally incapable of just saying "Thank you," make it an innocuous, "Thanks, I hadn't considered that." Or, "Thanks. You've given me something to think about."

After one week, I guarantee you will have significantly reduced the number of pointless arguments you engage in at work or at home. If you continue this for several weeks, at least three good things will happen.

First, you won't have to think about this sort of neutral response; it will become automatic—as easy as saying, "God bless you" when someone sneezes.

Second, you will have dramatically reduced the hours you devote to contentious interfacing. When you don't judge an idea, no one can argue with you.

Third, people will gradually begin to see you as a much more agreeable person, even when you are not in fact agreeing with them. Do this consistently and people will eventually brand you as a welcoming person, someone whose door they can knock on when they have an idea, someone with whom they can spitball casual ideas and not end up spitting at each other.

If you can't self-monitor your judgmental responses, "hire" a friend to call you out and bill you hard cash every time you make a judgmental comment. It could be your spouse at home, your assistant, or a buddy at work. If you're docked $10 for each incident of gratuitous judgment, you'll soon feel the same pain you've been inflicting on others—and stop.

Habit #4 Making destructive comments

Destructive comments are the cutting sarcastic remarks we spew out daily, with or without intention, that serve no other purpose than to put people down, hurt them, or assert ourselves as their superiors. They are different from comments that add too much value—because they add nothing but pain.

They run the gamut from a thoughtless jab in a meeting ("That wasn't very bright") to gratuitous comments about how someone looks ("Nice tie"—with a smirk) to elaborately planned critiques of people's past performances that everyone but you has forgotten. ("Do you remember the time you . . .")

Press people to list the destructive comments they have made in the last 24 hours and they will quite often come up blank. We make destructive comments without thinking—and therefore without noticing or remembering. But the objects of our scorn remember. Press them and they will accurately replay every biting comment we've made at their expense. That's a statistical fact. The feedback I've collected says that "avoids destructive comments" is one of the two items with the lowest correlation between how we see ourselves and how others see us. In other words, we don't think we make destructive comments, but the people who know us disagree.

One of my clients told me that for his fortieth birthday, his colleagues and friends held a "roast" where the evening's theme required everyone to recite one biting remark that he had made over the years at their expense. An interesting gambit: They were making fun of the birthday boy by revisiting the times he had made fun of them. It was a raucous, hilarious evening.

"Here's the thing," said my client. "Of the dozens of nasty funny comments I heard that night, I didn't remember saying one of them. That's how thoughtless they were. Also, my friends didn't hate me for it. They may be called 'destructive' comments but in my group they didn't do any destruction. People considered it a part of who I am, and it wasn't a problem."

He was right; it wasn't. That's the other interesting thing about destructive comments. We think it's common but statistically it's only a problem in 15 percent of my clients. That doesn't mean the other 85 percent of the world is not guilty of making destructive comments. We all make them every day. It indicates that only 15 percent of us do it to the point where it *is* a problem with our colleagues.

What you need to find out is whether that 15 percent includes you.

That's when the real problem begins—because once the

comment leaves your lips, the damage is done and it's very hard to undo. You can't take it back. No matter how fervently you apologize—and even if the apology is accepted—the comment lingers in the memory.

One of my clients was having a casual downtime conversation with his assistant about eye color (of all things!).

"What color are your eyes?" he asked, squinting to peer at her eyes.

"They're blue. Can't you see that they're blue?" she said.

"Well, they're not really blue," he said.

"Yes they are," she insisted. "They're a sparkling blue."

"Let's put it this way," he snorted. "If your eyes were diamonds, they'd be selling at Zales, not Harry Winston."

She was visibly crushed by this cruel, gratuitous jab.

The aftermath of this episode is instructive. Within moments of uttering these words, my client erased them from his memory. But his assistant didn't. Even though the comment came at her expense, she replayed the exchange to all her friends—as proof that her boss was a jerk. She replayed it to me when I interviewed her for feedback about her boss. She was making the point that, although she loved working for her boss, he habitually made destructive comments, which she didn't love.

How do we stop making destructive comments? That was my problem several years ago. I was running a small consultancy with a dozen employees. As a feedback professional, I naturally experimented on myself. I had my staff do a full 360 degree evaluation of my behavior. The feedback said I was in the 8th percentile on "avoids destructive comments"—meaning that 92 percent of the people in the world are better at it than I was. I had failed a test that I wrote!

My specific challenge (and I'm not proud of this) was *not* that I made nasty comments to people directly. I would do it when they weren't in the room. This was a problem for me as a manager. In an environment where everyone's preaching the value of teamwork and reaching out in the organization, what happens to the quality of teamwork and cooperation when we stab our coworkers in the back in front of other people? It does not go up. And I wanted the business to succeed.

So I talked to my staff. I said, "I feel good about much of my feedback. Here's one thing I want to do better: Quit making destructive comments. If you ever hear me make another destructive comment about another person, I'll pay you $10 each time you bring it to my attention. I'm going to break this habit."

Then I launched into an emotional pep talk, encouraging them to be honest and diligent about "helping" me. Turns out it wasn't necessary. In fact, they would trick me into making nasty comments because they wanted the $10. They'd mention names of people guaranteed to bring up some bile—and I took the bait each time. They mentioned a colleague named Max and I said, "Can you believe he has a Ph.D? He has no idea what he's talking about." Ten bucks. A customer called and I remarked, "He's too cheap to pay." Ten bucks. By noon, I was down $50. I locked myself in my office and refused to speak to anyone for the rest of the day. Of course, hiding helps you avoid the issue; it doesn't help you fix it. But the financial pain got me thinking in the right direction. The next day my nasty comments cost me $30. The third day, $10. This policy was in force in our office for several weeks. And it cost me money. But eventually I brought my score up to the 96th percentile. I don't make destructive comments anymore—at least not so it's a problem.

My experience proves a simple point: Spend a few thousand dollars and you will get better!

Destructive comments are an easy habit to fall into, especially among people who habitually rely on candor as an effective management tool. Trouble is, candor can easily become a weapon. People permit themselves to issue destructive comments under the excuse that they are true. The fact that a destructive comment is true is irrelevant. The question is not, "Is it true?" but rather, "Is it worth it?"

What you need to see is that we all spend a great deal of time filtering our truth-telling during the course of each day. I'm not only referring to the little white lies (e.g., complimenting someone's haircut rather than saying it looks ridiculous) that we employ to smooth out each day's routine social exchanges. We instinctively avoid destructive comments when it's a survival issue. We know the difference between honesty and full disclosure. We may think our boss is a complete ass, but we are under no moral or ethical obligation to express that—to the boss's face or to anyone else for that matter.

You need to extend this survival instinct not only up the organization but across and down as well.

Warren Buffett advised that before you take any morally questionable action, you should ask yourself if you would want your mother to read about it in the newspaper.

You can apply a similar test to help you avoid destructive comments. Before speaking, ask yourself:

1. Will this comment help our customers?
2. Will this comment help our company?
3. Will this comment help the person I'm talking to?
4. Will this comment help the person I'm talking about?

If the answer is no, the correct strategy does not require a Ph.D. to implement. Don't say it.

Habit #5 Starting with "No," "But," or "However"

A few years ago the CEO of a manufacturing company hired me to coach his COO. The COO was talented, but stubborn and opinionated.

The first time I met with the COO to go through his direct reports' feedback, his reaction was, "But Marshall, I don't do that."

"That one is free," I said. "Next time I hear 'no,' 'but,' or 'however' it's going to cost you $20."

"But," he replied, "that's not . . ."

"That's $20!"

"No, I don't . . ." he refuted.

"That's $40!"

"No, no, no," he protested.

"That's 60, 80, 100 dollars," I said.

Within an hour, he was down $420. It took another two hours before he finally understood and said, "Thank you."

A year later I knew the COO was getting better when a woman at the company gave a presentation to top management about how few women were in the company's upper ranks (always an explosive issue that makes men jumpy and defensive). After listening to her fundamental argument, the CEO said, "You're making some very interesting points, but . . ."

The COO stood up and cut his boss off. "Excuse me. I think the correct response is, 'Thank you.'"

The CEO glared at him, then smiled and said, "You're right. Thank you." He turned back to the woman and asked her to continue.

When you start a sentence with "no," "but," "however," or any variation thereof, no matter how friendly your tone or how many cute mollifying phrases you throw in to acknowledge the other person's feelings, the message to the other person is *You are wrong.* It's not, "I have a different opinion." It's not, "Perhaps you are misinformed." It's not, "I disagree with you." It's bluntly and unequivocally, "What you're saying is wrong, and what I'm saying is right." Nothing productive can happen after that. The general response from the other person (unless he or she is a saint willing to turn the other cheek) is to dispute your position and fight back. From there, the conversation dissolves into a pointless war. You're no longer communicating. You're both trying to win.

There aren't too many cheap, surefire, simple, guaranteed 100 percent accurate peeks into the competitive makeup of our colleagues and friends. But the following drill fits the bill. For one week monitor your coworkers' use of "no," "but," and "however": Keep a scorecard of how many times each individual uses these three words to start a sentence.

At the very least, you'll be shocked at how commonly used these words are.

If you drill a little deeper, patterns will emerge. You'll see how people inflict these words on others to gain or consolidate power. You'll also see how intensely people resent it, consciously or not, and how it stifles rather than opens up discussion.

I monitor my clients' use of "no," "but," and "however" instinctively now, the same way an orchestra conductor hears musicians playing sharp or flat. Without even thinking, I keep count of their usage. It's such an important indicator that I do it on autopilot. If the numbers pile up in an initial meeting with a client, I'll often interrupt him or her to say, "We've been talking for 40 minutes. Do you realize in that time you have started 17 responses with either no, but, or however?"

The client is *never* aware of it. That's the moment a serious talk about changing behavior begins.

If this is your interpersonal challenge, you can do this for yourself just as easily as I do it for my clients.

Stop trying to defend your position and start monitoring how many times you begin remarks with "no," "but," or "however." Pay extra-close attention to those moments when you use these words in sentences whose ostensible purpose is *agreement* with what the other party is saying. For example, "That's true, however . . ." (Meaning: You don't think it's true at all.) Or the particularly common opener, "Yes, but . . ." (Meaning: Prepare to be contradicted.)

As in almost any one of these exercises to stop annoying behavior, in addition to self-monitoring, it's easy to monetize the solution. Do what I did with the manufacturing COO. Ask a friend or colleague to charge you money every time you say "no," "but," or "however."

Once you appreciate how guilty you have been, maybe then you'll begin to change your "winning" ways. (Irony intended.)

That said, it's still a challenge.

A few years ago I taught a class at a telecom headquarters. One of the men in my class mocked me when I mentioned this problem we have with "no," "but," and "however." He thought it was easy not to use the words. He was so sure of himself that he offered $100 for each time he used them. I made a point of sitting with him during the lunch break. I asked him where he was from, and he replied Singapore.

"Singapore?" I said. "That's a great city."

"Yeah," he replied, "it's great but . . ."

He caught himself and reached into his pocket for cash, saying, "I just lost $100, didn't I?"

That's how pervasive the urge to be right can be. "No," "but," and "however" creep into our conversations even when the discussion is trivial, even when we should be hyperaware of our word choices, even when it costs us $100.

Habit #6 Telling the world how smart we are

This is another variation on our need to win. We need to win people's admiration. We need to let them know that we are at least their intellectual equal if not their superior. We need to be the smartest person in the room. It usually backfires.

Many of us do this covertly and unwittingly all day long.

We do it whenever we agree with someone offering us some practical advice, whenever we nod our heads impatiently while people are talking, whenever our body language suggests that we are not hearing something we haven't heard before. (Are those your drumming fingers I hear?)

We do this more overtly when we tell someone, "I already knew that."

(Alternative phrasings run the gamut from the gently chiding, "I think someone told me that," to the sarcastic, "I didn't need to hear that," to the downright arrogant, "I'm five steps ahead of you.") The problem here is not that we're merely boasting about how much we know. We're insulting the other person.

What we are really saying is, "You really didn't need to waste my time with that information. You think it's an insight that I haven't heard before. But I agree with you and totally understand what you are saying. You mistake me, the ever so wise and lovely me, for someone who needs to hear what you are saying right now. I am not that person. You are confused. You have no idea how smart I am."

Imagine if someone actually said all that to your face. You'd think they were a jackass. But that's what people hear (and think) when you say, "I already knew that." You're better off hearing them out and saying nothing at all.

The paradox is that this need to demonstrate how smart we are rarely hits its intended target.

A friend was interviewing for a research assistant's job with a psychology professor. The professor was writing a book on genius and creativity. During the course of the interview, the subject turned to great geniuses—specifically Mozart. The professor boasted that he had read everything he could find about Mozart. This is typical of academics; they are exceedingly proud of their intellects and never pass up a chance to tell the world how smart they are. But this professor went a step further. To prove his depth of knowledge he challenged my friend to ask him any question about Mozart.

My friend demurred, a little surprised at the strange turn the job interview had taken. But at the same time, his brain was working overtime. Classical music and opera, as luck would have it, were his great passion. He, in fact, knew more than most people about Mozart.

"Go ahead," said the professor, "don't be shy. I can handle it."

My friend begged off again, although by now he was running potential questions through his mind. Where was Mozart born? When did he die? What was his sister's name? (All too easy.)

"Indulge me," the professor insisted. "Unless of course you don't know enough to ask a question."

That rhetorical slap in the face clinched it for my friend.

"Okay," he said, "name thirteen Mozart operas."

To a self-proclaimed Mozart fanatic, identifying thirteen operas (Mozart composed at least 20 of them) should have been a snap—like asking a presidential historian to name all the vice presidents. Alas, the professor could only name nine.

An awkward moment in the interview, thought my friend, feeling both sheepish and triumphant. There *was* a smart person in the room, but he wasn't the one boasting about it.

To the professor's credit, he didn't hold it against my friend. He offered him the job on the spot.

To my friend's credit, he declined.

Being smart turns people on. Announcing how smart you are turns them off.

So, how do you tone down the need to tell the world how smart you are?

The first step is recognizing our behavior. Have you ever done this? Your assistant dashes into your office with a document that needs your immediate attention. What your assistant doesn't know is that you've already been alerted to the situation a few minutes earlier by another colleague. What do you do? Do you accept the document and thank your assistant, omitting the fact that you already are up to speed on the matter? Or do you find some way to make your assistant aware that you are privy to the information?

In my experience, this seemingly insignificant moment is a litmus test for our excessive need to tell people how smart we are.

If you can let the moment pass with a simple "Thank you," you're doing fine.

If you're like most people, though, you won't let it go so easily. You'll find a way to communicate that you are a step ahead of your assistant. The manner in which you do this may vary from a simple, "I already knew that," to a dismissive, "Why are you bothering me with this?" But either way, the damage is done.

The implication is that your assistant has just wasted your time, that your assistant has confused you with someone who is *not up to speed* on all things vital and urgent, that your assistant has no clue how smart you really are.

Stopping this behavior is not hard—a three-step drill in which you (a) pause before opening your mouth to ask yourself, "Is anything I say worth it?" (b) conclude that it isn't, and (c) say, "Thank you."

If you can stop yourself in this minor moment with some-one who works closely with you and presumably knows you well—in other words, when nothing is at stake and you don't have to flex your muscles—you have the skill to stop telling the world how smart you are. After all, if you can resist the urge in a really comfortable moment when you are in a dominant posi-tion, you will certainly hesitate in other situations when you are not so dominant and comfortable. Think about it. If your CEO walked into your office brandishing the same document, would you tell him or her in the same contemptuous tone that you "already knew that"?

Habit #7 Speaking when angry

Anger has its value as a management tool, I guess. It wakes up sleepy employees. It raises everyone's metabolism. It delivers the clear message that you give a damn—which employees need to hear on occasion. But at what price?

Emotional volatility is not the most reliable leadership tool. When you get angry, you are usually out of control. It's hard to lead people when you've lost control. You may think you have a handle on your temper, that you can use your spontaneous rages to manipulate and motivate people. But it's very hard to predict how people will react to anger. They will shut down as often as they will perk up.

Whenever I hear managers justify anger as a management tool, I wonder about all those other leaders who do not need anger to make their subordinates toe the line. Without anger to strike fear in the troops, how do these steady composed leaders ever get anything accomplished?

But the worst thing about anger is how it stifles our ability to change. Once you get a reputation for emotional volatility, you are branded for life. Pretty soon that is all people know about you. For example, basketball coach Bob Knight won three NCAA titles at Indiana University and is only one of two coaches in college history with 800 or more victories. By any measure, he's one of the greatest coaches of all time. But he also has a well-documented history of arguing with referees and tossing chairs across the court. That reputation overwhelms Knight's record. When people think of Bob Knight, their first thought is his volcanic temper, not his won-lost record.

It's the same in the workplace. We save a special place in our minds for our chronically angry colleagues. No matter what else they do, we brand them as easily combustible. When we talk about them, the first words out of people's mouths are, "I hear he has a temper."

That hothead image is tough to live down. Given the fact that our efforts to change are judged not by us but by the people around us, you may need years of calm, collected behavior to shake such a reputation.

How do you stop getting angry?

I don't have a definitive answer. Anger management is not the subject of this book, and even if it were, I doubt if I could shut down your rages at life's injustices and follies. But I can make you appreciate that (a) you're probably not angry at the proverbial "other guy" and (b) there's a simple way to lose your reputation for getting angry.

On the first point, when I have to deal with anger in my line of work, it's invariably one-on-one rage—the anger that one human being induces in another. It's my job to show clients that anger is rarely someone else's fault. It's a flaw that's solely our own.

A Buddhist legend tells of a young farmer who was covered with sweat as he paddled his boat up the river. He was going upstream to deliver his produce to the village. He was in a hurry. It was a hot day and he wanted to make his delivery and get home before dark. As he looked ahead, he spied another vessel, heading rapidly downstream toward his boat. This vessel seemed to be making every effort to hit him. He rowed furiously to get out of the way, but it didn't seem to help.

He yelled at the other vessel, "Change direction, you idiot! You are going to hit me. The river is wide. Be careful!" His screaming was to no avail. The other vessel hit his boat with a sickening thud. He was enraged as he stood up and cried out to the other vessel, "You moron! How could you manage to hit my boat in the middle of this wide river? What is wrong with you?"

As he looked at the other vessel, he realized that there was no one in the other boat. He was screaming at an empty vessel that had broken free of its moorings and was going downstream with the current.

The lesson is simple. *There is never anyone in the other boat.* When we are angry, we are screaming at an empty vessel.

All of us have people in our lives who drive us crazy, whom we hate with a passion. We may have spent countless hours reliving the moments when this person was unfair, unappreciative, or inconsiderate to us. Even remembering this person bumps up our blood pressure.

It's obvious that the best course of action for dealing with people like this is to not let them make us angry. Getting angry doesn't improve the situation and life's too short to waste on feeling bad. A sage would say that the person making us so angry cannot help who he is. Getting mad at him for being who he is makes as much sense as getting mad at our desk for being a desk. If we had his parents, his genes, and his background, we would be him. That's easier said than done, but it comes closer to the real issue: More often than not, we might as well be him because we are really angry at ourselves.

As to the second point, I can help you lose your reputation

as a person who gets angry with one simple piece of advice. It is this: *If you keep your mouth shut, no one can ever know how you really feel.*

That's asking a lot, I know. You have to suppress your natural inclination and bite your tongue. But once you appreciate the payoff of saying nothing—that if you're silent, you cannot make an ass out of yourself or make an enemy out of someone else—then you might have a chance of getting better.

I learned this after spending a week at a retreat at a small monastery in Plum Village, France, a few years ago. Our guide was the Vietnamese Buddhist monk, Thich Nhat Hanh. Each day Thich Nhat Hanh encouraged us to meditate on a variety of topics. One day the topic was anger. He asked us to think of a time in our lives when we had become angry and lost control. Then he asked us to analyze who was responsible for our unattractive behavior.

I thought of my daughter Kelly when she was in her teens. She came home wearing a large brightly colored article of jewelry called a navel ring. These are common among the younger set, along with tattoos in hard-to-reach places of the human anatomy. There is no use having a navel ring if people can't see it! So Kelly had also acquired a heroically skimpy outfit designed to highlight the navel ring (and nearly everything else about her abdomen).

A navel ring on a daughter is one of those moments that truly tests a father's tolerance and love. But for me it was a little more complicated, I guess. I reacted with something less than enthusiasm. In fact, I devolved into a raving, ranting caricature of an angry father.

As I meditated on this event in the quiet confines of the monastery, I wondered, "What was I thinking about?" I realized that my first thought was that someone would see my daughter and think, "What a cheap-looking, trashy kid! Who are her parents?"

My second thought was worse. What if one of my friends saw her and thought, "I can't believe Marshall allows his kid to parade around town like that."

Who was I concerned about in this case? Kelly or me? Was the bigger problem her navel ring or my ego?

If I had to do it over again, I would still suggest she lose the navel ring. (One week of enlightenment in France is good, but not *that* good!) However, I would stop reacting with anger and making a fool out of myself. I may be raging like a lunatic inside. But if I stop speaking when angry, no one has to know about it.

The next time you start to speak out of anger, look in the mirror. In every case, you'll find that the root of your rage is not "out there" but "in here."

Habit #8 Negativity, or "Let me explain why that won't work."

We all know negative people—or what my wife calls "nega-trons"—in the workplace. They're the people who are constitutionally incapable of saying something positive or complimentary to any of your suggestions. Negativity is their default response. You could walk into their office with the cure for cancer and the first words out of their mouth would be, "Let me explain why that won't work."

That, in my experience, is the telltale phrase of negativity. I cite it as a major annoyance because it's emblematic of our need to share our negative thoughts even when they haven't been solicited.

"Let me explain why that won't work" is not quite the same as adding too much value—because no value is being added.

It's not like overusing "no," "but," and "however," because we're not hiding our negativity under the mask of agreement.

Nor is it the same as passing judgment on someone else's ideas—because we're not rating or comparing anything. We're not saying it's good, better, or best.

It's clearly not the same as making destructive comments—because it's not overtly nasty.

"Let me explain why that won't work" is unique because it is pure unadulterated negativity under the guise of being helpful.

We employ it (or its variations such as "The only problem with that is . . .") to establish that our expertise or authority is superior to someone else's. It doesn't mean that what we say is correct or useful. It's simply a way of inserting ourselves into a situation as chief arbiter or senior critic. The only problem with that (to coin a phrase) is how little we like or respect our critics. They're annoying. And over time, we treat them as if they're carrying avian flu. We avoid them. We stop working with them. We refuse to help them.

I used to know a woman named Terri who ran a lecture bureau in New York City. Two or three times a year she would book me to speak to a corporate group. I'd talk about leadership and helping people change. At the end of each speech, invariably one or two people in the audience would come up to me, hand me their cards, and invite me to speak to their group in the near future. Apparently, I was delivering a message that they thought other people would want to hear.

I could have handled the details of the speaking appearance myself, I suppose, but because the invitation occurred on a date that Terri had set up for me, I felt obliged to turn it over to her. I thought it was only right that she negotiate for me and earn her commission. I'd call her up immediately after the appearance.

She'd ask how the event turned out. Was the host pleased? That sort of thing.

I'd say, "Great. In fact, a couple of people want me to speak to their groups."

Then I'd read the contact information off their business cards so she could follow up with them.

Without fail, Terri's first response was always some variation on "Let me explain why that won't work."

The company had a history of paying low fees, so they couldn't afford me. (Message: I was too expensive.)

The company's employees were yokels who didn't need to hear my message or were too ignorant to "get it." (Message: I was too sophisticated.)

The company would abuse my time; they'd want me to stay all day, including dinner, costing me an extra travel day. (Message: I'd be overworked.)

When Terri responded this way, I'd hold the receiver out and stare at it, dumbfounded. Here I was throwing easy money at her, and she was coming up with bogus reasons to shoot me down. Perhaps she thought she was protecting me from a potentially "bad deal." But in trying to prove to me that she knew more about her business than I did, she only proved that she didn't understand me at all. I don't overcharge clients. My message is simple, not complicated. And I'm not afraid of work; if clients want me to stick around all day, I take it as a compliment, not an abuse of my time.

It made me wonder if I really wanted Terri "presenting" me to the world.

Eventually I realized that I could have been forwarding Terri an invitation for me to host the Academy Awards and she would have found a way to put a negative spin on the opportunity. I stopped working with her.

If negativity is your flaw, my first impulse would be to have you monitor your statements the moment someone offers you a helpful suggestion. If you've read this far, you know that I firmly believe that paying attention to *what we say* is a great indicator of what we're doing to turn people off. If you catch yourself frequently saying, "Let me tell you why that won't work," you know what needs fixing.

But in this case, the more revealing clue would be to take a personal inventory of how your colleagues deal with you.

How often do they come to you with helpful suggestions—without you having to ask?

How often do they knock on your door and sit down to shoot the breeze or give you a heads-up about a development that may affect you?

How does the floor traffic around your desk compare with other colleagues? Are you a popular item, or are you beginning to gather dust on the shelf? If you get even the vaguest sense that there is an imaginary "Do Not Enter" sign outside your office, you've just become a little smarter about what you must change.

When the issue is negativity, I prefer this form of observational feedback to mere monitoring of speech patterns. Checking what you say doesn't automatically tell you what other people think of you. You may be overly negative, but your colleagues may be capable of living with it. But seeing how people relate to you provides proof that *your flaw is serious,* that it matters to people, that it's a problem.

Habit #9 Withholding information

In the age of knowledge workers, the cliché that information is power is truer than ever—which makes withholding information even more extreme and irritating.

Intentionally withholding information is the opposite of adding value. We are deleting value. Yet it has the same purpose:

To gain power. It's the same old need to win, only more devious. And it appears in more forms than merely playing our cards close to our vest. You see it in people who exaggerate the virtue of keeping a secret; they use it as an excuse to leave you out of the information flow. You see it in people who answer every question with a question; they believe revealing *anything* puts them at a disadvantage. You see it in its passive-aggressive incarnation in people who don't return your phone calls or answer your e-mails or only give partial answers to your queries.

If you don't understand why it annoys people, reflect on how you felt about the following events:

- A meeting you weren't told about
- A memo or e-mail you weren't copied on
- A moment when you were the last person to learn something

The problem with not sharing information—for whatever reason—is that it rarely achieves the desired effect. You may think you're gaining an edge and consolidating power, but you're actually breeding mistrust. In order to have power, you need to inspire loyalty rather than fear and suspicion. Withholding information is nothing more than a misplaced need to win.

What I'm describing here is not just the willful poison-sowing refusal to share information, the way people behave when they want to divide and conquer. I'm not sure I have the skill or patience to alter that Machiavellian behavior.

What I'd prefer to focus on are all the unintentional or accidental ways we withhold information.

We do this when we're too busy to get back to someone with valuable information.

We do this when we forget to include someone in our discussions or meetings.

We do this when we delegate a task to our subordinates but don't take the time to show them exactly how we want the task done.

One of my neighbors asked his teenaged son to wash his Lexus SUV. The son pulled out the water hose, filled a bucket with soapy water, and went to work with a sponge. Problem was, the sponge was one of those two-sided designs, one side scratchy, the other soft. By the time the father came out to inspect the results, the son had scrubbed away a good deal of the Lexus's shiny enamel finish. The Lexus's once-gleaming surface looked like an ice skating rink after a hockey game. The father was enraged. His Lexus was ruined. How could his son be so stupid?

"Don't you know how to do something as simple as washing a car?" he asked between snorts of rage.

But as my neighbor thought about it (and as he saw that his son was embarrassed and upset), he said something wise. "Son, I'm not mad at you. I'm mad at myself—because I should have told you how to do this job properly. I never taught you how to wash a car, and that's my fault."

Whatever tension hovered over that scene in the family driveway at that moment instantly disappeared when my neighbor realized that he had left some vital information out of his son's basic education. The son felt relieved. The father was no longer upset, either at his son or at the sorry condition of his Lexus. It's now a running family joke whenever someone sees a sponge.

More often than not, we don't withhold information out of malice. We do it because we're clueless. That's a good thing. Willful maliciousness is not a "flaw" that we can fix here. But cluelessness is easy to change.

I was advising a friend who was having trouble with his assistant. They weren't meshing as a team, he told me. But he didn't know why or how to fix the problem. All he had to go on was a vague feeling that "our timing is off."

Before I talked to his assistant, I asked him, "What would your assistant say is your biggest flaw as a boss?"

"That I don't communicate enough with her," he answered. "I don't share information. I leave her out of the loop."

"Anything else?" I inquired.

"No, that's it," he said. "Isn't that enough?"

"Do you think she's right?" I asked.

"Yes."

Interesting, I thought. You don't hear too many bosses taking all the blame for some interpersonal dysfunction.

Then I asked his assistant why they didn't mesh. She agreed. Her boss didn't share information well.

Because he was a friend, and I was helping him pro bono, I did something I don't normally do. I pretended to be a consumer researcher who tracks how people use a company's product all day. In this case, I tagged along with him from the moment he walked into work and observed his behavior with his assistant until he left work.

What I saw explained everything. He arrived at the office about fifteen minutes before his assistant. The first thing he did was check his e-mails. Then his cell phone rang and he answered it. During this conversation, his assistant arrived at her desk. She poked her head in to say good morning. He waved while still talking. When he ended the call, he turned to his computer screen and jotted down some notes and answered a few e-mails. His assistant popped in to say that one of his accounts was on the line. Did he want to take that call? He did. Three other calls came in during this twenty-minute conversation. When he hung up, he returned those calls—all the while scanning his computer for incoming e-mails. This pattern continued all morning.

By noon I had seen enough.

"Is this what it's like around here every day?" I asked.

"Pretty much," he said.

My friend, indeed, was guilty of keeping his assistant in the dark. But he wasn't doing so maliciously or, for that matter, intentionally. His work life was like a haphazard fire drill. He was so distracted, so disorganized, so busy responding to calls and putting out fires that he never had time to sit down with his assistant for a daily debriefing.

If he had, I suspect it would have solved their information sharing issue.

I also suspect that's a big reason why so many of us withhold information. It's not that we want to keep people in the dark. It's simply that we're too busy. We mean well. We have good intentions. But we fail to get around to it. As a result we become bad at sharing information—whether it comes in the form of a news bulletin, or a heads-up, or instruction that teaches people how to do something that we don't have time to do ourselves. Over time it begins to look as if we are *withholding* information.

Being bad at sharing information doesn't mean we are willfully withholding it. The two are not exactly the same thing. But the net result is the same in the eyes of the people around us.

How do you stop withholding information?

Simple answer: Start sharing it.

That's what my friend did. He made sharing information a higher priority in his busy day. He scheduled time to debrief his assistant on what he was up to. And he made that time inviolate. It couldn't be cancelled or postponed or interrupted by a phone call.

If this is your issue, I advise the same solution. In doing so, you will not only improve your communication, but you'll be proving that you care about your coworkers—demonstrating that what they think matters to you. It's not often that we get such an obvious two-for-the-price-of-one solution to our interpersonal challenges. But making the subtle shift from withholding to sharing information is one of them.

Habit #10 Failing to give proper recognition

This is a sibling of withholding information. In withholding your recognition of another person's contribution to a team's success, you are not only sowing injustice and treating people unfairly but you are depriving people of the emotional payoff that comes with success. They cannot revel in the success or accept congratulations—because you have choked off that option. Instead they feel forgotten, ignored, pushed to the side. And they resent you for it. If you really want to tick people off, don't recognize their contributions.

In depriving people of recognition, you are depriving them of closure. And we all need closure in any interpersonal transaction. Closure comes in many forms—from the emotional complexity of paying our last respects to loved ones before they die to something as pro forma as saying, "You're welcome" when someone else says, "Thank you." Either way, we expect closure.

Recognition is all about closure. It's the beautiful ribbon wrapped around the jewel box that contains the precious gift of success you and your team have created. When you fail to provide that recognition, you are cheapening the gift. You have the success but none of the afterglow.

This happens at work and at home.

In training programs, when I ask participants, "How many of you think you need to do a better job of recognizing others for their great work?" without fail eight out of ten people raise their hands.

When I ask them why they fail at recognition, the answers say more about the people responding than the people who aren't being recognized. "*I* just got too busy." "*I* just expected everyone to do great work." "*I* never realized how important it was to them." "*I* was never recognized for my great work—why should they be?"

Note the aggressive use of the first person singular pronoun. It's a hallmark of successful people; they become great *achievers* because of their intense focus on themselves. *Their* career, *their* performance, *their* progress, *their* needs. But there's a difference between being an achiever and a leader. Successful people become great *leaders* when they learn to shift the focus from themselves to others.

One of my clients taught me a wonderful technique for improving in the area of providing recognition.

1. He first made a list of all of the important groups of people in his life (friends, family, direct reports, customers, etc.).
2. He then wrote down the names of every important person in each group.
3. Twice a week, on Wednesday morning and Friday afternoon, he would review the list of names and ask himself, "Did someone on this page do something that I should recognize?"
4. If the answer was "yes" he gave them some very quick recognition, either by phone, e-mail, voice mail, or a note. If the answer was "no" he did nothing. He didn't want to be a phony.

Within one year this executive's reputation for providing positive recognition improved from poor to excellent. He was amazed at how little time this took.

Of all the interpersonal slights we make in our professional or private lives, not providing recognition may be the one that endures most deeply in the minds of the slighted. Except for . . .

Habit #11 Claiming credit that we don't deserve

Claiming credit is adding insult to the injury that comes with overlooked recognition. We're not only depriving people of the credit they deserve, but we are hogging it for ourselves. It's two crimes in one.

Imagine those moments in your life—whether as a school-kid or an adult in the workplace—when you did something wonderful and waited for the praise and congratulations. And waited. And waited. It happens all the time. The world isn't always paying attention when we excel. People have their own agendas to pursue. If it happens when we're kids, we sulk and whimper about being overlooked. "It's not fair!" we whine. But as we mature, we learn to handle the neglect. "It's the way of the world," we tell ourselves. It doesn't alter the fact that we did something special—even if we're the only ones to know it. We move on to something else.

But even the most highly evolved human being would have a tough time grinning and bearing when neglect turns to larceny. That's what it is when someone claims credit that they do not deserve: theft. It's as if they're stealing our ideas, our performances, our self-esteem, our life. We didn't like it when it happened to us as children (and the stakes generally involved little more than our teachers' approval). But we actively hate it when it happens to us as adults (in part because the stakes in terms of our careers and financial rewards are so much greater). When someone you work with steals the credit for a success that you created, they're committing the most rage-inducing interpersonal "crime" in the workplace. (This is the interpersonal flaw that generates more negative emotion than any other in my feedback interviews.) And it creates a bitterness that's hard to forget. You can forgive someone for not recognizing your stellar performance. You can't forgive that person for recognizing it and brazenly claiming it as his or her own. If it's happened to you, you know how hard it is to shed that bitter taste.

Now turn the tables. Imagine you're the perpetrator rather than the victim.

If you look closely, you'll see that claiming credit that we don't deserve is another sibling of the need to win. You wouldn't claim someone else's résumé or college degree as your own. That's because those achievements are well-documented. Your claim can be challenged. But when it comes to determining exactly who came up with the winning phrase in a meeting or who held together an important client relationship during a rocky phase, the evidence gets fuzzy. It's hard to say who deserves the credit. So, given the choice between grasping the credit for ourselves or leaving it for someone else to claim, we fall into the success traps described in Chapter 3—I can succeed, I will succeed, I have succeeded, I choose to succeed—and give ourselves the benefit of the doubt. We claim more credit than we have earned, and slowly begin to believe it. In the meantime, the victims of our injustice are seething. If you know how you feel as a victim, you should know how people feel about you for doing the same. It's not a pretty picture, is it?

There's no telling what a group can achieve when no one cares who gets the credit. We know this in our bones. We know it because we remember how good we felt about our colleagues when they accorded us the credit we deserved.

So why don't we reciprocate when someone else deserves the credit?

I don't have the answer for that. Even if we can legitimately blame our parents or our upbringing or some petty slight in high school for our credit hogging, that doesn't begin to solve the problem. It's focusing on the past (which we cannot change) rather than arming ourselves with concrete actionable ideas for the future.

The best way to stop being a credit hog is to do the opposite. Share the wealth. Here's a simple drill that will transform you from a credit miser to a credit philanthropist.

For one day (or longer if you can handle it) make a mental note of every time you privately congratulate yourself on an achievement, large or small. Then write it down. If you're like me, you'll find that you pat yourself on the back more often than you think during a normal day—for everything from coming up with a big idea for a client to showing up on time for a meeting to dashing off a clever note to a colleague.

"Hmm," we think as we survey our beautiful handiwork. "We did good."

There's nothing wrong with these private thoughts. This pleasure that we take in our own performance is what keeps us merrily motivated as we chug our way through a long, arduous day. I wouldn't be surprised if one day yielded two dozen episodes of self-congratulation for each of us.

Once you've assembled the list, take apart each episode and ask yourself if it's *in any way possible* that someone else might deserve the credit for "your" achievement.

If you showed up on time for a meeting across town, is it because you are heroically punctual and thoughtful? Or was it because your assistant hounded you that morning about the meeting and actually chased you off a phone call and made sure you were out the door to get across town in sufficient time?

If you came up with a good idea in a meeting, did it spring unbidden from your fertile imagination? Or was it inspired by an insightful comment from someone else in the room?

As you go through your list, consider this make-or-break question: If any of the other people involved in your episodes were looking at the situation, would they accord you as much credit as you are claiming for yourself? Or would they hand it out to someone else, perhaps even themselves?

It's possible as you review your list that you conclude you deserve *all* the credit. But I doubt even the most self-involved among us would see things this myopically. We have a strong bias to remember events in a light most favorable to us. This drill exposes that bias and makes us consider the possibility that someone else's perspective is closer to the truth.

Habit #12 Making excuses

When Bill Clinton published his best-selling memoir in 2004, he knew he would have to deal with the Monica Lewinsky scandal during his second term. He did so by *explaining* it as a personal failure, a yielding to private demons. "Once people reach the age of accountability, no matter what people do to them," he said, "that is not an excuse for any mistakes they make. On the other hand, one does seek to understand why he or she makes the mistakes they make. I was involved in two great struggles at the same time: a great public struggle over the future of America with the Republican Congress and a private struggle with my old demons. I won the public one and lost the private one. I don't think it's much more complicated than that. That's not an excuse. But it is an explanation, and that's the best I can do."

Bill Clinton understood the distinction—and not just

because his behavior was inexcusable. There simply is no excuse for making excuses.

When you hear yourself saying, "I'm sorry I'm late but the traffic was murder," stop talking at the word "sorry." Blaming the traffic is a lame excuse—and doesn't excuse the fact that you kept people waiting. You should have started earlier. What's the worst that could happen? You arrive ahead of schedule and have to wait a few minutes in the lobby? Are you really worried about having to say, "I'm sorry I'm early but I left too soon and the traffic was nowhere near as bad as I anticipated."

If the world worked *that* way, there would be no excuses.

I like to divide excuses into two categories: blunt and subtle.

The blunt "dog ate my homework" excuse sounds like this: "I'm sorry I missed our lunch date. My assistant had it marked down for the wrong day on my calendar."

Message: See, it's not that I forgot the lunch date. It's not that I don't regard you as important, so important that lunch with you is the unchangeable, nonnegotiable highlight of my day. It's simply that my assistant is inept. Blame my assistant, not me.

The problem with this type of excuse is that we rarely get away with it—and it's hardly an effective leadership strategy. After reviewing thousands of 360-degree feedback summaries, I have a feel for what direct reports respect and don't respect in their leaders. I have never seen feedback that said, "I think you are a great leader because I love the quality of your excuses." Or, "I thought you were messing up, but you turned me around when you made those excuses."

The more subtle excuses appear when we attribute our failings to some inherited DNA that is permanently lodged within us. We talk about ourselves as if we have permanent genetic flaws that can never be altered.

You've surely heard these excuses. Maybe you've used them to describe yourself:

"I'm impatient."

"I always put things off to the last minute."

"I've always had a quick temper."

"I am horrendous at time management. I've been told for years by my coworkers and spouse that I waste time on pointless projects and discussions. I guess that's just the way I am."

It's amazing how often I hear otherwise brilliant, successful people make willfully self-deprecating comments about themselves. It's a subtle art because, in effect, they are stereotyping themselves—as impatient, or hot-tempered, or disorganized—and using that stereotype to excuse otherwise inexcusable behavior.

Our personal stereotyping may have its origins in stories that have been repeated for years—often from as far back as childhood. These stories may have no basis in fact. But they imprint themselves in our brains, and establish low expectations that become self-fulfilling prophecies. We behave as if we wanted to prove that our negative expectations were correct.

I'm a good example of this. Growing up in Valley Station, Kentucky, I might naturally have become involved in cars, tools, and mechanical things. My dad owned a two-pump gas station. Many of my friends liked to work on cars and race them on Saturday nights at the drag strip.

As a child, however, I gained a different set of expectations from my mother. Almost from birth, she told me, "Marshall, you are extremely smart. In fact, you are the smartest little boy in Valley Station." She told me that I wasn't just going to go to college—I could go to graduate school!

She also said, "Marshall, you have no mechanical skills, and you will never have any mechanical skills for the rest of your life." (I think this was her way of making sure I wouldn't pump gas and change tires at the service station.)

It's interesting how my mother's imprinting and expectations affected my development. I was never encouraged to work on cars or be around tools. (As a teenager in the 1960s, I thought a universal joint was something that hippies smoked.) Not only did my parents assume that I had no mechanical skills, my friends knew it, too. When I was 18 years old, I took the U.S. Army's Mechanical Aptitude Test and scored in the bottom second percentile of the entire nation. So, it was true.

Six years later, however, I was at UCLA, working on my Ph.D. One of my professors asked me to write down things I did well and things I couldn't do. On the positive side I jotted down "research" and "writing" and "analysis" and "speaking" (which was a not-so-subtle way of writing "I am smart"). On the negative side, I wrote, "I have no mechanical skills. I will never have any mechanical skills."

The professor asked me how I knew I had no mechanical skills. I explained my life history and told him about my dismal showing on the Army test.

"How are your mathematical skills?" he asked.

I proudly replied that I had scored a perfect 800 on the SAT Math 1 achievement test.

He then asked, "Why is it that you can solve complex mathematical problems, but you can't solve simple mechanical problems?"

Then he asked, "How is your eye-hand coordination?"

I said that I was good at pinball and had helped pay my college expenses by shooting pool, so I guessed that it was fine.

He asked, "Why is it that you can shoot pool but you can't hammer nails?"

That's when I realized that I did not suffer from a genetic defect. I was just living out the expectations that I had chosen to believe. At that point, I was old enough to know better. It was no longer just my family and friends reinforcing my belief that

I was mechanically hopeless. And it wasn't the Army test, either. I was the one who kept telling myself, "You can't do this!" I realized that as long as I kept saying that, it was going to be true.

The next time you hear yourself saying, "I'm just no good at . . . ," ask yourself, "Why not?"

This doesn't just refer to our aptitudes at mathematics or mechanics. It also applies to our behavior. We excuse our tardiness because we've been running late all our lives—and our parents and friends let us get away with it. The same with any of the other annoying habits we've been describing. Passing judgment, making destructive comments, refusing to share information? These are not genetic flaws! We weren't born that way, no matter what we've been brought up to believe.

Likewise the next time you hear one of your coworkers try to worm their way out of accepting responsibility by saying, "I'm just no good at . . . ," ask them, "Why not?"

If we can stop excusing ourselves, we can get better at almost anything we choose.

Habit #13 Clinging to the past

There is a school of thought among psychologists and behavioral consultants that we can understand a lot about our errant behavior by delving into our past, particularly our family dynamics. This is the school that believes, "When it's hysterical, it's historical."

If you're a perfectionist or constant-approval seeker, it's because your parents never said you were good enough. If you operate above the rules and feel you can do no wrong, it's because your parents doted on you and inflated your importance. If you freeze around authority figures, it's because you had a controlling mother. And so on.

That school is on permanent recess here.

I don't have much patience with "therapy" that clings to the past—because going backwards is not about creating change. It's about understanding.

One of my earliest clients used to spend hours telling me, "Marshall, you don't understand. Let me explain why I have these issues. Let me explain my mother and father." It was one long unendurable whine. Finally, I reached into my pocket for a coin and said, "Here's a quarter. Call someone who cares."

Don't get me wrong. There's nothing wrong with understanding. Understanding the past is perfectly admissible if your issue is *accepting the past.* But if your issue is *changing the future*, understanding will not take you there. My experience tells me that the only effective approach is looking people in the eye and saying, "If you want to change, do this."

But even with the blunt talk, clients who cling to the past—who want to *understand* why they are the way they are—remain my toughest assignments. It takes me a long time to convince them that they can't do anything about the past. They can't change it, or rewrite it, or make excuses for it. All they can do is accept it and move on.

But for some reason, many people enjoy living in the past, especially if going back there lets them blame someone else for anything that's gone wrong in their lives. That's when clinging to the past becomes an interpersonal problem. We use the past as a weapon against others.

We also cling to the past as a way of contrasting it with the present—usually to highlight something positive about ourselves at the expense of someone else.

Do you ever find yourself beginning a long self-serving story with the phrase, "When I was your age . . ."?

What's really going on here?

When we make excuses, we are blaming someone

or something beyond our control as the reason for our failure. Anyone but ourselves. But sometimes we blame other people not as an excuse for our failure, but as a subtle way of highlighting our successes. It's no more attractive than making excuses, but we usually require a really smart person whom we love to point it out to us.

I learned this from my daughter, Kelly.

She was seven years old. We were living in a nice house in San Diego (still my home). One day, annoyed over a professional setback, I came home and took out my annoyance on Kelly. I trotted out the sorriest, most pathetic speech any parent can give a child, the one that begins, "When I was your age . . ." Inevitably, it's a self-pitying lecture that points out how difficult and miserable the parent's childhood was in comparison with the childhood the parent is now providing for his or her children.

I started yammering about growing up in Kentucky in a gas station and how we didn't have money and how hard I had to work to become the first person from my family to graduate from college. Contrasting this, of course, with all the wonderful things Kelly had.

She patiently listened to my diatribe, instinctively letting me vent. When I was finished, she said, "Daddy, it's not my fault you make money."

That stopped me in my tracks. I realized, "She's right." How could I expect her to know what it's like to be poor— when I was damn sure she never would be? I chose to work hard and make money. She didn't. In effect, I was bragging about how hard I had it and how clever I was to have triumphed over such great adversity—and masking that boasting by dumping my frustrations on her. Fortunately, she called me on it.

Stop blaming others for the choices you made—and that goes with double emphasis for the choices that turned out well.

Habit #14 Playing favorites

I have reviewed custom-designed leadership profiles at more than 100 major corporations. It's my job to rewrite them. These documents typically feature boilerplate language that describes the leadership behavior each company desires. Such chestnuts include "communicates a clear vision," "helps people to develop to their maximum potential," "strives to see the value of differing opinions," and "avoids playing favorites."

Not one profile has ever included the desired behavior that read "effectively sucks up to management." Although given the dedication to fawning and sucking up in most corporations—and how often such behavior is rewarded—it probably should. While almost every company says it wants people to "challenge the system" and to "be empowered to express your opinion" and "say what you really think," there sure are a lot of performers who are stuck on sucking up.

Not only do companies say they abhor such comically servile behavior, but so do individual leaders. Almost all the leaders I have met say that they would never encourage such a thing in their organizations. I have no doubt that they are sincere. Most of us are easily irritated, if not disgusted, by derriere kissers. Which raises a question: If leaders say they discourage sucking up, why does it dominate the workplace? Keep in mind that these leaders are generally very shrewd judges of character. They spend their lives sizing up people, taking in first impressions and recalibrating them against later impressions. And yet, they still fall for the super-skilled suck-up. They still play favorites.

The simple answer is: We can't see in ourselves what we can see so clearly in others.

Perhaps you are thinking now, "It's amazing how leaders send out subtle signals that encourage subordinates to mute their criticisms and exaggerate their praise of the powers that be. And it is surprising how they cannot see it in themselves. Of course, this doesn't apply to me."

Maybe you're right. But how can you be so sure you're not in denial?

I use an irrefutable test with my clients to show how we all unknowingly encourage sucking up. I ask a group of leaders, "How many of you own a dog that you love?" Big smiles cross the executives' faces as they wave their hands in the air. They beam as they tell me the names of their always-faithful hounds. Then we have a contest. I ask them, "At home, who gets most of your unabashed affection? Is it (a) your husband, wife or partner; (b) your kids; or (c) your dog?" More than 80 percent of the time, the winner is the dog.

I then ask the executives if they love their dogs more than their family members. The answer is always a predictable but resounding no. My follow-up: "So why does the dog get most of your attention?"

Their replies all sound the same: "The dog is always happy to see me." "The dog never talks back." "The dog gives me unconditional love, no matter what I do." In other words, the dog is a suck-up.

I can't say that I am any better. I love my dog, Beau. I travel at least 180 days a year, and Beau goes bonkers when I return home from a trip. I pull into the driveway, and my first inclination is to open the front door, go straight to Beau, and exclaim, "Daddy's home!" Invariably, Beau jumps up and down, and I hug him and pat him and make a huge fuss over him. One day my daughter, Kelly, was home from college. She watched my typical love fest with Beau. She then looked at me, held her hands in the air like little paws, and barked, "Woof woof."

Point taken.

If we aren't careful, we can wind up treating people at

work like dogs: Rewarding those who heap unthinking, unconditional admiration upon us. What behavior do we get in return? A virulent case of the suck-ups.

The net result is manifestly obvious. You're encouraging behavior that serves you, but not necessarily the best interests of the company. If everyone is fawning over the boss, who's getting work done? Worse, it tilts the field against the honest, principled employees who won't play along. This is a double hit of bad news. You're not only playing favorites but favoring the wrong people!

Leaders can stop encouraging this behavior by first admitting that we all have a tendency to favor those who favor us, even if we don't mean to.

We should then rank our direct reports in three categories.

First, how much do they like me? (I know you can't be sure. What matters is how much *you think* they like you. Effective suckups are good actors. That's what fawning is: acting.)

Second, what is their contribution to the company and its customers? (In other words, are they A players, B, C, or worse?)

Third, how much positive personal recognition do I give them?

What we're looking for is whether the correlation is stronger between one and three, or two and three. If we're honest with ourselves, our recognition of people may be linked to how much they seem to like us rather than how well they perform. That's the definition of playing favorites.

And the fault is all ours. We're encouraging the kind of behavior that we despise in others. Without meaning to, we are basking in hollow praise, which makes us hollow leaders.

This quick self-analysis won't solve the problem. But it does identify it—which is where change begins.

Habit #15 Refusing to express regret

Expressing regret, or apologizing, is a cleansing ritual, like confession in church. You say, "I'm sorry"—and you feel better.

That's the theory at least. But like many things that are fine in theory, it's hard for many of us to do.

Perhaps we think apologizing means we have lost a contest (and successful people have a practically irrational need to win at everything).

Perhaps we find it painful to admit we were wrong (we rarely have to apologize for being right).

Perhaps we find it humiliating to seek forgiveness (which suggests subservience).

Perhaps we feel that apologizing forces us to cede power or control (actually the opposite is true).

Whatever the reasons, refusing to apologize causes as much ill will in the workplace (and at home) as any other interpersonal flaw. Just think how bitter you have felt when a friend failed to apologize for hurting you or letting you down. And how long that bitterness festered.

If you look back at the tattered relationships in your life, I suspect many of them began to fray at the precise moment when one of you couldn't summon the emotional intelligence to say, "I'm sorry."

People who can't apologize at work may as well be wearing a t-shirt that says, "I don't care about you."

The irony, of course, is that all the fears that lead us to resist apologizing—the fear of losing, admitting we're wrong, ceding control—are actually erased by an apology. When you say, "I'm sorry," you turn people into your allies, even your partners.

I picked up on this paradox when I began studying Buddhism in graduate school. As a Buddhist I believe that we reap what we sow. If you smile at people, they will smile back. If you ignore them, they will resent you. If you put your fate in their hands—i.e., cede power to them—they will reward you.

But I didn't "get it" until I was 28 years old and found myself in New York City, dining alone at Le Perigord, a tony French restaurant on Manhattan's East Side. I had never been to a restaurant like this, where the flower arrangements required separate tables, the cutlery had the heft of an ax, and the waiters were dressed in black tie and sported impenetrable French accents. I confessed to the waiter that I was intimidated by the surroundings, that I only had one hundred dollars, tip included, to spend on the meal, and that I couldn't read the menu, which was hand-written in French.

"Would you please bring me the best one-hundred-dollar meal you have," I asked.

I am convinced that the meal I was served that night—not only the extra courses, the cheese tray, and the constant refills of my wine glass, but also the ridiculously solicitous service—was worth at least 50% more than my hundred-dollar budget. I admitted I was a rube, and the staff responded by treating me like the Sun King.

This experience instilled in me the conviction that if you put all your cards in someone else's hands that person will treat you better than if you kept the cards to yourself. I'm sure this is what Benjamin Franklin believed when he said, "To gain a friend, let him do you a favor."

You see this principle at work in the first step I help every successful person take in order to become more successful. I teach them to *apologize*—face to face—to every coworker who has agreed to help them get better.

Apologizing is one of the most powerful and

resonant gestures in the human arsenal—almost as powerful as a declaration of love. It's "I love you" flipped on its head. If love means, "I care about you and I'm happy about it," then an apology means, "I hurt you and I'm sorry about it." Either way, it's seductive and irresistible; it irrevocably changes the relationship between two people. It compels them to move forward into something new and, perhaps, wonderful together.

The best thing about apologizing, I tell my clients, is that it forces everyone to let go of the past. In effect, you are saying, "I can't change the past. All I can say is I'm sorry for what I did wrong. I'm sorry it hurt you. There's no excuse for it and I will try to do better in the future. I would like you to give me any ideas about how I can improve."

That statement—an admission of guilt, an apology, and a plea for help—is tough for even the most cold-hearted among us to resist. And when you employ it on coworkers it can have an alchemical effect on how they feel about you and themselves.

My client Beth was the highest-ranking woman at a Fortune 100 company. Her bosses loved her. So did her direct reports. By contrast she was loathed by some of her peers. When I surveyed her coworkers I learned that she had a particularly toxic relationship with a hard-boiled division chief named Harvey. Beth was a smart, know-it-all young hotshot brought in by the CEO to stir things up. Harvey, however, saw her as arrogant and felt she didn't respect the company's history and traditions. The two of them were in a perpetual turf war, and it brought out the worst side of her personality: Her mean, vindictive streak. We agreed that this is the behavior she would change.

The first thing I had Beth do was apologize—to Harvey. I could see her bristle at the suggestion. I told her, "If you can't do this, you can't get better. And by the way, I'm outta here. I can't help you." The thought of yielding to Harvey was so distasteful to her that I actually scripted out the apology. I didn't want any misgivings or hesitations to creep in and pollute the apology (which would destroy the effect). To Beth's credit she followed the script.

She said, "You know, Harvey, I've got a lot of feedback here and the first thing I want to say is that I'm positive about a lot of it. The next thing I want to say is that there are some things at which I want to be better. I've been disrespectful to you, the company, and the traditions in the company. Please accept my apologies. There is no excuse for this behavior and . . ."

Harvey cut her off before she could finish her apology. She looked at him with alarm, poised for another fight, until she noticed that he had tears in his eyes. The first thing he said was, "You know, Beth, it's not just you. It's me. I have not been a gentleman in the way I've treated you. I know that this was hard for you to tell me these things and they are not all your problems. This is my problem, too. We can get better together."

That's the magic in this process. When you declare your dependence on others, they usually agree to help. And during the course of making you a better person, they inevitably try to become better people themselves. This is how individuals change, how teams improve, how divisions grow, and how companies become world-beaters.

Now that you know *why* apologizing works, we'll deal with the mechanics of actually doing it more thoroughly in Chapter 7.

Habit #16 Not listening

This is certainly one of the most common complaints I hear in my professional life. People will tolerate all sorts of rudeness, but the inability to pay attention holds a special place in their hearts—perhaps because it's something all of us should be able to do with ease. After all, what's it take to keep our ears open, our eyes looking at whoever's talking, and our mouths shut?

When you fail at listening you're sending out an armada of negative messages. You're saying:

- I don't care about you.
- I don't understand you.
- You're wrong.
- You're stupid.
- You're wasting my time.
- All of the above.

It's a wonder people ever talk to you again.

The interesting thing about not listening is that, for the most part, it's a silent, invisible activity. People rarely notice you doing it. You can be not listening because you're bored, or distracted, or busy composing what you want to say—and no one will know it.

The only time people actually see that you're not listening to them is when you're displaying extreme impatience. You want them to hurry up and get to the point. People notice that. And they rarely think better of you for it. You may as well be shouting, "Next!" at them.

That's what happened when I worked with a group of executives who comprised the top management team of one of the world's most respected research and development organizations. Their problem: Retaining young talent. Their flaw: During presentations everyone in senior management had developed the annoying habit of looking at their watches, motioning for junior scientists to move it along, and repeating over and over, "Next slide. Next slide." This annoying habit explained the problem.

Have you ever tried to make a presentation while a manager grunted at you and kept telling you to move it along? Well, that's how the junior scientists at this company felt.

Senior management's challenge: listening patiently while junior scientists made presentations.

It's easy to see why the bosses were so impatient. They were all brilliant. They all sported advanced degrees from MIT and Harvard. As a result, they found it hard to sit still while those below them on the pecking order talked because (a) they often felt they already knew what they were about to hear and (b) their minds worked so fast that they could comprehend any message by filling in the blanks themselves. When I told this story to the head of another pharmaceutical company, he ruefully admitted, "I was worse. Instead of, 'Next slide!' I said, 'Last slide. Last slide.'"

The executives learned that they had to change—because the world had changed. In the old days, the junior scientists at a major corporation might not have had a better option for employment. It was a choice between one big company and another.

As the executives slowly learned, as they watched talent walk out the door, times change. Today these junior scientists have the option of working in small start-ups or venturing out on their own. They're not hostages to a bunch of old men in white shirts. They can wear blue jeans to work. They can have beer blasts on Fridays. In many cases, they can get very rich at a very young age.

The reality for leaders of the past and leaders in the future is that *in the past very bright people would put up with disrespectful behavior, but in the future they will leave!*

When you find yourself mentally or literally drumming your fingers while someone else is talking, stop the drumming. Stop demonstrating impatience when listening to someone.

Stop saying (or thinking) "Next!" It's not only rude and annoying, but it's sure to inspire your employees to find their next boss.

Habit #17 Failing to express gratitude

Dale Carnegie liked to say that the two sweetest words in the English language were a person's first and last name. He maintained that using them liberally in conversation was the surest way to connect with a person and disarm them. After all, who doesn't like to hear their name on other people's lips?

I'm not sure Dale was right. To me, the two sweetest words in the language are "Thank you." They're not only disarming and pleasant to the ear, but they help us avoid so many problems. Like apologizing, thanking is a magical super-gesture of interpersonal relations. It's what you say when you have nothing nice to say—and it will never annoy the person hearing it.

There's really no art to saying, "Thank you." You shape your mouth in the appropriate manner, flex your vocal cords, and let the two monosyllabic words float past your lips and out upon the grateful appreciative ears of anyone within shouting distance.

Yet people still have a tough time executing this rudimentary maneuver. Whether they're receiving a helpful suggestion or unwanted advice or a nice compliment, they get confused about how to respond. They have too many options. They can dispute the comment, question it, fine-tune it, clarify it, criticize it, amplify it. They'll do practically everything but the right thing: Say "Thank you."

Has this ever happened to you? You're at a party. It doesn't matter if you're a man or woman. You see a female neighbor wearing a stunning dress. You tell her, "You look great, Barbara. That's a gorgeous dress."

Instead of saying thank you, she turns into a flustered schoolgirl. "Oh, this old thing?" she says. "It's just some rag I found in the closet."

You tune out. She's going on and on about the dress, but you're looking at her in puzzlement. You've just handed her a sweet compliment, and she's arguing with you! In effect, she's saying, "You are confused if you think this is a beautiful dress. It is nothing compared to the other really beautiful dresses in my closet. If you were smarter, you would know that this pathetic old rag is hardly conclusive evidence of my exquisite sartorial taste."

Of course, she doesn't mean it that harshly. But that's the chilling effect of not saying thank you. You create a problem where none should exist.

I try to teach people that, if they don't know what to say, their default response to any suggestion should be, "Thank you."

I was watching golfer Mark O'Meara playing in the Skins Game with his buddy Tiger Woods. The Skins Game is a made-for-TV event where the golfers wear microphones, so you can hear everything they say. Golf is a game of etiquette. Golfers say "nice shot" throughout the round. Every time someone would say "nice shot" to O'Meara, he'd respond, "Thank you. I appreciate that." He never wavered. He must have said it fifty times during the match.

That's not hard to understand. O'Meara was getting positive feedback from his playing partners. What else is there to say? But even if he were getting negative feedback—"Tough shot, Mark!"—I'd recommend the same response. "Thank you. I'll try to do better next time."

I'm not sure how many people would do that. It means

letting go of our overwhelming need to win, to be right, to add value, to come out on top.

What's needed is a slight tweak in our mindset for accepting other people's comments. My friend Chris Cappy, an expert in executive learning, has a saying that put this into perspective for me. No matter what someone tells him, he accepts it by reminding himself, "I won't learn less." What that means is when somebody makes a suggestion or gives you ideas, you're either going to *learn more* or *learn nothing*. But you're not going to *learn less*. Hearing people out does not make you dumber. So, thank them for trying to help.

If you examine the alternative, you'll see that almost any response to a suggestion other than "thank you" has the potential to stir up trouble. Intentionally or not, you appear as if you are attacking the person talking to you.

The troublemaking phrase I always look out for is, "I'm confused"—because it is so subtle and dishonest. Have you ever had this happen to you? You make a sincere suggestion to your boss: "Boss, have you ever considered . . . ?" The boss looks at you and says, "I'm confused by what you're telling me."

The boss doesn't mean he's confused. He's saying *you're confused*—which is another way of saying, "You're wrong."

What the boss should say is, "Thank you. I had never considered that." It's almost irrelevant whether the boss gives the idea any further thought. The critical issue is that saying "thank you" keeps people talking to you. Failing to say "thank you" shuts them down.

We all know this instinctively. From our earliest years we're taught that "please" and "thank you" are the basics of etiquette. That's why it's mystifying when so many people fail to appreciate the power of thanking. A bigger mystery to me is why we delay expressing gratitude. We believe we have to wait for the perfect moment—as if only a grand theatrical thank you will do the job properly. The trouble is, we rarely know when that perfect moment comes. This belief makes no sense.

I was talking with one of my clients about the lost art of expressing gratitude.

He claimed it was one of his strong points.

As proof, he told me a story about his wife. He had always wanted his own private-office-cum-library at home. He talked about it for years, but never had the time or energy to do all the work required for a major home renovation. But his wife did.

She found an architect to design the addition, hired a contractor, arranged the home improvement loan with the bank, shuttled the plans through the local building board's tortuous approval process, and then oversaw the entire project as workers tore down walls, laid down a foundation, and built the new addition.

"Why are you telling me this?" I asked.

"Because the room is almost done and I haven't thanked her yet. I'm planning to do so with a big gift for her when it's finished."

"Why don't you thank her now?" I asked.

"Because I want to wait. It'll be more impressive when the job is done."

"That may be true," I said. "But do you think she'll resent it if you thank her now and thank her again with a bigger gesture when the job is completed? Do you think she'll resent you for thanking her *twice*?"

Gratitude is a skill that we can never display too often. And yet for some reason, we are cheap and chary with gratitude—as if it were rare Bordeaux wine that we can serve only on special occasions. Gratitude is not a limited resource, nor is it costly. It is as abundant as air. We breathe it in but forget to exhale.

Of all the behavioral challenges we are covering here, this one should be the easiest to conquer. Pick something to be grateful for. Find the "guilty" party. Tell him or her, "Thank you." Do it now.

Everything else you need to know about expressing gratitude can be found in Chapter 10.

Habit #18 Punishing the messenger

Punishing the messenger is like taking the worst elements of *not giving recognition* and *hogging the credit* and *passing the buck* and *making destructive comments* and *not thanking or listening*—and then adding *anger* to the mix.

It manifests itself in big and little ways.

It's not merely the unjust retaliatory action we take against a whistleblower or the angry tirade we heap upon an employee who tells us something we don't enjoy hearing.

It's also the small responses we make throughout the day whenever we are inconvenienced or disappointed. Until someone points it out to us, we're not aware how we punish the messenger all day long.

It's the momentary snort of disgust you exhale when your assistant reports that the boss is too busy to see you. It's not your assistant's fault that the boss is avoiding you. But that's not how your assistant interprets your disgust.

It's the expletive you neglect to delete in a meeting when a subordinate announces that a deal fell apart. If you had calmly asked, "What went wrong?" no damage would be done. The subordinate would explain what happened and everyone in the room would be wiser for it. However, that little flash of temper evident in your expletive sends a different signal. It says if you want to tick off the boss, surprise him with bad news.

It's not just bad news, however. It's all the times that people give us a helpful warning about something—a red light up ahead when we're driving, the fact our socks don't match as we head out the door in the morning, whatever—and we bite their heads off or argue with them for trying to help us.

If your goal is to stop people from giving you input—of all kinds—perfect your reputation for shooting the messenger.

On the other hand, if your goal is to stop this bad habit, all you need to say is, "Thank you."

For example, I'm on the road nearly every week of the year, but I'm religious about being home for weekends. As a result, I'm almost always in a car on Sunday afternoon or Monday morning heading to the airport. I do this so frequently that I've become very adept at putting off my departure for the airport until the last possible minute. Not surprisingly, I am usually in a mad rush to get there. On one particular drive to the airport, my wife, Lyda, was sitting in the front seat. My two children, Kelly and Bryan, were sitting in the back seat. As usual, I was late, driving too fast, and not paying attention. Lyda (who is, to make things worse, a licensed clinical psychologist with a Ph.D.) said, "Look out! There's a red light up ahead!"

Being a trained behavioral science professional, a person who teaches *others* the value of encouraging input, I naturally screamed at her. "I know there's a red light! Don't you think I can see? I can drive as well as you can!"

When we arrived at the airport, Lyda, for some peculiar reason, abandoned her usual farewell ministrations. She neglected to kiss me goodbye or, for that matter, say anything at all. She walked around the car, slid behind the wheel, and drove off.

Hmmm, I thought, I wonder if she's mad at me?

During the six-hour flight to New York, I did a cost-benefit analysis. I asked myself, "What was the cost of her saying, 'There is a red light up ahead'?" Zero. "What was the potential benefit? What could have been saved?" Many benefits came to mind, including—my life, her life, the lives of our children, and the lives of other innocent people.

When someone gives us something that has a huge potential benefit and costs absolutely nothing, there's only one adequate response: "Thank you!"

I landed in New York feeling guilt and shame. I called Lyda and told her my cost-benefit story. I said, "The next time that you help me with my driving, I am just going to say, 'Thank you.'"

"Sure you will!" she said (sarcasm free of charge).

"Just watch. I am going to do better!"

A few months passed, and I had long forgotten this incident. Again, I was racing to the airport, not paying attention, when Lyda said, "Look out for the red light!" My face turned crimson. I started breathing hard. I grimaced and then yelled, "Thank you!"

I am a long way from perfect. But I am getting better!

The next time someone offers you advice or "helps you" with something as important as your driving, don't punish the messenger. Don't say a word. Stop whatever you're thinking of saying—unless it's "Thank you!"

Habit #19 Passing the buck

Passing the buck is one of those terrifying hybrid flaws. Take a healthy dose of *needing to win* and *making excuses*. Mix it with *refusing to apologize* and *failing to give proper recognition*. Sprinkle in a faint hint of *punish the messenger* and *getting angry*. And what you end up with is passing the buck. Blaming others for our mistakes.

This is the behavioral flaw by which we judge our leaders—as important a negative attribute as positive qualities such as brainpower, courage, and resourcefulness. A leader who cannot shoulder the blame is not someone we will follow blindly into battle. We instinctively question that individual's character, dependability, and loyalty to us. And so we hold back on our loyalty to him or her.

Unlike most of the other flaws listed here, which are subtle and masked by clever rhetoric, passing the buck is one of those obviously unattractive personal habits—as obvious as belching in public. When we pass the buck, everyone notices—and no one is impressed. When was the last time someone said to you, "We think you're a great leader because we love your ingenuity at avoiding responsibility." Or, "It seemed like you were making a lot of silly mistakes, but you changed my mind when you passed the buck and demonstrated that someone else was to blame."

Passing the buck is the dark flip side of claiming credit that others deserve. Instead of depriving others of their rightful glory for a success, we wrongfully saddle them with the shame of our failure.

What's strange about passing the buck is that unlike the other flaws listed here, which we're rarely aware of, we don't need other people to point out that we're passing the buck. We're well aware of it. We know we must shoulder the blame for a failure, but we can't bring ourselves to do it. So we find a scapegoat.

In other words, we know we're guilty of an interpersonal "crime" but we do it anyway.

This was the challenge when I worked one-on-one with a media executive named Sam. Sam was a rising star at his company, but the CEO who hired me said there was something lacking in the man's leadership skills. My job was to find out why people didn't like following Sam's lead.

It didn't take me long to figure out what and why after I

canvassed his colleagues. Sam had impeccable taste in spotting talent. He had exquisite social skills, which helped in dealing with high-maintenance producers and writers. He had a golden touch when it came to giving the green light to one project over another. It seemed that he could do no wrong. And he liked to promote that aura of infallibility. His invincible self-image, in fact, explained his meteoric rise to a senior position at the company. He was clearly a winner, someone who would go far.

But that sense of infallibility was also Sam's Achilles heel. A person who thinks he can do no wrong usually can't admit that he's wrong. The feedback on Sam said that he was always missing in action when one of his projects ran into trouble or an idea flopped. As good as he was at picking winners, he was a genius at pinning the blame on someone else when the occasional loser materialized.

This was his form of passing the buck. Needless to say, it didn't endear him to his staff or impress them with his leadership skills.

When I sat down with him to go over the feedback, he said, "I don't need to hear the results. I know what you've learned. People say I'm not good at accepting responsibility."

"That's right," I said. "People think you pass the buck. As a result, you're losing their respect. You'll never get to the top of this or any other company with that behavior. How come you know this about yourself and still do it?"

Sam was silent. Even now, with the feedback on the table, Sam had a tough time admitting he was wrong. But there were only him and me in the room. There was no one else to scapegoat.

I looked around his office, which was dotted with baseball memorabilia, and decided to ease him into the discussion with a baseball analogy.

"No one is perfect," I said, stating the obvious. "None of us is right all the time. In baseball, of the more than million major league games played, fewer than 30 have been perfect games. No hits, no walks, no batters reaching first base. Even the greatest hitters in their best years, such as Ty Cobb or Ted Williams, made an out at the plate 60 percent of the time. What makes you think you have to be better than Ted Williams?"

"I guess I need to be perfect," said Sam. "So I dump any imperfection on someone else."

We spent the next hour discussing the paradox that Sam's sense of infallibility made him look even more fallible to his colleagues. Sam thought he was preserving his reputation for making good decisions, everyone else thought he was passing the buck. It was such an unattractive quality that it cancelled out all of Sam's positives.

The irony, of course, is that infallibility is a myth. No one expects us to be right all the time. But when we're wrong, they certainly expect us to own up to it. In that sense, being wrong is an opportunity—an opportunity to show what kind of person and leader we are. Consumers judge a service business not so much when it does things right (consumers expect that) but rather by how the business behaves in correcting a foul-up. It's the same in the workplace. How well you own up to your mistakes makes a bigger impression than how you revel in your successes.

Once Sam could see that passing the buck was jeopardizing his career, the process of change could begin. It wasn't a difficult process, but it took time. Sam had to apologize to all his coworkers for his behavior in the past. He promised to do better in the future. He asked his coworkers to help him change and give him ideas that would make him a better leader. He asked them to point out any incident where he was deflecting responsibility. He thanked them for doing so, even when he wasn't sure they were right. And he had to do all this consistently. Any backsliding and all of Sam's efforts to change would be undone. Over time, as Sam doggedly pursued this strategy, his reputation for passing the buck began to vanish. Eighteen months later when I conducted my last review of his colleagues, Sam's scores on accepting responsibility were close to perfect.

If passing the buck is your challenge, you're probably already aware that you're doing it. My goal here is to make you see that you're not fooling anyone—except perhaps yourself—and that no matter how much you think you're saving your hide, you're actually killing it.

Habit #20 An excessive need to be "me"

Each of us has a pile of behavior which we define as "me." It's the chronic behavior, both positive and negative, that we think of as our inalterable essence.

If we're the type of person who's chronically poor at returning phone calls—whether it's because we're overcommitted, or we're simply rude, or we believe that if people *really* need to talk to us they'll call again until they get through—we mentally give ourselves a pass every time we fail to get back to callers. "Hey, that's me. Deal with it." To change would be going against the deepest, truest part of our being. It would be inauthentic.

If we are incorrigible procrastinators who habitually ruin other people's timetables, we do so because we're being true to "me."

If we always express our opinion, no matter how hurtful or noncontributory it may be, we are exercising our right to be "me."

You can see how, over time, it would be easy for each of us

to cross the line and begin to make a virtue of our flaws—simply because the flaws constitute what we think of as "me." This misguided loyalty to our true natures—this excessive need to be me—is one of the toughest obstacles to making positive long-term change in our behavior. It doesn't need to be.

Some years ago I worked with a top executive whose chief documented roadblock was that he wasn't very good at giving positive recognition to his staff.

As I went over his scores with him, I said, "This is quite remarkable. You have some of the highest scores I've ever seen in seven key areas, and then there's this one area—giving positive recognition—which *nobody* thinks you're good at."

"What do you want me to do? Go around praising people who don't deserve it?" he asked. "I don't want to look like a phony."

"Is that your excuse? You don't want to look like a phony?" I asked.

"Yes, that's what I'm saying."

We went back and forth on this for a while as he desperately defended why he scored so miserably on giving positive recognition. He had high standards and people didn't always meet them. He didn't like to hand out praise indiscriminately because it cheapened the value of praise when it was legitimately earned. He thought singling out people could weaken the team. On and on this went in a dazzling display of sophistry and rationalization.

I finally stopped him and said, "No matter what you say, I don't believe you have a problem with handing out praise. Nor is it that you think doing so means you're a phony. The real problem is your self-limiting definition of who you are. You define phony as anything that isn't . . . *me*! When you hand out praise, you're thinking, 'This isn't me.'"

So I started to work with him to answer the question, "Why isn't this you?"

His scores proved that he had many qualities that defined him very positively—and he accepted them. My job in helping him change was to make him see that he could add one more definition of himself—that he could see himself as a boss who is good at giving recognition.

I asked him, "Why can't this be you, too? Is doing so immoral, illegal, or unethical?"

"No."

"Will it make people feel better?"

"Yes."

"Will they perform better as a result of this positive recognition?"

"Probably."

"Will that help your career?"

"Probably."

"So why don't you start doing it?"

"Because," he laughed, "it wouldn't be me."

That was the moment when change became possible—when he realized that this stern allegiance to his definition of himself was pointless vanity. If he could shed his "excessive need to be me," he wouldn't see himself as a phony. He could stop thinking about *himself* and start behaving in a way that benefited *others*.

Sure enough, when he let go of this devotion to "me," all his other rationalizations fell by the wayside. He began to see that his direct reports were actually talented hard-working people who did indeed deserve his periodic praise. He began to see that congratulating people, patting them on the back, singling out their contributions warmly in a meeting, writing "Good job!" on a report—even when the performance wasn't 100% perfect—didn't damage his reputation as a demanding boss. The payoff in terms of improved morale and performance was enormous. Within a year, his scores for giving positive recognition were on a par with his other scores—all because he had lost his excessive need to be "me."

The irony of all this wasn't lost on him either. The less he focused on himself and the more he considered what his staff were feeling, the more it benefited him. His reputation as a manager soared. His career did too.

It's an interesting equation: Less me. More them. Equals success.

Keep this in mind when you find yourself resisting change because you're clinging to a false—or pointless—notion of "me." It's not about you. It's about what other people think of you.

CHAPTER 5

The Twenty-First Habit: Goal Obsession

THERE'S A REASON I have given goal obsession a special stand-alone place in this section on our interpersonal challenge. By itself, goal obsession is not a flaw. Unlike adding value or punishing the messenger or any of the other twenty annoying habits, goal obsession is not transactional; it's not something you do to another person. But it is often the root cause of the annoying behavior. Goal obsession turns us into someone we shouldn't be.

Goal obsession is one of those paradoxical traits we accept as a driver of our success. It's the force that motivates us to finish the job in the face of any obstacle—and finish it perfectly.

A valuable attribute much of the time. It's hard to criticize people for wanting to do things 100 percent right (especially when you consider the sloppy alternative). But taken too far, it can become a blatant cause of failure.

In its broadest form, goal obsession is the force at play when we get so wrapped up in achieving our goal that we do it at the expense of a larger mission.

It comes from misunderstanding *what we want in our lives*. We think we'd be truly happy (or at least happier) if only we made more money, or lost thirty pounds, or got the corner office. So, we pursue those goals relentlessly. What we don't appreciate until much later is that in obsessing about making money, we might be neglecting the loved ones—i.e., our family—for whom we are presumably securing that money; in obsessing about our weight with extreme diets we might actually end up doing more harm than good to our bodies; in pursuing the corner office we might trample upon the colleagues at work whose support and loyalty we will need later on to *stay in* that corner office or move even higher. We start out with a road map heading in one direction but end up in the wrong town.

It also comes from misunderstanding *what others want us to do*. The boss says we have to show ten percent revenue growth for the year, so when it appears we will miss that target, goal obsession forces us to adopt questionable, less than honest methods of hitting the target. In other words, the honorable pursuit of a difficult goal set by someone else transforms us into cheaters. If you examine it more closely, we're not really obsessed with hitting the ten percent growth; our true goal is pleasing our boss. The only problem is that we either don't see this or we refuse to admit it to ourselves. Is it any wonder our values get mixed up? Goal obsession has warped our sense of what is right or wrong.

As a result, in our dogged pursuit of our goals we forget our manners. We're nice to people if they can help us hit our goal. We push them out of the way if they're not useful to us. Without meaning to, we can become self-absorbed schemers.

Consider a marketing executive named Candace with whom I worked. By all accounts, Candace was the poster child for "having it all." She was 38 years old, with a happy marriage and two healthy perky children at home. She was so energetic and capable that the company gave her two personal assistants. Her staff admired her for her creativity and poise—and for the breakthrough results she produced. She delivered the numbers—and then some. Her office was littered with "Marketing Executive of the Year" plaques and tributes from the industry trade magazines. Her CEO considered her his eventual successor.

So, what's wrong with this picture? Candace had a problem retaining her talented staff. A lot of them asked to be transferred to other parts of the company or simply left. My job was to figure out why people didn't want to stick around working for such an obvious star.

When I talked to Candace's colleagues, no one was willing to fault her powerful ambition. They praised her for the fact that she set very clear goals for herself. She wanted to be a "superstar" in her field—and she was well on the way to achieving that goal. But that goal obsession had worn away some of the warmth in Candace's otherwise sunny, optimistic personality. She was becoming hard and cold to her subordinates. As one staffer told me, "You could chill a six-pack of beer next to her heart."

When I dug a little deeper, the universal complaint about Candace was that she always had to be front and center in every success. She hogged the spotlight. It wasn't that Candace withheld praise or recognition. If one of her staff came up with a great marketing campaign, Candace would shower him or her with praise. But she would always take center stage when she reported the success to her superiors.

That was her flaw. Goal obsession had turned Candace into someone who claimed credit for everything, even when she didn't deserve it.

If I could make her see that her goal of being a star—as opposed to being an effective leader—was misguided, then everything else would fall into place. She wouldn't be so desperate to purloin credit from her peers and staff. She could learn to accept that *their* triumphs said something positive about her as a leader.

As I say, this is why I've given goal obsession its own special corner. It's not a flaw. It's a creator of flaws. It's the force that distorts our otherwise exemplary talents and good intentions, turning them into something we no longer admire.

It's one thing to pursue your dreams—but not if that pursuit turns a dream into a nightmare.

Take the movie *The Bridge on the River Kwai* and the lead character, Colonel Nicholson, which won Alec Guinness the Best Actor Academy Award. In it, Guinness plays a prisoner of war in Burma who is compelled to lead his fellow prisoners in building a bridge for their Japanese captors. Nicholson is an officer of high integrity, dedicated to excellence, a great leader of men—and thus well trained to complete any mission he is given. So he doesn't just build a bridge, he builds a beautiful bridge. At film's end, he finds himself in the painful position of defending the bridge from attack by fellow officers who want to destroy it to prevent Japanese trains from using it. There's a chilling moment of realization, right before he detonates the bridge, when he utters the famous line, "What have I done?" He was so focused on his goal—build the bridge—that he forgot the larger mission was winning the war. That's goal obsession. Our quest for a successful outcome may end up doing more harm than good to our organizations, our families, and ourselves.

The canyons of Wall Street are littered with the victims of goal obsession. I asked one hard-driving deal maker, "Mike, why do you work all of the time?" He replied, "Why do you think? Do you think I love this place? I am working so hard because I want to make a lot of money!"

I continued my inquiry, "Do you really need this much money?"

"I do now," Mike grimaced. "I just got divorced for the third time. With three alimony checks each month, I am almost broke."

"Why do you keep getting divorced?" I asked.

The answer came out as a sad sigh. "All three wives kept complaining that I worked all of the time. They have no idea how hard it is to make this much money!"

This sort of classic goal obsession would be laughable if the irony—or more accurately the failure to appreciate the irony—weren't so painful.

One of the most ironic examples of goal obsession was the "Good Samaritan" research done by Darley and Batson at Princeton in 1973. In this widely-referenced study, one group of theology students was told that they were to go across campus to deliver a sermon on the topic of the Good Samaritan. As part of the research, some of these students were told that they were late and needed to hurry up. They believed people would be waiting for them to arrive. Along their route across campus to the chapel, Darley and Batson had hired an actor to play the role of a "victim" who was coughing and suffering. Ninety percent of the late students in Princeton Theology Seminary ignored the needs of a suffering person in their haste to get across campus. As the study reports, "Indeed, on several occasions, a seminary student going to give his talk on the parable of the Good Samaritan literally stepped over the victim as he hurried on his way!"

My guess is that few, if any, of these seminary students were "bad people." Like Colonel Nicholson, they probably were ethical, well-meaning people who deeply believed in the value of helping others. But goal obsession clouded their judgment.

What happened to Candace, Colonel Nicholson, Mike, and the seminary students?

They were chasing the spotlight. They were under pressure! They were in a hurry! They had deadlines! They were going to do something that they thought was important! Other people were depending upon them!

These are the classic conditions that can lead to goal obsession. Great follow through. Terrific discipline. Awesome goal obsession. Short-sighted goal.

A recipe for disaster.

Candace was climbing to the top, but stomping on her supporters to get there. Colonel Nicholson was building a bridge, but not winning a war. Mike was making money, but losing a wife. The seminary students were on time for a sermon, but not practicing what they preached.

The solution is simple, but not easy. You have to step back, take a breath, and look. And survey the conditions that are making you obsessed with the wrong goals.

Ask yourself: When are you under time pressure? Or in a hurry? Or doing something that you have been told is important? Or have people depending upon you?

Probable answer: All the time. These are the classic conditions of the goal obsessed. We confront them every minute of every day. They do not go away. This makes it all the more important to reflect upon our work, match it up against the life we want to live, and consider, "What am I doing?" and, "Why am I doing this?"

Ask yourself, "Am I achieving a task—and forgetting my organization's mission?"

Are you making money to support your family—and forgetting the family that you are trying to support?

Are you on time to deliver a sermon to your staff—and forgetting to practice what you're preaching?

After all this effort and display of professional prowess, you don't want to find yourself at a dead end, asking, "What have I done?"

How We Can Change for the Better

In which we learn a seven-step method for changing our interpersonal relationships and making these changes permanent

TAKE A BREATH.

Did I scare you in the previous section? Did I paint a picture of a workplace so dense with fractured personalities that you're wondering if you should go back to work tomorrow?

It's not that bad.

If you step back and look at most of these interpersonal flaws, they revolve around two familiar factors: information and emotion.

The journalist/novelist Tom Wolfe has a theory he calls *information compulsion*. He says that people have an overwhelming need to tell you something that you don't know, even when it's not in their best interest. Journalists would have a hard time surviving without information compulsion. People wouldn't call them with tips on a good story, or agree to be interviewed, or spill secrets about their company, or hand out delicious quotes.

The same compulsion blossoms into full flower in our daily lives. It's the reason we like to dazzle our friends at dinner parties with the esoterica we know (even when we suspect we may be overstaying our welcome), or why coworkers like to gossip around the water cooler (even when they know that their chatter may get back to the people they're prattling about), or why friends tell us in excessive detail about their health or their love lives (even though they close their ears when the tables are turned). It's the reason "that's too much information" has entered everyday speech. We all have an overwhelming need to display and share what we know. And we do it excessively.

Study the twenty annoying habits and you'll see that at least half of them are rooted in information compulsion. When we add value, or pass judgment, or make destructive comments, or announce that we "already knew that," or explain "why that won't work" we are compulsively sharing information. We're telling people something they don't know. We're convinced that we're making people smarter or inspiring them to do better, when we're more likely to achieve the opposite effect. Likewise, when we fail to give recognition, or claim credit we don't deserve, or refuse to apologize, or don't express our gratitude, we are withholding information.

Sharing or withholding. They're two sides of the same tarnished coin.

The other habits are rooted in a different kind of compulsion, one that's centered on emotion. When we get angry, or play favorites, or punish the messenger, we are succumbing to emotion—and displaying it for all the world to see.

Information and emotion. We either share them or withhold them.

There's nothing wrong with that. The world would be a more dangerous and less interesting place if we didn't understand how to either share information or withhold it. It's good to share information that helps people. Likewise, it's good to withhold it when it harms people (that's why many secrets *should* be kept). The same goes for emotion. Worth sharing sometimes. Other times, not worth it at all.

At the risk of complicating this with too much information, I would add another dimension here. When dealing with information or emotion, we have to consider if what we're sharing is *appropriate*.

Appropriate information is anything that unequivocally helps the other person. But it veers into inappropriate when we go too far or risk hurting someone. Discussing a rival company's good fortune can be positive if it gets your people working harder, but it's usually inappropriate information when it soils other people's reputations. Instruction is usually appropriate, to a point. It's the difference between someone giving you simple directions to their house and telling you every wrong turn you can make along the way. The latter is inappropriate. At some point, with too many details and red flags, you will get lost, confused, or wary of making the trip at all.

The same with emotion. Love is often an appropriate emotion. Anger is not appropriate. But even saying "I love you" can be inappropriate if we employ it too often or at awkward moments. And conversely, anger can be a useful tool if we parse it out in small doses at opportune moments.

When sharing information or emotion, we have to ask *is this appropriate* and *how much should I convey*?

I realize these are broad generalizations involving delicate subject matter. But they will give some context to understand these challenges. We are not lancing deep-rooted psychological "tumors" here. We're asking blunt questions about basic behavior.

Is it appropriate?

How much should I convey?

You can do a lot worse than pause and pose these questions as guidelines for anything you do or say as you follow the instructions in this section's seven chapters. From feedback to feedforward, I will show you how to identify your specific flaws, how to determine if they matter, and how to change your annoying behavior so that you are not only better for it but also so that your colleagues notice the change (very important).

CHAPTER 6

Feedback

A Brief History of Feedback

Feedback has always been with us, ever since the first man knelt down at a pool of water to get a drink and saw his face reflected in the water's surface. Formal up-the-ladder feedback designed to help managers didn't appear until the middle of the previous century—with the first suggestion box. The feedback that matters to me is a more recent development of the last 30 years. It's commonly called 360-degree feedback, because it is solicited from everybody at all levels of the organization. Until something better comes along, confidential 360-degree feedback is the best way for successful people to identify what they need to improve in their relationships at work.

Successful people only have two problems dealing with negative feedback. However, they are big problems: (a) they don't want to hear it from us and (b) we don't want to give it to them.

It's not hard to see why people don't want to hear negative feedback. Successful people are incredibly delusional about their achievements. Over 95 percent of the members in most successful groups believe that they perform in the top half of their group. While this is statistically ridiculous, it is psychologically real. Giving people negative feedback means "proving" they are wrong. *Proving* to successful people that they are wrong works just about as well as *making* them change. Not gonna happen.

Feedback generally doesn't break through to successful people even when we adopt the eminently sane guideline of *depersonalizing* the feedback. That is, talk about the *task*, not the *person*. This is easy in theory. But successful people's identities are often so closely connected to what they do that it's naive to assume they will not take it personally when receiving negative feedback about the most important activity in their lives.

Basically, we accept feedback that is consistent with our self-image and reject feedback that is inconsistent.

It's also easy to see why we don't want to give feedback. In big organizations, successful people have power over us—over our paycheck, our advancement, our job security. The more successful these people are, the more power they have. Combine that power with the fairly predictable "kill the messenger" response to negative feedback and you can see why emperors will continue to rule without clothes. (Spot quiz: When was the last time your efforts to prove the boss wrong worked as a career-enhancing maneuver?)

I have other issues with traditional face-to-face negative feedback—and almost all of them boil down to the fact that it focuses on the past (a failed past at that), not a positive future. We can't change the past. We can change the future. Negative feedback exists to prove us wrong (or at least many of us take it that way). Feedback can be employed by others to reinforce our feelings of failure, or at least remind us of them—and our reaction is rarely positive. (Spot quiz: When your spouse or partner reminds you of all your shortcomings, how well do you accept this trip down memory lane?)

More than anything, negative feedback shuts us down. We close ranks, turn into our shell, and shut the world out. Change does not happen in this environment.

But enough about what's wrong with feedback. I'm not trying to prove that negative feedback creates dysfunction. Feedback is very useful for telling us "where we are." Without feedback, I couldn't work with my clients. I wouldn't know what everyone thinks my client needs to change. Likewise, without feedback, we wouldn't have results. We couldn't keep score. We wouldn't know if we were getting better or worse. Just as salespeople need feedback on what's selling and leaders need feedback on how they are perceived by their subordinates, we all need feedback to see where we are, where we need to go, and to measure our progress.

We need honest, helpful feedback. It's just hard to find. But I have a foolproof method for securing it.

The Four Commitments

When I work with a coaching client, I always get confidential feedback from many of my client's coworkers at the beginning of the process. The fewest I have ever interviewed is eight and the most is thirty-one. My average is about fifteen. The number of interviewees depends upon the company's size and the executive's job. Before I begin these interviews, I involve my client in determining who should be interviewed. Each interview lasts about an hour and focuses on the basics: What is my client doing right, what does my client need to change, and how my (already successful) client can get even better!

Today, all of my personal coaching clients are either CEOs or executives who have the potential to be CEOs in major corporations. If my client is the CEO, I get his or her opinion on who should be interviewed. If my client is not the CEO, the CEO must also approve my list of interviewees. (I don't want the CEO to feel that I left out important people.) One reason so many people deny the validity of feedback is that they believe that the feedback was delivered by the "wrong people." Since my clients pick their raters, it is hard for them to deny the validity of the feedback.

I have been asked if my clients ever just "pick their friends" and ignore valuable feedback from people who may be critical. In theory I see how this could happen, but I've never had this experience.

As part of my interview process, I enlist each of my client's coworkers to help me out. I want them to assist, not sabotage the change process. I let the coworker know how my process works by saying, "I'm going to be working with my client for the next year or so. I don't get paid if he doesn't get better. 'Better' is not defined by me. It's not defined by my client. 'Better' is defined by you and the other coworkers who will be involved in this process."

The raters usually respond well to that. People like hearing that they are the customer and they have the power to determine if I get paid. After all, if change happens, the raters taste victory with a dramatically improved boss and work environment.

I then present these coworkers with four requests. I call them The Four Commitments. I need them to commit to:

1. Let go of the past.
2. Tell the truth.
3. Be supportive and helpful—not cynical or negative.
4. Pick something to improve yourself—so everyone is focused more on "improving" than "judging."

Almost every coworker agrees to my four requests. In a couple of cases, coworkers have just said "no." They felt that they could not "let go" of the past and help my client try to get better. In these cases they had psychologically "written off" my client. Since all of the interviews are confidential, I don't tell this to my client. I only request that the coworkers not participate in the final feedback report. If we aren't going to try to help our colleagues, why should we be allowed to judge them?

As you contemplate changing your behavior yourself—without my hands-on assistance—you will need to do the same with your colleagues. Here's how you can get the people you know to commit to helping you.

First commitment: Can they let go of the past? Whatever real or imagined sins you have committed against people in the past, they are long past correction. You can't do anything to erase them. So, you need to ask people to let go of the past. This is simple, but it is not easy. Most of us have never forgiven our mothers and fathers for not being the perfect parents. We cannot forgive our children for not being the ideal kids. We don't forgive our spouse for not being the perfect partner. Quite often, we can't forgive ourselves for not being the perfect us. But you have to get this first commitment. Without it, you can't shift people's minds away from critic toward helper. As a friend wisely noted, "Forgiveness means letting go of the hope for a better past!"

Second commitment: Will they swear to tell the truth? You don't want to work your butt off for a year, trying to get better based on what people have told you that you were doing wrong—and then find out that they *didn't really mean it*. That they were jiving you, that they were only saying what they thought you wanted to hear. That's a waste of time. I'm not naive. I know people can be dishonest. But if you solicit—no, demand—honesty from people, you can proceed with the confidence that you're going in the right direction—and that you won't get a rude surprise at the end.

Third commitment: Will they be supportive, without being a cynic, critic, or judge? This is asking a lot of people, especially if they are in a subordinate position to you. People are just as likely to suspect or resent their superiors at work as respect and admire them. So you have to remove any and all of their judgmental impulses from the equation. Do that and people are much more inclined to be helpful. At some point, they realize that if you get better, they have won something too. They get a kinder, gentler, better boss.

Fourth commitment: Will they pick one thing they can improve in themselves? This is the subtlest commitment, but it only sounds like you're asking a lot from your colleagues. What you're actually doing is creating parity, even a bond, between you and the other person. Imagine if you walked into work one day and announced that you were going on a diet. Most people would respond to that announcement with a massive yawn. But what if you announced your plans and also asked a colleague to help you—for example, to help you monitor your eating habits and stay on track? Since most people like to help their friends, you'd probably get a much more involved and sincere response to your objective. Finally, what if you add the compelling reciprocal twist of saying, "Now, what would you like to change in yourself? I'd like to return the favor and help you"? If you do that, you won't have any problem enlisting support. Suddenly, both you and the other person have become equals: fellow humans engaged in the same struggle to improve.

Imagine if you were in a marriage in which both you and your spouse were unhappy being, say, 25 pounds overweight. What if one of you decided to go on a diet and shed those excess pounds? Wouldn't your chances of succeeding increase if you could enlist your spouse to join you on the diet? Suddenly, you'd both be involved in planning the day's meals, you'd both be goading each other to maintain the discipline. You'd both be checking the scale to see how you're hitting your targets. That's certainly a lot better than sticking with your regimen at the dinner table while your other half continues eating the foods that packed on the excess weight in the first place. The two of you are going in opposite directions. That's an unpromising formula for getting where you want to go; one of you will be miserable, more likely both.

This fourth commitment is the final piece in making the process a two-way exchange.

And it is crucial if you want people to stick with you through the 12- to 18-month process. I learned this early on with my clients. When I had to figure out who to talk to for initial feedback, it seemed like common sense to me that the client should pick the people rating his performance. After all, these colleagues were the people telling me what this fellow needed to change. Wouldn't they be in the best position to tell me if and when he was getting better? So I had to draft them into the process and get *them* to play on my terms too. I told each coworker about my client's plan to change and I asked him or her to commit to help him. I was being scientifically rigorous and practical. I wanted the folks filling out the *first* report card to fill out *all* the report cards. It would make the results more valid and credible. However, it took me a little trial and error to appreciate the massive side benefits of getting other people involved—especially the part where they committed to changing something too. It enriched the entire experience. The client not only changed for the better because he was getting support from his coworkers, but the coworkers changed too because of what they learned by supporting him. This is a rich and subtle dynamic, proving that *change is not a one-way street. It involves two parties: the person who's changing and the people who notice it.*

As you begin your personal self-reclamation project, don't slough off this fourth commitment. Put equal emphasis on changing yourself *and* the people who will determine whether any change has occurred. You and the people helping you are both equal parts of a delicate equation. You can't ignore the "other guy" in any interpersonal transaction and think you're accomplishing something "interpersonal" or engaged in a "transaction."

Then, and only then, are you ready to solicit feedback about yourself.

Finding a bunch of people to tell us the truth about ourselves is not hard. You just have to know where to look.

I didn't go through this listing of the four commitments to impress you with the rigor of my methodology. It's the criteria you should be applying once you've decided on the people you want to provide feedback.

First on your list should probably be your best friend. We all have a best friend at work—someone with whom we don't compete, who has no agenda when it comes to our success, who has our interests at heart. By definition, this person fills the four commitments:

If he's our best friend, he surely isn't bitter about something in our mutual past, so he won't keep bringing up the past or hold it against us.

He's comfortable with leveling with us. He has no reason to lie. He'll consider telling us the raw unvarnished truth a badge of honor.

He's there to support us.

And he'll be willing to play along and get into the change process with us.

That would be my first choice. But it doesn't have to be yours.

Make a list of the last dozen or so people with whom

you've had professional contact. They could be colleagues, subordinates, customers, clients, even long-term competitors. As long as they're people who can make legitimate observations about your behavior, they're eligible. Then run the four commitments against each name. If any of them qualify on all four commitments, they're as good a place to start getting feedback as any.

Treat it as if you're conducting voir dire to assemble a trial jury—because that in effect is what's going on here.

Remember, this process (especially at the beginning) is not supposed to be difficult. Getting feedback is the easy part. Dealing with it is hard.

Stop Asking for Feedback and Then Expressing Your Opinion

Years ago I was riding an elevator with a famous trial lawyer who was well into his 80s at the time (but still practicing law). The elevator doors opened and a man smoking a cigarette got on. (This was in the early 1980s, before smoking was universally banned.) The lawyer panicked. He was allergic to smoke and he vainly tried to jump off the small cramped elevator so he wouldn't have to breathe the smoke. Too late. The doors closed.

"Are you okay?" the smoker asked the lawyer.

"You know, you're not supposed to smoke on elevators," he told the man. "It's against the law."

The man said, "What are you, a lawyer?" He was in no mood to apologize or put out the cigarette. He was clearly prepared to argue with the lawyer, to defend his right to smoke.

"I don't believe this," said the lawyer. "You're acting as if I'm wrong—that you're the victim because I happen to be in the elevator while you're breaking the law."

It was one of those small but outrageous moments that remind you how defensive people can be, whether they are right or wrong—especially if they're wrong.

I think about that elevator ride every time someone asks me for my advice and then after I give it, they render a less-than-glowing verdict about the quality of my advice. "I can't believe it," I say, with the lawyer's words ringing in my ears. "You asked me for my opinion and now you're arguing with me."

It's no different than our behavior when we argue with someone who's giving us advice, offering feedback, or otherwise trying to help us. And we do that every time we ask for feedback and unthinkingly respond by expressing our opinion. When we ask a friend, "What do you think I should do in this situation?" we are setting up the expectation that we want an answer—and that we will give the answer full consideration and quite possibly use it. We are not announcing that we're initiating an argument.

But that's exactly what we're doing when we ask for feedback from someone and then immediately express our opinion. This is certainly true when our opinion is negative ("I'm not sure about that. . . ."). Whatever we say, however softly we couch it, our opinion will sound defensive. It will resemble a rationalization, a denial, a negation, or an objection.

Stop doing that. Treat every piece of advice as a gift or a compliment and simply say, "Thank you." No one expects you to act on every piece of advice. If you learn to listen—and act on the advice that makes sense—the people around you may be thrilled.

Feedback Moments: How to Get Good Feedback on Your Own

I realize few of you have the resources to hire a professional to do the "fieldwork" of getting great feedback.

When I work with executives I spend my first hours on the job conducting a 360-degree feedback review. I don't want to drape the process in complexity and mystery. It's really simple. With the client's help, I identify all the people he or she works with who see his or her interpersonal challenges on a daily basis. These are the raters. I qualify them with my four commitment questions. And I have them fill out a leadership questionnaire. Sometimes the questions are customized to reflect the company's values and objectives (at GE, for example, there's a high premium placed on cooperation and sharing information across boundaries whereas at another company the premium value might be customer satisfaction).

The questions are simple. Does the executive in question:

- Clearly communicate a vision.
- Treat people with respect.
- Solicit contrary opinions.
- Encourage other people's ideas.
- Listen to other people in meetings.

That sort of thing. I ask people to rate their colleague on a numerical scale. From that, a statistical picture emerges, usually revealing one or two problem areas that we need to address. Surveys show that about 50% of corporate America uses something like this in evaluating employee performance and attitudes. If, somehow, this format has eluded you, I've included a 72-question leadership survey in an appendix to give you a picture of how professionals in this field operate.

But I'm not asking you to become a "feedback professional" here. I have to do it this way because I'm a newcomer at every company I work in. I don't have any history with the client. I've never worked with him. All I know before I meet the client is what his or her boss has told me about him. So I have no alternative but to canvass the troops.

That said, if you've worked in a corporate environment large enough to have three employees in its human resources department, you've probably been a participant in something resembling 360-degree feedback.

Even if you haven't, we're all familiar with feedback—whether or not we label it as such.

We've all endured performance appraisals from our bosses. That's feedback.

We've all gone through salary reviews. That's the most direct feedback.

If we're in sales, we've all read customer surveys of our performance. That's feedback.

We've sat through quarterly sales meetings as our figures are stacked up against our quotas and projections. That, too, is feedback.

We're being told all day long how we're doing. And the reason we accept this feedback and actually attempt to respond to it (e.g., if we're down in sales, we'll try harder to bring the figures up) is that we *accept the process*: An authority figure "grades" us and we are motivated to do better because of it.

It's not like that with interpersonal behavior, which is vague, subjective, unquantifiable, and open to wildly variant interpretations. But that doesn't make it less important. It's my contention—and it's the bedrock thesis of this book—that interpersonal behavior is the difference-maker between being great and near-great, between getting the gold and settling for the bronze. (The higher you go, the more your "issues" are behavioral.)

So, how do we get this much-needed feedback if we have neither the skill nor resources nor opportunity to poll our peers on what they really think about us? We know what feedback is. We don't know how to get it.

Basically, feedback comes to us in three forms: Solicited, unsolicited, and observation. Each of them works well, but not for everyone. Let's look closely at all three to see which one's right for you.

Solicited Feedback, or Knowing How to Ask

Solicited feedback is just that. We solicit opinions from people about what we're doing wrong. Sounds simple, no? I am not always so optimistic.

I'm not saying that you, working on your own, cannot replicate my feedback retrieval methods. It's quite possible that you could corral a dozen people who know you, qualify them with the four commitment test, and have them fill out a questionnaire about what you could be doing better.

My only concern is that we cannot be sure that you will (a) ask the right people, (b) ask the right questions, (c) interpret the answers properly, or (d) accept them as accurate. This harks back to my big issue with negative feedback: We don't want to hear it and people don't want to give it.

In my experience the best solicited feedback is *confidential* feedback. It's good because nobody gets embarrassed or defensive. There are no emotional issues, because you do not know who to blame or retaliate against for attacking you. In the best cases, you have no sense of being attacked at all. You're merely ingesting honest commentary—which you requested!—from blind but well-meaning sources.

The only problem: This is virtually impossible for one person working alone to pull off. To maintain the confidentiality (and avoid the emotionality) you need an unbiased third party to do the polling—someone like me.

Absent that, you have to ask people one-on-one. But that too is fraught with obstacles.

In my experience there are a hundred wrong ways to ask for feedback—and one right way. Most of us know the wrong ways. We ask someone, "What do you think of me?"

"How do you feel about me?"

"What do you hate about me?

"What do you like about me?"

These are all variations of the same encounter group question designed to elicit honest feelings between people. Well, we're not running encounter groups here.

These types of questions are particularly pernicious in power relationships where the boss is asking the bossed, "What do you think of me?" In a power relationship you have all kinds of issues that influence the answer—because the answer has consequences. People will not tell the truth if they think it will come back to haunt them—and in a power relationship subordinates have no guarantee that the unvarnished truth won't anger the boss, send them back to the end of the line, or worse, get them fired.

When you think about it, these "what do you think of me?" encounter group questions are actually irrelevant. In the workplace you don't have to like me; we don't have to be buddies who hang out together after work. All we have to do is work well together. How we really "feel" about each other is practically moot.

Think about your colleagues at work. How many of them are your friends? For how many of them would you be willing to articulate your true *feelings*? How many of them have you actually thought about in terms of *feelings*? The answer, I suspect, is not that many. A small minority. And yet you probably work well together with a majority of your colleagues. That disconnect—between the small number of *friends* and the larger number of *colleagues* with whom you work well—should convince you once and for all that what people feel or think about you is not the key to getting better.

In soliciting feedback for yourself, the only question that works—the only one!—must be phrased like this: "How can I do better?"

Semantic variations are permitted, such as, "What can I do to be a better partner at home?" or, "What can I do to be a better colleague at work?" or, "What can I do to be a better leader of this group?" It varies with the circumstances. But you get the idea. Pure unadulterated issue-free feedback that makes change possible has to (a) solicit advice rather than criticism, (b) be directed towards the future rather than obsessed with the negative past, and (c) be couched in a way that suggests you will act on it; that in fact you are trying to do better.

Unsolicited Feedback, or the Blindside Event

If we're lucky, every once in a while something or someone comes along who opens our eyes to our faults—and helps us strip away a delusion or two about ourselves. It doesn't happen often, but when it does, we should consider ourselves lucky and grateful.

Psychologists have all sorts of schemata to explain us to ourselves. One of the more interesting ones is a simple four-pane grid known as the Johari Window (named after two real characters, Joe and Harry). It divides our self-awareness into four parts, based on what is known and unknown about us to other people and what is known and unknown about us to ourselves.

As you can see from the illustration on the following page, the stuff that is known about us to others is *public* knowledge. What's known to us and unknown to others is *private*. What's unknown to ourselves and others is, well . . . *unknowable* and, therefore, not relevant.

The interesting stuff is the information that's known to others but unknown to us. When that information is revealed to us, those are the "road to Damascus" moments that create dramatic change. They are the moments when we can get blindsided by how others really see us, when we discover a truth about ourselves. These blindside moments are rare and precious gifts. They hurt, perhaps (the truth often does), but they also instruct.

I've had a few in my life, but the most significant blindside event came when I was a 28-year-old Ph.D. candidate at UCLA. Back then, in the late 1960s, the era of free love and Woodstock, I thought of myself as being just a little more insightful, more "hip," than the people around me. I believed that I was intensely involved in things like deeper human understanding, self-actualization, and uncovering profound meaning. I was a student in a small class led by a very wise teacher, Dr. Bob Tannenbaum. Tannenbaum was a revered figure not only at UCLA but in psychology circles around the world. He had invented the term "sensitivity training" and had published the most influential papers on the subject. He was a god to me.

In Bob's class we were encouraged to discuss anything we wanted. I took this as a license to rail against the shallow, materialistic citizens of Los Angeles. For three weeks I delivered a monologue about how "screwed up" people in Los Angeles were—with their sequined blue jeans, gold Rolls-Royces, and manicured mansions. "All they care about is impressing others.

They do not understand what is deep and important in life." (It was easy for me to be an expert on the people of Los Angeles. I had, after all, grown up in a small town in Kentucky.)

After enduring my babble for three weeks, Bob asked, "Marshall, who are you talking to?"

"I am speaking to the group," I answered.

"To whom in the group are you talking?"

"I am talking to everybody," I said, not quite sure where Bob was going with this line of interrogation.

Bob said, "I don't know if you realize this, but each time you have spoken you have looked at only one person. You have addressed your comments toward only one person. And you seem interested in the opinion of only one person. Who is that person?"

"That's interesting. Let me think about it," I said. Then (after careful consideration) I said, "You."

Bob said, "That's right. *Me.* There are twelve other people in this room. Why aren't you interested in any of *them*?"

Now that I had dug myself into a hole, I decided to dig even faster. I said, "Dr. Tannenbaum, I think you can understand the true significance of what I am saying. I think that you can truly understand how 'screwed up' it is to run around trying to impress people all the time. I believe that you have a deeper understanding of what is *really* important in life."

Bob asked, "Marshall, is there any chance that for the last three weeks all you have been trying to do is impress me?"

I was stunned by Bob's obvious lack of insight. "Not at all!" I said. "You haven't understood one thing I have said! I have been explaining to you the folly of trying to impress other people. You've totally missed my point and frankly, I am disappointed in your lack of understanding."

He stared at me, scratched his beard, and concluded, "No, I think I understand."

I looked around and saw twelve people scratching their faces and thinking, "Yes, we understand."

I hated Bob Tannenbaum for six months. I devoted a lot of energy into figuring out *his* problems and understanding why *he* was confused. After a half-year of this stewing, it dawned on me that the person with the issue about impressing other people wasn't Bob Tannenbaum or the citizens of Los Angeles. The person with the real issue was me. I looked in the mirror and didn't like the person staring back at me.

I still shudder with shame at the memory of how fatuous I was back then. But we need these painful unsolicited feedback episodes, when others reveal how the world really sees us, in order to change for the better. Without the pain, we might not discover the motivation to change.

This was a blindside event for me not only because it exposed my shallow self-involvement, but it taught me two great lessons that have literally shaped my professional work.

1. It is a whole lot easier to see our problems in others than it is to see them in ourselves.
2. Even though we may be able to deny our problems to ourselves, they may be very obvious to the people who are observing us.

This is the simple wisdom of the Johari Window: What is unknown to us may be well-known to others. We can learn from that.

As human beings we almost always suffer from the disconnect between the self we think we are and the self that the rest of the world sees in us. The lesson that I learned from Dr. Tannenbaum is that the rest of the world usually has a more accurate perspective than we do.

This is the value of *unsolicited feedback*. And in many ways when I work one-on-one with people, I am re-creating that painful realization inspired by Dr. Tannenbaum. I'm trying to blindside them by making them peer through that fourth window to see what is known to others but unknown to them.

If we can stop, listen, and think about what others are seeing in us, we have a great opportunity. We can compare the self that we want to be with the self that we are presenting to the rest of the world. We can then begin to make the real changes that are needed to close the gap between our stated values and our actual behavior.

Although he is no longer with us, I still say, "Thank you, Dr. Tannenbaum."

Observational Feedback, or Seeing Your World Anew

One of my clients—let's call him Barry—told me about one of the more important insights he had at work; it involved a senior executive who was about a half notch above him in the organizational hierarchy.

It's important to know that, because Barry handled a couple of accounts that were near and dear to the CEO, Barry had a slightly closer relationship with the CEO than anyone else in the company. He traveled with the CEO and talked to the CEO at least once a day. Barry's access to the CEO was so good that some of his peers—who weren't as tight with the CEO—resented him for it. They felt that because of his perceived "special relationship" with the CEO, Barry could always go around them and get his way by sucking up to the CEO. It wasn't necessarily true; certainly not to Barry, who had never felt that the CEO had favored him over others. It was envy, pure and simple. But it's important to know that this dynamic may have colored

KNOWN TO OTHERS

Blind Spots
Unknown to us
Known to Others

Public Knowledge
Known to us
Known to Others

UNKNOWN TO SELF   KNOWN TO SELF

Unknowable
Unknown to us
Unknown to Others

Private Knowledge
Known to us
Unknown to Others

UNKNOWN TO OTHERS

Barry's relationship with his peers. The only strange thing was that Barry had no clue that some of his peers felt that way. He thought they liked him.

Then one day he had a "feedback moment."

In a group meeting Barry noticed that a senior executive named Peter was making a pointed effort to ignore him. Whenever Barry spoke, Peter would look away—as if the sound of Barry's voice was causing him pain. Nobody else in the room noticed this, but Barry did. So he started paying attention to Peter's behavior for the rest of the meeting. And what Barry saw confirmed the first clue. When Peter spoke, he would look around the room making eye contact with everyone—except Barry. Even when the discussion turned to one of Barry's responsibilities, Peter would look away. Everything he said and did gave the impression that Peter wished Barry would simply disappear.

That's when it hit Barry.

"Oh my," he thought, "Peter, who has the power to block some of my initiatives, hates my guts."

"Until that moment," Barry told me, "I had no idea. I thought we were colleagues. I thought we worked well together."

I submit that the subtle signals Barry picked up qualify as significant feedback. Observational feedback—unsolicited, less than explicit, hard to prove—but important feedback nevertheless. Because it taught Barry that he had a fractured collegial relationship that needed immediate attention.

I'm pleased to report that Barry responded brilliantly to this feedback. Instead of being defensive about it—as many of us would be if we learned that someone was harboring a deep animus toward us—he opted to turn the other cheek and begin a campaign to win Peter back to his side.

"I had options in dealing with Peter," said Barry. "I could treat him with kid gloves. Work around him. Ignore him. Start a campaign to undermine *him*. Or I could show him that I'm his friend, not his enemy, because I needed his support. I decided to make him my friend. I would direct business leads his way and go out of my way to bring deals to his division. I would keep him in the loop on everything that touched him and me—by following up and getting his input about stuff I'm working on. I would seek out his advice, show him respect, and hope he responded by no longer ignoring me."

It took Barry more than a year, but this excellent behavior converted the hatred into a working relationship. The two men didn't become instant drinking buddies (that would be asking too much), but Peter no longer hated Barry. More important, they worked well together.

I mention this because it demonstrates (a) that feedback from one person, however abstruse and vague, can be just as important as formal feedback from a group, and (b) not all feedback comes from asking people (solicited) or hearing what they volunteer. Some of the best feedback comes from what you observe. If you accept it and act on it, it's no less valid than people telling you the same thing at point-blank range.

Even if we're only half paying attention, we take in observational feedback all day long.

We shake hands with a neighbor at a party and notice that he doesn't look us in the eye. (Hmmm, we think, what's that all about?)

Coming home after work, we stroll into our living room and our 12-year-old daughter immediately leaves to go upstairs to her room. (Hmm, we think, what did we do to tick her off?)

We try to contact a client or customer and he doesn't return the call. (Hmm, we think, someone's displeased with us.)

Every day, people are giving us feedback, of a sort, with their eye contact, their body language, their response time. Interpreting this casual observational feedback can be tricky; learning that something's not right is not the same as learning what's wrong and how we can fix it.

The good news is that these feedback moments are plentiful and, with some simple drills, we can manipulate them so that patterns emerge to tell us everything we need to know to get started. Here are five ways you can get feedback by paying closer attention to the world around you.

1. Make a list of people's casual remarks about you.

I heard a creativity teacher give her class the following assignment. She sent them out in the street and for one hour had them write down everything they observed people doing in a busy public place. At the end of the hour, each student had compiled more than 150 observations. Then she had them do it again for an hour, except they were only allowed to write down observations *that they found interesting*. The lists were considerably shorter. Suddenly, a man walking across the street wasn't interesting, but a man tossing away a candy wrapper on the pavement—i.e., committing the crime of littering—was. She was trying to make the point that there's a difference between observing and observing *with judgment*.

It's the same in each of our lives. We observe all the time. But we don't often observe with a purpose or with judgment.

For one day, write down all the comments that you hear people make to you about you. For example, "Oh, that was really smart, Marshall." Or, "You're late, Marshall." Or, "Are you listening to me, Marshall?" Any remark that, however remotely, concerns you or your behavior, write it down. At the end of the day, review the list and rate each comment as positive or negative. If you look at the negatives, maybe some patterns will emerge. Perhaps a number of remarks will focus on your tardiness, or your inattention, or your lack of follow up. That's the beginning of a feedback moment. You're learning something about yourself without soliciting it—which means that the comment is agenda-free. It's honest and true.

Then do it again the next day and the next.

Do it at home too, if you want.

Eventually, you'll compile enough data about yourself—without any of your friends and family members being aware that they're giving you feedback—to establish the challenge before you.

When a friend of mine tried this for a week—at work and at home—the remark that popped up most often on his negative list was, "Yes, you said that." In effect people were telling him, "I heard you the first time," which suggested that people found his chronic repetition to be annoying.

An easy issue to fix, but he might never have learned it if he hadn't kept the list and searched for a persisting negative. If you have the courage to face the truth, you can do the same.

2. Turn the sound off.

I sometimes have clients conduct the following exercise. When they're in a team and starting to get bored, I ask them to pretend they're watching a movie with the sound off. They can't hear what anyone is saying. It's an exercise in sensitizing themselves to their colleagues' behavior. They must ask themselves what's going on around them. One of the first things they see is no different than what they hear with the sound on: People are promoting themselves. Only with this newfound sensitization, they see how people *physically* maneuver and gesture to gain primacy in a group setting. They lean forward toward the dominant authority figure. They turn away from people with diminished power. They cut rivals off with hand and arm gestures. It's no different than what people are doing with the sound on except that it's even more obvious with the sound off.

You can do the same for yourself and treat it as a feedback moment. Turn the sound off and observe how people physically deal with you. Do they lean toward you or away? Do they listen when you have the floor or are they drumming their fingers waiting for you to finish? Are they trying to impress you or are they barely aware of your presence? This won't precisely tell you what your specific challenge may be, but if the indicators are more negative than positive, you'll know that you aren't making quite the overwhelming impression on your colleagues that you may have hoped for. You'll know you have some work to do.

A variation on this drill is making sure you are the earliest person to arrive at a group meeting. Turn the sound off and observe how people respond to you as they enter. What they do is a clue about what they think of you. Do they smile when they see you and pull up a chair next to you? Do they barely acknowledge your presence and sit across the room? Note how each person responds to you. If the majority of people shy away from you, that's a disturbing pattern that's hitting you over the head with some serious truth. You have some serious work to do.

The "sound off" drill doesn't quite tell you what you need to change. But at least you'll know where to start asking, "How can I do better?" You can begin with the people in the room.

3. Complete the sentence.

The eminent psychologist Nathaniel Brandon taught me how to apply his sentence completion technique, which is a wonderful exercise for digging deep into creative thought but also works for helping people change.

Pick one thing that you want to get better at. It could be anything that matters to you—from getting in shape to giving more recognition to lowering your golf handicap. Then list the positive benefits that will accrue to you and the world if you achieve your goal. For example, "I want to get in better shape. If I get in shape, one benefit to me is that . . ." And then you complete the sentence.

It's a simple exercise. "If I get in shape, I will . . . live longer." That's one benefit. Then keep doing it. "If I get in shape, I'll feel better about myself." That's two. "If I get in shape, I'll be a better role model for my family and friends." And so on until you exhaust the benefits.

What's interesting about the sentence completion exercise is that as you get deeper into it the answers become less corporately correct and more personal. You start off by saying, "If I become better organized, the company will make more money . . . , my team will become more productive . . . , other people will enjoy their jobs more . . . , and so on." By the end, however, you're saying, "If I become more organized, I'll be a better parent . . . , a better spouse . . . , a better person."

I employed this once with a general in the U.S. Marine Corps. He was a typical hard-nosed Marine who resisted the exercise at first. I'm not sure why. But eventually he relented and played along, saying he wanted to "become less judgmental." As he began, I could see the proud Marine part of him resisting. He completed the first sentence with a cynical crack about "If I become less judgmental, I won't have so much trouble dealing with the clowns at headquarters." The second sentence was another sarcastic comment. The third time was less sarcastic. By the sixth sentence, I could see tears in his eyes. "If I become less judgmental," he said, "maybe my children will talk to me again."

This may seem like a loopy backward way of giving yourself good feedback. You start with the suggestion and then determine if it's important. But it works. As the benefits you list become less expected and more personal and meaningful to you, that's when you know that you've given yourself some valuable feedback—that you've hit on an interpersonal skill that you really want and need to improve. That's when you confirm that you've picked the right thing to fix.

4. Listen to your self-aggrandizing remarks.

I don't want to get too psychological here, but have you ever listened to a friend brag about how punctual he is—"You can count on me. I'm always on time."—when you know that being on time is the last thing you can expect from him?

Have you ever heard friends boast about how organized they are, when you know they are unmade beds?

Or how good they are at follow up when everyone thinks their responsiveness is a joke?

In one of those odd bits of reverse psychology, it seems that the stuff people boast about as their strengths more often than not turn out to be their most egregious weaknesses.

None of us is immune to this phenomenon. If it's true about our friends, it's probably true about us. Listen to yourself. What do you boast about? It's quite possible that if you assess this alleged "strength" as closely as your friends do, it's really a weakness. You shouldn't be bragging about it at all. In a perverse way, you've given yourself some of the most honest feedback of all.

I don't want to twist this into knots of psychobabble, but the same lesson might be on display when you make *self-deprecating* remarks.

When a colleague at a meeting starts off by saying, "Maybe I'm no expert on inventory control . . ." you can be sure that the comments that follow will suggest that he does think of himself as an expert on inventory control.

When a friend launches into an argument by saying, "I probably wasn't paying attention . . ." you can be sure that he's planning to show you that he was paying closer attention than you ever suspected.

The one that really perks up my ears is, "I don't have any ego invested in this." You know immediately that the issue is all about ego.

These pseudo-self-deprecating remarks—the ones we say about ourselves but don't believe—are the rhetorical devices and debating tricks of everyday communication that allow us to get an edge on our rivals. Nothing wrong with that. To a student of intracorporate warfare, such self-deprecation from others should put you on high alert. Whatever they say, you know they believe the opposite.

The same could be said of each of us. We should be on high alert when we hear ourselves make self-deprecating remarks—because they might be giving us feedback about ourselves. When you hear yourself make an offhand self-deprecation such as, "I'm not very good at thanking people," it's quite possible that you don't believe it. But it's also possible that it's true, that you're saying something piercingly honest about yourself which you're not yet admitting: You don't thank well.

As I say, I don't want to twist every comment we hear and make into knots. But self-deprecation, pseudo or otherwise, can be one of those honest feedback moments that makes a signal sound in our brain. "Pay attention," it tells us. "This might be something worth *observing*."

5. Look homeward.

Remember the movie *Wall Street* and the character Gordon Gekko? Michael Douglas won an Academy Award for Best Actor for his portrayal of this rude, larcenous wheeler-dealer. Well, I worked with a real-life investment banker who could have inspired the Gekko character.

The man I coached—let's call him Mike—wasn't amoral and unethical like Gekko, but he had some competitive fires burning within his soul that made him treat people like gravel in a driveway. They were the pebbles; he was the SUV. When I finished surveying Mike's colleagues about his interpersonal flaws, Mike's score for treating direct reports and colleagues with respect was an astounding 0.1 percent. That is, out of one thousand managers rated, he was dead last!

But Mike put up equally astounding numbers with his trades. He contributed such vast profits to the firm that the CEO promoted him to the firm's management committee. This should have been the apex of Mike's young career. But it exposed his bad side as well. The firm's leaders, who had been insulated from Mike's behavior, were suddenly in a position to get a firsthand dose of his "lead, follow, or get out of the way" style. In meetings they saw that there was no tollbooth between Mike's brain and mouth. He was surly and offensive to everyone. He would even mouth off to the CEO (his biggest supporter) in meetings. The CEO called me in to work with Mike, to "fix him."

The most obvious thing about Mike when I met him was his delight in his success. He was making more than $4 million a year, so professional validation was coursing through his veins like jet fuel. I suspected that breaking through to Mike by challenging his performance at work would be tough. He was producing and he knew it. So, the first thing I did was sit him down and tell him, "I can't help you make more money. You're already making a lot. But let's talk about your ego. How do you treat people at home?"

He said he was totally different at home, a great husband and father. "I don't bring my work home," he assured me. "I'm a warrior on Wall Street, but a pussycat at home."

"That's interesting," I said. "Is your wife home right now?"

"Yes," he said.

"Let's give her a call and see how different she thinks you are at home than at the office."

We called his wife. When she finally stopped laughing at her husband's statement, she concurred that Mike was a jerk at home, too. Then we got his two kids on the line, and they agreed with their mother.

I said, "I'm beginning to see a pattern here. As I told you, I can't help you make more money. But I can get you to confront this question: Do you really want to have a funeral where you're the featured attraction and the only attendees are people who came to make sure you're dead? Basically, that's where you're headed."

For the first time, Mike looked stricken. "They're going to fire me, aren't they?" he asked.

"Not only are they going to fire you," I said, "but everyone will be dancing in the halls when you go!"

Mike thought a minute, and then said, "I'm going to

change, and the reason I'm going to change has nothing to do with money and it has nothing to do with this firm. I'm going to change because I have two sons, and if they were receiving this same feedback from you in twenty years, I'd be ashamed."

Within a year, his scores in terms of treating people with respect shot up past the 50th percentile—meaning that he was above the already-high company norm. He probably deserved even better, since he started so far down in the ditch. He also doubled his income, although I cannot claim a direct cause-effect connection for that.

The lesson: *Your flaws at work don't vanish when you walk through the front door at home.*

The moral: Anybody can change, but they have to want to change—and sometimes you can deliver that message by reaching people where they live, not where they work.

The action plan for leaders (and followers): If you want to really know how your behavior is coming across with your colleagues and clients, stop looking in the mirror and admiring yourself. Let your colleagues hold the mirror and tell you what they see. If you don't believe them, go home. Pose the same question to your loved ones and friends—the people in your life who are most likely to be agenda-free and who truly want you to succeed. We all claim to want the truth. This is a guaranteed delivery system.

These five examples of observed feedback are stealth techniques to make you pay closer attention to the world around you.

When you make a list of people's comments about you and rank them as negative or positive, you're tuning in the world with two new weapons: Judgment and purpose.

When you turn off the sound, you're increasing your sensitivity to others by counterintuitively eliminating the precious sense of hearing.

When you try the sentence completion technique, you're using retrograde analysis—that is, seeing the end result and then identifiying the skill you'll need to achieve it.

When you challenge the accuracy of your self-aggrandizing remarks, you're flipping your world upside down—and seeing that you're no different from anyone else.

Finally, when you check out how your behavior is working at home, you realize not only what you need to change but why it matters so much.

The logic behind these drills is simple: If you can see your world in a new way, perhaps you can see yourself anew as well.

Although we've spent a lot of time on feedback here, keep in mind that it is only the baseline of our activity. We are only at the beginning.

If I were an orthopedic surgeon, feedback would be like an MRI. I need the MRI to show deep-tissue damage and identify what's broken. But I still need to perform an operation to fix the problem and the patient still needs weeks of diligent rehabilitation to get better.

If I were an advertising executive, feedback would be the part where the agency studies the data about the client's product. Who's buying it? Why? What's its market share against competing products? But this research feedback isn't a great commercial. I still have to come up with that on my own.

If I were a politician running for office, feedback would be the polling data telling me what's on voters' minds. But I still have to run for election on my own. I still have to convince voters that I'm the right person to deal with their issues. I still have to win votes. Feedback won't do *that* for me.

Feedback tells us what to change, not how to do it. But when you know what to change, you're ready to start changing yourself and how people perceive you. You're ready for the next step: telling everyone you're sorry.

CHAPTER 7

Apologizing

The Magic Move

If it isn't obvious by now, I regard apologizing as the most magical, healing, restorative gesture human beings can make. It is the centerpiece of my work with executives who want to get better—because without the apology there is no recognition that mistakes have been made, there is no announcement to the world of the intention to change, and most important there is no emotional contract between you and the people you care about. Saying you're sorry to someone writes that contract in blood.

In *Harvey Penick's Little Red Book*, there is a brief story titled "The Magic Move." It's Penick's indelible description of the cornerstone of the golf swing—the weight transfer from left to right foot as we take the club back and then the transfer back to the left foot as we bring our right elbow down and swing the club through the ball. If you learn this, says Penick, "you will hit the ball as if by magic."

Well, apologizing is my "magic move." It's a seemingly simple tactic. But like admitting you were wrong, or saying, "Thank you," it's tough for some people to do—but brilliant for those who can.

I can't think of a more vivid example of the magic move's cleansing power than Richard Clarke testifying before the 9/11 commission. Clarke spent hours talking about terrorism to the commissioners, but almost all of his testimony, much of it controversial, was overwhelmed by one moment—when he addressed the 9/11 families to say, "Your government failed you, those entrusted with protecting you failed you, and I failed you." It's an apology that Frank Rich of the *New York Times* suggested "is likely to join our history's greatest hits video reel, alongside Joseph Welch's 'Have you no sense of decency, sir?'"

Some thought Clarke was grandstanding, or that he had no right to apologize, or that he had injected an overwrought emotionality into the otherwise clinical proceedings. But I applauded, because Clarke was doing something that both parties needed. In effect, he was saying, "We can't redo the past. But the worst is behind us, and I am still so sorry." The apology gave him and the people he was addressing a sense of closure, however faint and bittersweet. Closure lets you move forward.

Clarke's apology was replayed on television for days. I'm puzzled that anyone was surprised by the emotional wallop packed into his mea culpa. It's what I try to get my clients to do without thinking. Sometimes the message takes longer to get through than I prefer.

That's what happened with a senior manager named Ted with whom I worked in the late 1990s. Ted was the standard-issue success story: a smart, personable, hard-working, deliver-the-numbers-and-live-the-values type, cherished by his bosses, admired by his colleagues, and loved by his direct reports. There was one recurring flaw in this otherwise perfect picture: Ted was disastrous on follow-up with clients and colleagues. It took years for this flaw to get noticed, which explained why all of Ted's relationships started out ecstatically but eventually drifted into conflict. He alienated the people closest to him—not out of malice or arrogance but out of passive neglect. He failed to return their calls. He would never make the first move to check up on them to see how they were doing. He would only pay attention to them if there was business to be done. This is the kind of benign hurtful pattern that emerges only over time—because you only miss nurturing and caring in their absence. But it was a recurring pattern with Ted. Somewhere along the way, he had to learn how to show people he cared for them as human beings, that he was their friend with or without a deal at stake.

We helped Ted change for the better at work—by applying the magic moves of apologize, advertise, and follow-up. That's not the point though.

Ted and I kept in touch (mostly me calling him, of course), but one day in March 2004 he phoned with exciting news.

"Marshall," he said, "you would have been proud of me. I totally screwed up one of my closest friendships."

"Okay," I hesitated. "And the reason I should be proud of you is . . ."

"Because I apologized and saved the friendship," he said.

The story goes like this: Ted's best friend for 20 years was his neighbor Vince. Over the course of two weeks, Vince had called Ted five times and Ted never called back. (Apparently, the correctives Ted had learned to apply on the job had not quite sunk in in his home life.) Vince, a volatile Sicilian who valued loyalty and friendship above all else, was hurt and stopped talking to Ted. Ted noticed but couldn't bring himself to contact Vince and apologize. Their respective wives tried to arrange a rapprochement: They decided Ted would write a contrite letter to Vince and all would be well. But Ted messed that up too. Because of business and out-of-town trips, several weeks went by without Ted writing the letter that Vince was now expecting. Finally, Vince boiled over and wrote Ted a stinging letter outlining all the slights and offenses that had poisoned their friendship—not returning phone calls, ignoring him at a dinner party, never initiating contact. (This sounds like a soap opera, but bear with me.)

This pained Ted enormously, to the point that he immediately wrote Vince a reply. I quote it here in its entirety because it is a model apologia.

> Dear Vince,
>
> As Vito Corleone said when he sat down with the Five Families, "How did it come to this?"
>
> I read your letter a few minutes ago and, in a first effort to change—i.e., being more responsive—I am writing to address the charges. As I see it, there are three.
>
> To the first count of not calling you back, you are right, absolutely right. It is rude. It is not how a friend, or even a solid citizen, behaves. I should know better. It sends an unfortunate and incorrect message that I don't care about you. (If it makes you feel better, I am democratic about this particular failing. I don't call back my mother, my brother, and my in-laws. My wife says, "Me too." This is hardly something to brag about—just a minuscule point of honor on my part to assure you that you are not in the bottom half of some imaginary call-back priority list. Apparently, I don't have one. I treat everyone equally—which is to say, rudely.) For this I apologize to you. And I will change that.
>
> To the second count of being a poor host when you were at my house, I certainly did not intend to ignore you or leave you out of the conversation. That said, what I remember is not the point. It's what you felt that matters, and this is especially pertinent when the issue is hospitality extended or withheld. As Boston Celtics coach Red Auerbach used to say about coaching his players, "It's not what you say, it's what they hear." You

obviously didn't enjoy the evening, and for that I apologize. I like to think of myself as a decent and caring and generous host, and I will take your comments as a signal to do better.

To the third count of my never initiating a phone call to friends, again you are right, absolutely right. Some people, as you say, like to work at friendship. Others don't.

Of all the charges you level at me, the third is the one that pains me most—because it is true and because it is so easily fixed. You are not the first to point this out. I guess I could wander back into my childhood to figure out why I act this way, but looking backward, seeking out scapegoats, is a fool's errand. I'm 52 years old. I can't blame my mother or my upbringing or that lousy tuna sandwich in third grade. All I can do is promise to fix my behavior, one step at a time—by taking my cues from you, by doing the things you say a good friend does. Hopefully, my rehabilitation starts with you.

The evidence notwithstanding, I do value our friendship. Tremendously. We have too many years of laughs and good times and neighboring and genuine caring for each other to let our friendship slip away because I am a schmuck in an area where you least value that kind of behavior. All I can ask is your forgiveness. If you can grant me that, I do not expect us to return to things the way they were. I think we should aim higher. I would want us to return to things as they should be, where I can aspire to the ideal of friendship that you have described in your honest, painfully honest, letter to me.

Shall we discuss this over a bottle of red?

A great letter, right? But not if it goes unread.

Vince sent it back unopened. The wives again interceded, begging Vince to read the letter. When he relented, the process of repairing the friendship was underway—because it is impossible to resist a heartfelt apology.

I always wonder about all those people who, like Ted in his former life, can't bring themselves to admit they're wrong or say they're sorry. How do they survive in the world? How do they mend damaged relationships? How do they show others what they're really feeling? How can they declare their willingness to alter their annoying ways without first saying, "I'm sorry"?

When I congratulated Ted on his handling of the situation, he said, "You know, if I hadn't gone through this at work I couldn't have apologized to Vince."

"Why can you do it now?" I asked.

"Because I know it works."

That may be a compelling reason to learn the magic move of apology, but the most compelling is this: *It is so easy to do.* All you have to do is repeat these words: "I'm sorry. I'll try to do better."

Try it sometime. It costs you nothing—not even your illusory pride—but the return on investment would make Warren Buffett green with envy. And it will change your life, as if by magic.

How to Apologize

Do you see a pattern here in the examples of Richard Clarke and Ted and Vince? The healing process begins with an apology.

It doesn't matter what we have done or what compels us to apologize. It could be the intense sorrow you feel for causing someone pain. Or the shame of neglecting someone who deserves your attention. Or the heartbreak of losing someone's affection for something you've done. Sorrow, pain, shame, heartbreak. These are powerful emotions, sometimes powerful enough to force an apology out of the hardest heart. But that's not the issue here. Cause and motive do not move me. Whatever forces an apology out of people who normally cannot do it, I'm for it.

Once you're prepared to apologize, here's the instruction manual:

You say, "I'm sorry."

You add, "I'll try to do better in the future." Not absolutely necessary, but prudent in my view because when you let go of the past, it's nice to hint at a brighter future.

And then . . . you say nothing.

Don't explain it. Don't complicate it. Don't qualify it. You only risk saying something that will dilute it. I remember back in 2001 when Morgan Stanley paid a $50 million fine to settle conflict-of-interest charges centering on the firm's research analysts writing favorable reports about companies doing business with the firm. The $50 million payment was supposed to help Morgan Stanley put the scandal behind them and move on to better days. As such, it certainly had the look and feel of an apology. But the firm's CEO, Phil Purcell, blew it the next day in a speech in which he sought to rationalize the fine. He said the firm paid it to get the issue over with; the firm really hadn't done anything wrong, and certainly wasn't as bad as other firms, which had paid even bigger fines. It sounded like he was boasting that his firm had paid the *smallest* fine. That's like bragging that you only served three years of jail time while your cellmates were in for ten.

The media, the Securities and Exchange Commission, and New York's Attorney General immediately leaped on Purcell for his remarks. No matter how much money the firm has, when you write a $50 million penalty check, that's a serious apology. You can't wink while you're apologizing. You can only say you're sorry and keep quiet.

If a sophisticated CEO can mess up a $50 million apology

by saying too much, imagine what havoc the rest of us can cause by voicing one word more than "I'm sorry" in our own displays of contrition.

When it comes to apologizing, the only sound advice is *get in and get out as quickly as possible*. You've got plenty of other things to do before you change for the better. The sooner you can get the apology over with, the sooner you can move on to telling the world.

CHAPTER 8

Telling the World, or Advertising

AFTER YOU APOLOGIZE, you must *advertise*. It's not enough to tell everyone that you want to get better; you have to declare exactly in what area you plan to change. In other words, now that you've said you're sorry, what are you going to do about it?

I tell my clients, "It's a lot harder to change people's perception of your behavior than it is to change your behavior. In fact, I calculate that you have to get 100% better in order to get 10% credit for it from your coworkers."

The logic behind this is, as I've explained in Chapter 3, cognitive dissonance: To recap, we view people in a manner that is consistent with our previous existing stereotypes, whether it is positive or negative. If I think you're an arrogant jerk, everything you do will be filtered through that perception. If you do something wonderful and saintly, I will regard it as the exception to the rule; you're still an arrogant jerk. Within that framework it's almost impossible for us to be perceived as improving, no matter how hard we try.

However, the odds improve considerably if you tell people that you are trying to change. Suddenly, your efforts are on their radar screen. You're beginning to chip away at their preconceptions.

Your odds improve again if you tell everyone how hard

you're trying, and repeat the message week after week.

Your odds improve even more if you ask everyone for ideas to help you get better. Now your coworkers become invested in you; they pay attention to you to see if you're paying attention to their suggestions.

Eventually the message sinks in and people start to accept the possibility of a new improved you. It's a little like the tree falling in the forest. If no one hears the thud, does it make a sound? The apology and the announcement that you're trying to change are your way of pointing everyone in the direction of the tree.

Don't Forget the "Dumb" Phase

Any marketer knows that there's no point in creating a great new product if you can't get the message out to the buying public. You have to tell the world, "Hey, I'm over here," and give them a reason to care.

That's the same rationale you must use as you undertake a serious personal initiative. You're about to create a new "you." Do you think people will buy that without a good advertising campaign?

It's not enough to merely let people know what you're doing. You're not running a "one day sale" here. You're trying to create a lasting change. You have to advertise *relentlessly*—as if it's a long-term campaign. You can't assume that people hear you the first time or the second time or even the third. You have to pound the message into your colleagues' heads through repetition that's as steady as a metronome—because people aren't paying as close attention to your personal goals as you are. They have other things on their minds; they have their own goals and challenges to deal with. As a result, your efforts to change may not get instant acceptance from your colleagues. You may have to fight your way through a "dumb phase."

I first heard this phrase as a dinner guest at the home of a wine expert. One of the other guests brought a 12-year-old bottle of red wine from one of the legendary vineyards of France. We were all eager to drink it, but our host politely suggested that it might not be the right time. It's 12 years old. It's ready, we insisted. So we opened the bottle, decanted it, poured it into sparkling crystals, swirled it in the glass, inhaled its profound bouquet, and then eagerly tasted it.

We put down our glasses and looked around at each other. We were all thinking the same thing. This wine has no flavor or character at all.

We tasted again.

Same opinion. The wine was totally bland, as if it had died in the bottle.

Finally, our oenophile host explained that some truly great wines, which can last for decades and tend to improve with age, go through a "dumb period" when the wine goes to sleep for a few years and then wakes up and improves dramatically in the bottle. It happens anywhere from age 6 to 18 years, depending on the wine. Our bottle was still in its dumb period. Like he said, we should have waited.

It's the same with any project you undertake at work, whether it's a campaign of personal change or an initiative that can transform your company. The best ideas are like great wines. They improve with age. But they can also go through a dumb period when they need time to settle and sink in.

Has the following ever happened to you? Your boss gives you a major assignment to find out what's going on at a trouble spot within your company. You do what any well-trained M.B.A. would do. You study the situation, identify the problem, report your findings and recommendations to the boss, outline a new approach, and turn it over to the appropriate people to implement the strategy.

A month goes by. Nothing happens. Another month. Still no progress. Six months later, the trouble spot remains unchanged.

What did you do wrong?

It's simple. You committed "one, two, three, seven."

You failed to appreciate that every successful project goes through seven phases: The first is assessing the situation; the second is isolating the problem; the third is formulating. But there are three more phases before you get to the seventh, implementation.

Unfortunately, a lot of people don't pay close attention to phases four, five, and six—the vital period when you approach your coworkers to secure the all-important political buy-in to your plans. In each phase you must target a different constituency. In phase 4, you woo up—to get your superiors to *approve*. In phase 5, you woo laterally—to get your peers to *agree*. In phase 6, you woo down—to get your direct reports to *accept*. These three phases are the sine qua non of getting things done. You cannot skip or skim over them. You have to give them as much, if not more, attention, as you do phases one, two, three, and seven. If you don't, you may as well be working alone in a locked room where no one sees you, hears you, or knows you exist. That's the guaranteed result of committing "one, two, three, seven."

What's true for getting people to solve a corporate problem is just as true for getting people to help you change for the better. It takes time and relentless persuasion for any idea to gain traction. Think of your "advertising" as recruiting colleagues up, over, and down to buy in to the concept. If you don't, you are committing "one, two, three, seven" on yourself. You can't get to seven without counting from one to six. Anything less is bad arithmetic.

Be Your Own Press Secretary

Wouldn't the world be a better place if we each had our own presidential press secretary to answer tough questions and "spin" our message all day long against any and all adversaries? (It would be great for us perhaps, but I'm not sure I want to live in a world where everyone is "spinning" everyone else.)

That said, there's something to be learned from the methods that politicians employ to stay in power.

Chief among these is staying on message—i.e., knowing what you want to say and then repeating it with extreme discipline and near-shamelessness, until it sinks in. If there's one thing we've learned in this noisy media age, it's that simple, un-nuanced messages break through the clutter and hit home with high impact. (I'm not saying that's always a good thing, but it's a fact of life. Deal with it.)

It's no different when you're attempting to change. Like a politician making headlines for introducing new legislation, if you have a new initiative at work, you have to do something dramatic to announce it. (Reagan taught us that.) For sheer drama, apologizing fits the bill. What could be more theatrical than telling people that you're sorry for some transgression and you'll try to do better in the future, especially people who think *you cannot change*?

Don't stop there. You can't just apologize and say you're trying to do better just once. You have to drill it into people repeatedly, until they've internalized the concept.

It's the reason politicians in a hard election campaign run the same ads over and over again. Repeating their message— relentlessly—works; it sinks the message deeper into our brains.

I don't want to push this political press secretary analogy too far. I'm not asking people to obfuscate or display selective memory or avoid questions, all of which are valuable weapons in the press secretary arsenal. All I'm saying is that you cannot rely on other people to read your mind or take note of the changed behavior you're displaying. It may be patently obvious to you, but it takes a lot more than a few weeks of behavioral modification for people to notice the new you.

That makes it all the more vital that you proactively control the message of what you're trying to accomplish. Here's how to start acting like your own press secretary.

- Treat every day as if it were a press conference during which your colleagues are judging you, waiting to see you trip up. That mindset, where you know people are watching you closely, will boost your self-awareness just enough to remind you to stay on high alert.
- Behave as if every day is an opportunity to hit home your message—to remind people that you're trying really hard. Every day that you fail to do so is a day that you lose a step or two. You're backsliding on your promise to fix yourself.
- Treat every day as a chance to take on all challengers. There will be people who, privately or overtly, don't want you to succeed. So shed the naiveté and be a little paranoid. If you're alert to those who want you to fail, you'll know how to handle them.
- Think of the process as an election campaign. After all, you don't elect yourself to the position of "new improved you." Your colleagues do. They're your constituency. Without their votes, you can never establish that you've changed.
- Think of the process in terms of weeks and months, not just day to day. The best press secretaries are adept at putting out the daily fires, but they're also focused on a long-term agenda. You should too. No matter

. what happens day to day, your long-term goal is to be
perceived as fixing an interpersonal problem—to the
point where it isn't a problem anymore.

If you can do this, like the best press secretaries, you'll have
your personal "press corps" eating out of your hands.

CHAPTER 9

Listening

JACK NICKLAUS SAID THAT 80 percent of a successful golf shot begins
with a proper grip and how you stand over the ball. In other
words, success is almost a foregone conclusion before you exert
one muscle.

It's the same with listening: 80 percent of our success in
learning from other people is based upon how well we listen. In
other words, success or failure is determined before we do
anything.

The thing about listening that escapes most people is that
they think of it as a passive activity. You don't have to do anything. You sit there like a lump and hear someone out.

Not true. Good listeners regard what they do as a highly
active process—with every muscle engaged, especially the brain.

Basically, there are three things that all good listeners do:
They think before they speak; they listen with respect; and
they're always gauging their response by asking themselves, "Is
it worth it?" Let's examine each one and see if it makes us better
listeners.

Think Before You Speak

The first active choice you have to make in listening is to think before you speak. You can't listen if you're talking. So keeping your mouth shut is an active choice (and as we know, for some people it's tougher to do than bench-pressing 500 pounds).

I don't know anyone better at it than Frances Hesselbein. Frances is one of my all-time heroes—someone I respect, admire, and love on a par with my wife and kids. She was the executive director of the Girl Scouts for 13 years during which she revived a sagging organization, increased enrollment, funding, and diversity, and balanced the budget. She has 17 honorary degrees. She received the Presidential Medal of Freedom in 1998 (America's highest civilian award). Peter Drucker called her the finest executive he's ever known.

Frances Hesselbein does a lot of things well. But she does one thing superbly above all else. She thinks before she speaks. As a result she is a world-class listener. If you asked her if this was a passive gesture, she would assure you that it requires great discipline, particularly when she is upset about what she's hearing. After all, what do most of us do when we're angry? We speak (and not in the carefully measured tones of a diplomat).

What do we do when we're upset? We talk.

What do we do when we're confused or surprised or shocked? Again, we talk. This is so predictable that we can see the other party almost cringe in anticipation of our harsh unthinking autoreflex response.

Not so with Frances Hesselbein. You could tell her the world was about to end and she would think before opening her mouth, not only about what she would say but how she would phrase it.

Whereas most people think of listening as something we

do during those moments *when we are not talking*, Frances Hesselbine knows that listening is a two-part maneuver. There's the part where we actually listen. And there's the part where we speak. Speaking establishes how we are perceived as a listener. What we say is proof of how well we listen. They are two sides of the same coin.

I defy you to argue that this approach is anything but a highly active, decisive choice. Telling your brain and mouth not to do something is no different than telling them to do it.

If you can master this, you can listen effectively.

Listen with Respect

To learn from people, you have to listen to them with respect. Again, not as easy to do as you might imagine. It too requires the use of unfamiliar muscles.

Has this ever happened to you? You're reading a book, watching TV, or shuffling papers while your significant other is talking to you. Suddenly you hear, "You're not listening to me."

You look up and say, "Yes I am." And calmly provide a verbatim playback of everything said to prove that you were listening and that your companion in life is . . . wrong.

What have you accomplished by this virtuosic display of your multitasking skills? Was it smart? No. Does your partner think more highly of you? Not likely. Is anyone impressed? Hardly.

The only thing going through your partner's mind is, "Gee, I thought you weren't listening. But now I realize it's a much deeper issue. You're a complete jerk."

This is what happens when we listen without showing respect. It's not enough to keep our ears open; we have to demonstrate that we are totally engaged.

Bill Clinton was the absolute master at this. My wife and I had several opportunities see the President in action in public forums. It didn't matter if you were a head of state or a bell clerk, when you were talking with Bill Clinton he acted as if you were the only person in the room. Every fiber of his being, from his eyes to his body language, communicated that he was locked into what you were saying. He conveyed how important you were, not how important *he* was.

If you don't think this is an active, practically aerobic piece of mental and muscular exertion, try it sometime in a receiving line of 500 people, all of whom regard this brief transaction with you as part of their lifetime highlight reel.

If you've never done it, listening with respect makes you sweat.

Ask Yourself, "Is It Worth It?"

Listening also requires us to answer a difficult question before we speak: "Is it worth it?"

The trouble with listening for many of us is that while we're supposedly doing it, we're actually busy composing what we're going to say next.

This is a negative two-fer: You're not only failing to hear the other person, you're orchestrating a comment that may annoy them, either because it misses the point, adds meaningless value to the discussion, or worst of all, injects a destructive tone into the mix. Not the desired result of listening. Keep it up and soon you won't have to worry about listening—because no one will be talking to you anymore.

When someone tells us something, we have a menu of options to fashion our response. Some of our responses are smart, some are stupid. Some are on point, some miss the point. Some will encourage the other person, some will discourage her. Some will make her feel appreciated, some will not.

Asking "Is it worth it?" forces you to consider what the other person will feel after hearing your response. It forces you to play at least two moves ahead. Not many people do that. You talk. They talk. And so on—back and forth like a beginner's chess game where no one thinks beyond the move in front of them. It's the lowest form of chess; it's also the lowest grade of listening. Asking, "Is it worth it?" engages you in thinking beyond the discussion to consider (a) how the other person regards you, (b) what that person will do afterwards, and (c) how that person will behave the next time you talk.

That's a lot of consequences emanating out of "Is it worth it?"

Think about the last time you floated an idea in a meeting and the most senior person in the room (assuming it wasn't you) ripped you for saying it. It doesn't matter whether your idea was dumb and the other person's response was brilliant—or vice versa. Just think about how you felt. Did you think more highly of the other person saying it? Did it make you appreciate anew that person's tremendous listening skills? Did it inspire you to go back to your work with fresh enthusiasm? Did it make you more eager to speak up the next time you were in a meeting with that person? I'd wager the answers are no, no, no, and no.

That's what happens when you respond without asking "Is it worth it?" People not only think you don't listen, but you have instigated a three-part chain of consequences: (1) they are hurt; (2) they harbor ill feelings toward the person who inflicted the hurt (i.e., they hate you); and (3) in the predictable response to negative reinforcement, they are less likely to repeat the event (i.e., they won't speak up next time).

Keep it up, and here's what will happen: Everyone will think you're an ass (a personal judgment, not necessarily damaging, but certainly not nice). They won't perform well for you (which damages your reputation as a leader). And they'll stop giving you ideas (which reduces your knowledge base). This is hardly the formula for leadership success.

One of my clients was the chief operating officer of a multi-billion dollar company (and now the CEO). His goal was to become a better listener and be perceived as a more open-minded boss. After working with him for 18 months, I asked him what was the major learning kernel he got out of the experience. He said, "Before speaking, I take a breath and ask myself one question, 'Is it worth it?' I learned that 50 percent of what I was going to say was correct—maybe—but saying it wasn't worth it."

He learned what Frances Hesselbein knew—that people's opinions of our listening ability are largely shaped by the decisions we make immediately after asking, "Is it worth it?" Do we speak or shut up? Do we argue or simply say, "Thank you"? Do we add our needless two cents or bite our tongue? Do we rate the comments or simply acknowledge them?

It's not up to me to tell you what to say in a meeting. All I'm saying is that you should consider if it's worth it—and if you believe it is, speak freely.

This is what my client absorbed. As a result, his scores for being a better listener and an open-minded boss skyrocketed. And he became the CEO.

The implications of "Is it worth it?" are profound—and go beyond listening. In effect, you are taking the age-old question of self-interest, "What's in it for me?" one step further to ask, "What's in it for him?" That's a profound consequential leap of thought. Suddenly, you're seeing the bigger picture.

As I say over and over again, this is simple stuff—but it's not easy. If you do it, everything will get better. So much of our interpersonal problems at work are formulaic. You say something that ticks me off. I lash back at you. Suddenly, we have an interpersonal crisis (otherwise known as a fight). It doesn't matter whether we're talking about global warming or whom to hire to make a widget. The content is irrelevant. What matters is how easily we slip into small behavioral patterns that create friction in the workplace—and how just as easily we could assume behavioral patterns that *don't* create friction. That's why simple disciplines—such as thinking before speaking, listening with respect, and asking, "Is it worth it?"—work. They don't require nuance. We just need to do them.

The Skill that Separates the Near-Great from the Great

Two lawyers are sitting at the bar at Spark's Steakhouse in New York City. One is my friend Tom, the other is his law partner, Dave. They're having a leisurely drink, waiting for their table to open up. They're in no rush. Spark's is the kind of place where you don't mind hanging around. It's a landmark steakhouse, with a huge dining room, a world-famous wine list, and a handful of New York's rich, powerful, or glamorous in attendance every night. (It's also notorious as the site where New York crime boss Paul Castellano was gunned down by John Gotti's henchmen.) On this night, the A-list name is superstar attorney David Boies, who has just walked in and immediately makes a beeline to the bar to say hello to lawyer Dave, whom he knows from previous trials. Boies joins Tom and Dave for a drink. A few minutes later Dave gets up to make a phone call outside. It turns into a very long call.

Boies remains at the bar, talking to my pal Tom for 45 minutes.

What the two lawyers discussed is not relevant here.

What's relevant is my friend Tom's recollection of the encounter.

"I'd never met Boies before," said Tom. "He didn't have to hang around the bar talking to me. And I have to tell you, I wasn't bowled over by his intelligence, or his piercing questions, or his anecdotes. What impressed me was that when he asked a question, he waited for the answer. He not only listened, he made me feel like I was the only person in the room."

I submit that Tom's last 13 words perfectly describe the single skill that separates the great from the near-great.

My friend Tom isn't easily impressed. He's vice chairman of a prosperous 300-lawyer firm in New York. His partner Dave is a highly skilled litigator. Boies, of course, is a legal superstar, the attorney the U.S. government hired to argue its antitrust case against Bill Gates and Microsoft, the same attorney Al Gore turned to in 2000 to argue his presidential election challenge in front of the U.S. Supreme Court.

Let's examine what happened at the bar. Tom stayed in his seat. Dave, for inexplicable reasons, disappeared to make a phone call outside. Boies, on the other hand, stuck around and made a lasting positive impression on Tom. There was no reason for him to treat Tom as his new best friend. The two attorneys have different practices; the chances that their paths would cross in court or that they could help each other is virtually nil. In other words, Boies wasn't thinking that there would be some future benefit in being nice to Tom. And yet, he still made my friend Tom feel like the most important person in the room. In showing interest, asking questions, and most important, listening for the answers without distraction, Boies was simply being himself, practicing the one skill that has made him an inarguably great success.

The ability to make a person feel that, when you're with that person, he or she is the most important (and the only) person in the room is the skill that separates the great from the near-great.

Television interviewers like Oprah Winfrey, Katie Couric, and Diane Sawyer, I'm told by people who've met them, have it. When they're talking to you, on camera or off, you feel as if you're the only one who matters to them. It's *the* skill that defines them.

A British acquaintance told me about an aging executive who could always be seen at London restaurants dining with the most beautiful women in the world. It wasn't his looks or animal magnetism. He was short, jowly, overweight, bald, and well into his seventies. But when my acquaintance asked one woman why she was so enthralled with this man, she answered, "He never takes his eyes off me. Even if the Queen walked in, he wouldn't be distracted. He would still be devoting his full attention to me. That's hard to resist."

As I say, Bill Clinton has this skill in spades. Whether you were meeting him for the first time in a receiving line, or dealing with him one-on-one in a private session, Clinton made a point of knowing something positive about you and, without making a big show of it, saying something to let you know he knew it. In effect, he was bragging about you *to you*. That's a very meaningful gesture. (Imagine how you'd feel if, instead of being forced to tell someone how swell you are, they pointed out your swellness to you and to everyone within earshot. Kinda nice, huh? Wouldn't you really respond to that person?) Couple that with a laser-like focus on what you had to say, and you understand why Clinton ascended far from his humble Arkansas origins.

I'm not sure why all of us don't execute this precious interpersonal maneuver all the time. We're certainly capable of doing so when it *really* matters to us.

If we're on a first date with a guy or girl whom we really want to impress, we will be paragons of attentiveness and interest. We will ask all the right questions, and we will pay attention to the answers with the concentration of a brain surgeon operating inside a patient's skull. If we're really smart, we will calibrate the conversation to make sure we don't talk too much.

If we're in a meeting with our boss, we will listen without interruption to every word she says. We will mark the boss's vocal inflections, seeing nuance and meaning that may or may not be intended. We will lock in on the boss's eyes and mouth, searching for smiles or frowns, as if they were significant clues about our career prospects. Basically, we are treating our boss as if she's the most important person in the room (because she is).

Likewise if we're on a sales call with a prospect who could make or break our year. We prepare by knowing something personal about the prospect. We ask questions designed to reveal the prospect's inclinations. We scan the prospect's face for clues about how badly he needs what we're selling. We are at Defcon Five in terms of attentiveness. Full alert.

The only difference between us and the super-successful among us—the near-great and the great—is that *the great ones do this all the time*. It's automatic for them. For them there's no on and off switch for caring and empathy and showing respect. It's always on. They don't rank personal encounters as A, B, or C in importance. They treat everyone equally—and everyone eventually notices.

The weird part here is that all of us, at every level of success, already know this. I've asked my clients point blank, "What interpersonal skill stands out in the most successful people you've met?" In one form or another, they always cite this "make the other person feel singularly special" ability—usually because (like my friend Tom) they're so impressed by people who make *them* feel that way.

So, I don't think I'm promulgating something new or hard to accept here. We already believe it.

The question is: Why don't we do it?

Answer: We forget. We get distracted. We don't have the mental discipline to make it automatic.

That's it in a nutshell.

Ninety percent of this skill is listening, of course. And listening requires a modicum of discipline—the discipline to concentrate. So I've developed a simple exercise to test my clients' listening skills. It's simple—as simple as asking people to touch their toes to establish how limber they are. I ask them to close their eyes and count slowly to fifty with one simple goal: They cannot let another thought intrude into their mind. They must concentrate on maintaining the count.

What could be simpler than that? Try it.

Incredibly, more than half my clients can't do it. Somewhere around twenty or thirty, nagging thoughts invade their brain. They think about a problem at work, or their kids, or how much they ate for dinner the night before.

This may sound like a concentration test, but it's really a listening exercise. After all, if you can't listen to yourself (someone you presumably like and respect) as you count to fifty, how will you ever be able to listen to another person?

Like any exercise, this drill both exposes a weakness and helps you get stronger. If I ask you to touch your toes and you can't, we've revealed that your muscles are tight. If you practice touching your toes each day, eventually you'll become more limber.

That's what this fifty-count exercise achieves. It exposes how easily distracted we can be when we're not talking. But it also helps us develop our concentration muscles—our ability to maintain focus. Do this exercise regularly and you'll soon be counting to 50 without interrupting yourself. This newfound power of concentration will make you a better listener.

After that, you're ready for a test drive.

Put this book down and make your next interpersonal encounter—whether it's with your spouse or a colleague or a stranger—an exercise in making the other person feel like a million bucks. Try to employ the tiny tactics we've outlined here.

- Listen.
- Don't interrupt.
- Don't finish the other person's sentences.
- Don't say "I knew that."
- Don't even agree with the other person (even if he praises you, just say, "Thank you").
- Don't use the words "no," "but," and "however."
- Don't be distracted. Don't let your eyes or attention wander elsewhere while the other person is talking.
- Maintain your end of the dialogue by asking intelligent questions that (a) show you're paying attention, (b) move the conversation forward, and (c) require the other person to talk (while you listen).
- Eliminate any striving to impress the other person with how smart or funny you are. Your only aim is to let the other person feel that *he or she* is accomplishing that.

If you can do that, you'll uncover a glaring paradox: *The more you subsume your desire to shine, the more you will shine in the other person's eyes.* I've seen this happen so many times, it's almost comical. I've watched two people have a discussion where one person is clearly doing all the talking while the other person patiently listens and asks questions. Later on, when I've asked the dominant talker what he thought of the other person, he never regards the other person's relative silence as evidence that he's dull, uninformed, and uninteresting. On the contrary, he invariably says, "What a great guy!"

You'd say the same thing about anyone who brought out

the best in you, who made you feel like the most important person in the room.

Please note that this test run is not an exercise in developing newfound charm, or learning the jargon of seduction, or using body language as subtle levers of persuasion. It's nothing more than an exercise in active listening. Active in the sense that there's a purpose to your listening. If your objective is to make people feel like a million bucks in your presence, you'll score a bull's-eye. You already know how to do it—on a first date, on a sales call, in a meeting with your boss. From now on, it's a matter of remembering to *do it all the time*.

CHAPTER 10

Thanking

Why Thanking Works

Thanking works because it expresses one of our most basic emotions: gratitude. Gratitude is not an abstraction. It's a genuine emotion, which cannot be expected or exacted. You either feel it or you don't. But when someone does something nice for you, *they expect gratitude*—and they think less of you for withholding it. Just think about the last time you gave someone a gift. If they forgot to thank you for it, how did you feel about them? Fine human being? Or ungrateful s.o.b.?

Gratitude is a complex emotion—and therefore can be complicated to express. It is frequently interpreted as submissive behavior, slightly humiliating. This may explain why parents must constantly remind their children to say, "Thank you." It's one of the last and hardest things to teach naturally rebellious kids.

One other thing: Saying "Thank you" is a crucial feature of etiquette and being mannerly. As with most rules of etiquette, it can become formulaic; it doesn't have to be sincere. We use the phrase all day long without thinking, often as a form of punctuation in conversation. For example, we'll say "thank you" on a phone call to end the conversation. We may not be conscious that "thank you" in this context really means "We're done here. Now please stop talking." But such is the polite power of "Thank you" that people always obey.

The best thing about saying "Thank you" is that it creates closure in any potentially explosive discussion. What can you say after someone thanks you? You can't argue with them. You can't try to prove them wrong. You can't trump them or get angry or ignore them. The only response is to utter two of the most gracious, inviting, and sweet words in the language: "You're welcome." It's music to anyone's ears.

Get used to saying, "Thank you." You're going to need this skill as we move on to the final two steps: follow-up and feedforward. But first, a series of thanking drills:

Give Yourself an A+ in Gratitude

I was flying to Santa Barbara, California. Suddenly, the plane took an enormous dip—one of those thrill-ride deep drops that make many passengers grab for the air sickness bag and the rest of us think about the afterlife. The pilot came on the speaker system and announced in his calm Chuck Yeager voice that we had a "minor problem." The landing gear wasn't working and we were going to circle the airport until we ran out of fuel so we could land more safely with the wheels up. It's always disconcerting to be circling in a plane waiting for it to run out of fuel. In those moments, when you're thinking, "I might die!" you begin to ponder your life. You ask yourself, "What do I regret?"

At least that's what I did. I thought about how many people have been good to me in my life. I never thanked them adequately.

I told myself, "If I ever get down on the ground, I will thank these people." This is not an uncommon thought. The number one regret children have when their parents die is that they never told them how much they appreciated all that the parents had done for them.

The plane landed safely. (Believe me, I thanked the pilot and crew.) When I got to my hotel room, the first thing I did was write gushy, mushy thank you notes to at least 50 people who had helped me in my life.

That was the moment I became a connoisseur of gratitude, a virtuoso at thanking. I'm always thanking people now in my e-mails, my letters, my seminars. The last thing I say on most phone calls is not "good-bye" but "thank you," and I really mean it. When it comes to gratitude, I'm a radical fundamentalist. I've even gone so far as to make a list of the top 25 people in both my personal and professional lives to whom I owed thanks. I had special certificates printed up with their names embossed in gold lettering saying, "Thank you. You're one of the top 25 people who have helped me have a great professional life."

I realize this is a bit extreme, but I make no apology for it. I have a lot of deficiencies, but gratitude is not one of them. I regard gratitude as an asset. Its absence is a major interpersonal flaw. I give myself an A+ in gratitude.

That should be your goal, too.

Here's an exercise to get you started (mercifully without the in-flight adrenaline rush of imminent death).

No matter how far along you are in life, think about your career. Who are the people most responsible for your success? Write down the first 25 names that come to mind. Ask yourself, "Have I ever told them how grateful I am for their help?" If you're like the rest of us, you probably have fallen short in this area.

Before you do anything else (including moving on to the next chapter of this book) write each of these people a thank you note.

This isn't just an exercise in making yourself and other people feel good (although that's a worthwhile therapeutic). Writing a thank you note forces you to confront the humbling fact that you have not achieved your success alone. You had help along the way.

More important, it forces you to identify your strengths and weaknesses. After all, when you thank people for helping you, you're admitting that you needed help in the first place— which is one way to pinpoint your deficiencies. If you didn't need to improve in a specific area, you wouldn't have needed another person's help. Think of it as a thank you note's side benefit; it helps you identify your old weak spots (which may still be weaker than you think).

As I write these words, it occurs to me that telling people to write thank you notes is obvious, almost trite. But it's incredible how neglected a practice thanking is. None of us can ever do it enough.

Eventually, you'll come to see that expressing gratitude is a talent—a talent that goes hand in hand with wisdom and self-knowledge and maturity.

A lawyer friend was arguing a case in front of a state supreme court justice. He didn't win the case, but afterwards the judge took him aside and praised him for the quality of writing in his briefs. "They were a pleasure to read," said the judge, "even if they weren't ultimately persuasive."

My friend thanked the judge and explained that he owed his writing skill to an English professor during his undergraduate years at Notre Dame. The professor had taken him aside and in a dozen sessions forced him to write succinctly.

"Did you ever thank him?" asked the wise judge.

"No," said my friend. "I haven't talked to him in twenty years."

"Maybe you should," said the judge.

That night he wrote to the professor, still teaching at Notre Dame, and told him the whole story in a thank you note.

A week later the professor wrote back, congratulating my friend on the timeliness of his note. The professor had been slogging through dozens of term papers, questioning the value of reading them and grading them. "Your note," he wrote, "reminded me that what I'm doing has worth."

That's the beauty and grace of a thank you note. If you can get an A+ in gratitude, nothing bad will ever come of it. Only good.

CHAPTER 11

Following Up

You Do Not Get Better without Follow-Up

Once you master the subtle arts of apologizing, advertising, listening, and thanking, you must follow up—relentlessly. Or everything else is just a "program of the month."

I teach my clients to go back to *all* their coworkers every month or so and ask them for comments and suggestions. For example, that first client who had a problem sharing and including his peers went to each colleague and said the following: "Last month I told you that I would try to get better at being more inclusive. You gave me some ideas and I would like to know if you think I have effectively put them into practice." That question forces his colleagues to stop what they're doing and, once again, think about his efforts to change, mentally gauge his progress, and keep him focused on continued improvement.

If you do this every month, your colleagues eventually begin to accept that you're getting better—not because you say so but because it's coming from *their* lips. When I tell you, "I'm getting better," I believe it. When I ask you, "Am I getting better?" and you say I am, then *you* believe it.

In the late 1970s and early 1980s, New York City's Mayor Ed Koch was famous for touring the five boroughs of New York and asking everyone he met, "How'm I doing?" To the untrained eye, Koch's question seemed like unbridled egotism, a weary hangover from the "Me Decade." Koch knew better. With the gut instinct of a master politician who understood people and perceptions, Koch was executing a crude but fairly sophisticated strategy of follow-up to create change, not only in the city but in its citizens' perception of their mayor.

By asking people, "How'm I doing?" he was advertising the fact that he was trying; that he cared.

By phrasing it as a question, rather than asserting, "I'm doing great," Koch was both including and involving the citizens, telling them in effect that his fate rested in *their* hands.

By repeating the question—turning "How'm I doing" into his personal slogan—Koch was imprinting his efforts in the citizens' minds and reminding them that improving New York City was an ongoing process, not an overnight miracle (which helps explain why he was New York's last three-term mayor).

Most important, "How'm I doing" forced Koch to "walk the talk." If he asked the question and people answered, "Not so great," he had to deal with the answer so he wouldn't hear it the next time he asked, "How'm I doing?"

Follow-up is the most protracted part of the process of changing for the better. It goes on for 12 to 18 months. Fittingly, it's the difference-maker in the process.

Follow-up is how you measure your progress.

Follow-up is how we remind people that we're making an effort to change, and that they are helping us.

Follow-up is how our efforts eventually get imprinted on our colleagues' minds.

Follow-up is how we erase our coworkers' skepticism that we *can* change.

Follow-up is how we acknowledge to ourselves and others that getting better is an *ongoing* process, not a temporary religious conversion.

More than anything, follow-up makes us do it. It gives us the momentum, even the courage, to go beyond understanding what we need to do to change and *actually do it,* because in engaging in the follow-up process, we are *changing*.

Why Follow-Up Works

Let me make an important admission: I didn't start out knowing this about the importance of follow-up. I was preparing training sessions at a Fortune 100 company when the Executive Vice President, perhaps with an eye on the training budget, asked me the perfectly reasonable question, "Does anyone who goes to these leadership development programs ever *really* change?"

I thought about it for a moment, and thought some more, then sheepishly answered, "I don't know."

I had trained thousands of people. I had received glowing reviews about my classes (although it occurred to me that the reviews only meant attendees *thought* my classes were valuable; it didn't prove their value). I had dozens of letters from people who believed they had changed (although I realized that didn't mean *anyone else* believed they had changed). I had worked with some of the best companies in the world and nobody had ever asked me that question. Worse, until that moment, it had never entered my mind.

This was a life-altering moment for me. Until then I had been one of the more successful practitioners of 360-degree feedback, a participative management concept that had workers evaluating their managers rather than the other way around. My personal contribution to the field was the notion of "custom feedback." I created surveys that answered the question, "What makes a great leader in *this particular organization*?" But even though I loved to crunch numbers, I had never gone back to these companies to see if my training sessions had had any effect or if people actually did what they promised to do in the training sessions. I assumed that if they understood the benefit of listening to wise, wonderful, and practical me, they would do what they were told.

Chastened by the executive vice president's piercingly obvious question, I became a follow-up grind for the next two years. I scoured all the research and went back to all my client corporations, assembling data that answered the question, "Does anyone really change?"

The numbers slowly grew into a statistically significant pile that involved eight major corporations, each of which invested millions of dollars a year in leadership development programs. In other words, they took the process of developing executives very seriously. My pool of respondents eventually numbered 86,000 participants.* As I studied the data, three conclusions emerged.

The first lesson: Not everyone responds to executive development, at least not in the way the organization desires or intends. Some people are trainable; some aren't. It's not because they don't want to get better. At the eight companies where hundreds of employees have gone through my leadership development training, I asked the participants at the end of each session whether they intended to go back to their job and apply what they had just learned. Almost 100 percent said yes. A year later I asked the direct reports of these same leaders to confirm that

* I outlined the complete methodology, statistical results, the companies involved, and my conclusions in "Leadership Is a Contact Sport: The Follow-Up Factor in Management Development," written with Howard Morgan, in *Strategy and Business*, Fall 2004.

their boss applied the lessons on the job. About 70 percent said yes and 30 percent said the boss had done absolutely nothing. This 70/30 split showed up with statistically elegant consistency in each of the eight companies I studied, and it didn't waver whether the executives involved were Americans, Europeans, or Asians. In other words, it reflects human nature, not cultural imprinting.

When I drilled a little deeper to find out why executives would go through training, promise to implement what they learned, and then *not do it,* the answer was incredibly mundane and, again, reflective of human nature. They failed to implement the changes *because they were simply too busy.* After the training session, they all returned to their offices to find piles of messages to return, reports to read and write, clients and customers to call. They were distracted by the day-to-day demands of their job.

This taught me a second lesson: There is an enormous disconnect between understanding and doing. Most leadership development revolves around one huge false assumption: If people understand, then they will do. That's not true. Most of us understand, we just don't do. For example, we all understand that being grossly overweight is bad for our health, but not all of us actually do anything to change our condition.

But this insight didn't really answer my question. It only indicated that 70 percent of all the people who *understand* will actually *do.* It didn't tell me whether the 70 percent who applied the lessons actually got better.

That's when I realized that follow-up was the missing link not only in my training concepts but also in getting people to change. Here I was, telling people that part of the process of changing for the better was following up with colleagues and asking, "How'm I doing?" But I had never followed up myself to measure the impact of my clients' follow-up. I rewired my objectives and began measuring people to see not only if they got better but why. My hunch about follow-up being the difference-maker paid off.

I traced five of my eight companies to measure the level of follow-up among their executives. Follow-up was defined as interaction between would-be "leaders" and their colleagues to see if they were, in fact, improving their leadership effectiveness. Follow-up ran through five scales—from "frequent interaction" to "little or none."

The results were astonishingly consistent. At one end of the spectrum, when leaders did little or no follow-up with their subordinates, there was little or no perceived change in the leaders' effectiveness. At the other extreme, when leaders consistently followed up, the perception of their effectiveness jumped dramatically.

My conclusion was swift and unequivocal: *People don't get better without follow-up. That was lesson three.*

In hindsight, it makes perfect sense—and echoes the Peter Drucker prediction that "the leader of the future will be a person who knows how to ask." If nothing else, these studies show that leaders who ask for input on a regular basis are seen as increasing in effectiveness. Leaders who don't follow up are not necessarily bad leaders. They are just not perceived as getting better.

In a way, our work reinforces a key insight from the famous Hawthorne Effect studies, which Harvard professor Elton Mayo conducted among factory workers at the Western Electric Hawthorne Works nearly 80 years ago. The Hawthorne Effect posits that productivity tends to increase when workers believe that their bosses are showing a greater interest and involvement in their work. In its most elemental form, it's the reason employees are more alert at their job when they know the boss is watching. In its more subtle forms, it's the reason entire factory floors work harder with greater morale when they see that their bosses care about their welfare.

The same dynamic was at work in my follow-up studies. Follow-up shows that you care about getting better. Following up with your coworkers shows that you value their opinions. Following up consistently, each month or so, shows that you are taking the process seriously, that you are not ignoring your coworkers' input. That's an important part of follow-up. After all, a leader who sought input from his coworkers but ignored it or did not follow up on it would quite logically be perceived as someone who did not care very much about becoming a better leader.

The whole experience taught me a fourth lesson: *Becoming a better leader (or a better person) is a process, not an event.* Historically, much of executive development has focused on the importance of an *event*—whether it's in the form of a training program, a motivational speech, or an intense executive retreat. My experience with the eight companies proves that real leadership development involves a *process* that takes time. It doesn't happen in a day. Nor can you "get it" in the form of a nitroglycerin tablet.

The process is a lot like physical exercise. Imagine having out-of-shape people sit in a room and listen to a speech on the importance of exercising, then watch some tapes on how to exercise, and perhaps then spend a few minutes simulating the act of exercising. Would you be surprised if all the people in the room were still unfit a year later? The source of physical fitness is not understanding the theory of working out. It is engaging in regular exercise.

Well, that pretty much sums up the value of executive development *without follow-up*. Nobody ever changed for the better by going to a training session. They got better by doing what they learned in the program. And that "doing," by definition, involves follow-up. Follow-up turns changing for the better into an ongoing process—not only for you but for everyone around you who is in the follow-up mix. When you involve other people in your continuing progress, you are virtually guaranteeing your continuing success. After all, if you go on a diet and know that someone who matters to you will check your weight at the end of each month, you're more likely to follow the diet and stay on it.

My Nightly Follow-Up Routine

Let me show you how follow-up works in my life.

I have a coach. His name is Jim Moore, a longtime friend who is a coaching professional. Every night wherever I am in the world, it's Jim's job as my coach to call me and ask me questions. They focus largely on my physical well-being and fitness. They're the same questions each night—and knowing that Jim will call and that I will have to answer the questions honestly is my method of following up on my goal of becoming a healthier individual.

The first question is always, "How happy are you?" Because for me it's most important to be happy. Otherwise, everything else is irrelevant. After that, the questions are:

1. How much walking did you do?
2. How many push-ups?
3. How many sit-ups?
4. Did you eat any high-fat foods?
5. How much alcohol did you drink?
6. How many hours of sleep did you get?
7. How much time did you spend watching TV or surfing the Internet?

8. How much time did you spend writing?
9. Did you do or say something nice for Lyda (my wife)?
10. Did you do or say something nice for Kelly and Bryan (my children)?
11. How many times did you try to prove you were right when it wasn't worth it?
12. How many minutes did you spend on topics that didn't matter or that you could not control?

That's it—my baker's dozen. I realize these questions may sound petty, even shallow. But I don't need help in the deep questions department. I spend most of my working hours talking to people about their relationships and helping them improve in areas that matter deeply to them. I get enough "depth" all day every day.

But I have a lifestyle that wreaks havoc on my physical well-being. I'm on the road, in airports, cars, conference centers, and hotel rooms 200 days a year. If my wife didn't remind me, I wouldn't know what time zone I'm in most days. I don't have the luxury of a "regular" home schedule where I can eat three square meals each day, sleep in my own bed each night, and follow a fitness regimen that could qualify as a "routine." There is no routine in my life other than the routine of being on the road.

The questions Jim asks me each evening deal with the stuff that's hard for me to do—that requires discipline. They're not petty or shallow to me. They matter. The nightly call is my form of enforced follow-up. (By the way, after I review my questions with Jim, he reviews his questions with me!)

And it works. I'm more disciplined about writing (this book is the proof). I've cut down on my weight, my caffeine consumption, and my time in front of the television. I'm also in better shape than I've been in decades.

As a connoisseur of follow-up's value, I'm not surprised. The key, however, is that *it involves another person besides me*. It's one thing to keep a log each night of the same questions and fill in the answers. That, to me, is not quite follow-up. It's more like entering data in a diary—and considerably less likely to breed ongoing success. (How many of us have started a diary but soon abandoned it?)

But injecting Jim into the mix—a friendly sympathetic human being whom, on the one hand, I do not want to disappoint (that's human nature) and who, on the other hand, provides constant encouragement and input—brings it more in line with the follow-up process I've been describing here. It helps me measure my progress. It reminds people that I'm making an effort to get better. In turn, it provides me with the steady recognition that I *am* getting better. When another person is involved, it's like giving yourself a mirror and being assured that you will like what you see.

You can do this too. You can have your own "Jim Moore." You might think that asking someone to call you each night—without paying them!—is a lot to ask of another human being. It is the rare individual who has the stamina and discipline to call us daily.

Is that so? Many of us perform a variation on this already in our lives.

I know lots of busy adults who, no matter where they are, call their aging parents at the end of each day to see how they're doing.

A group of busy mothers in my neighborhood who have banded together to run marathons and 10K races for charity call each other every night to lock in the time for the next day's run, to map out their training schedules, and to keep each other motivated.

The same with a group of colleagues who have become

yoga devotees. They're busy people but somehow they find the time to meet after work at the same yoga class five times a week and then they get together after class to talk about their lives.

We do this because we *care* about our parents, we're *serious* about running and want to excel at it, and we *enjoy* the change in our lives that yoga provides. So we become disciplined about it.

That rigor can—and should—be extended to follow-up in our own lives. After all, isn't changing our behavior and our interpersonal relationships as vital as taking care of our parents or maintaining our physical well-being?

Almost anyone in your life can function as your coach. It could be a spouse, or a sibling, or a son or daughter, or a colleague, or a best friend. It could even be your mother or father. They nagged you when you were a child. I'm sure they'd be delighted to "nag" you again—only this time with your permission.

Your only criteria for picking a coach are:

One, it shouldn't be a chore for your coach to get in touch with you (and with cell phones that's no longer an issue). You never want to have some technical problem as an excuse for not following up.

Two, your coach should be interested in your life and have your best interests at heart. You don't want someone yawning through your checklist as you answer whether you flossed or remembered to take your vitamins. For example, Jim Moore is an old friend, also from my home state of Kentucky. We enjoy talking to each other. It's not a burden for us to call each other.

Three, your coach can only ask the prescribed questions; he or she cannot judge your answers. (Warning: If your coach is a spouse or parent, suspending judgment might be asking a lot of them.)

After that, it's a simple process. Pick an issue in your life that you're not happy with and that you want to improve. Make a list of a dozen small daily tasks—nothing so major that it overwhelms the rest of your day—that you need to do to improve in your chosen area. And have your "Jim Moore" ask you about each task at the end of each day. That's it. As with any exercise, you won't see results immediately. But if you stick to it with daily follow-up, you will do all the tasks on your list. The results will appear. You will change. You will be happier. And people will notice.

CHAPTER 12

Practicing Feedforward

HERE'S WHERE WE ARE.

You've identified the interpersonal habit that's holding you back.

You've apologized for whatever errant behavior has annoyed the people who matter to you at work or at home. You've said, "I'm sorry. I'll try to do better." And they've accepted that.

You've continued to advertise your intention to change your ways. You've remained in steady contact with the people who matter, regularly reminding them that you're trying to do better. You do this by bringing up your objectives and asking point-blank, "How am I doing?"

You have also mastered the essential skills of listening and thanking. You can now listen to people's answers to your questions without judging, interrupting, disputing, or denying them. You do this by keeping your mouth shut except to say, "Thank you."

You've also learned how to be more diligent about follow-up, seeing the process as part of an ongoing, never-ending advertising campaign to (a) find out from others if you are, in fact, getting better and (b) remind people that you're still trying, still trying.

With these skills, now you're ready for feedforward.

As a concept, as something to do, feedforward is so simple I almost blush to dignify it with a name. Yet some of the simplest ideas are also the most effective. Since they're so easy to do, you have no excuse not to try them.

Feedforward asks you to do four simple steps:

1. Pick the one behavior that you would like to change which would make a significant, positive difference in your life. For example, *I want to be a better listener.*

2. Describe this objective in a one-on-one dialogue with *anyone* you know. It could be your wife, kids, boss, best friend, or coworker. It could even be a stranger. The person you choose is irrelevant. He or she doesn't have to be an expert on the subject. For example, you say, *I want to be a better listener.* Almost anyone in an organization knows what this means. You don't have to be an "expert" on listening to know what good listening means to you. Likewise, he or she doesn't have to be an expert on you. If you've ever found yourself on a long flight seated next to a perfect stranger and proceeded to engage in an earnest, heartfelt, and honest discussion of your problems with that stranger—or vice versa—you know this is true. Some of the truest advice can come from strangers. We are all human beings. We know what is true. And when a useful idea comes along, we don't care who the source is. (If you think about it, a stranger—someone who has no past with you and who cannot possibly hold your past failings against you or, for that matter, even bring them up—may be your ideal feedforward "partner.")

3. Ask that person for two suggestions *for the future* that might help you achieve a positive change in your

selected behavior—in this case, becoming a better listener. If you're talking to someone who knows you or who has worked with you in the past, the only ground rule is that there can be no mention of the past. Everything is about the future.

For example, you say, *I want to be a better listener. Would you suggest two ideas that I can implement in the future that will help me become a better listener?*

The other person suggests, *First, focus all your attention on the other person. Get in a physical position, the "listening position," such as sitting on the edge of your seat or leaning forward toward the individual. Second, don't interrupt, no matter how much you disagree with what you're hearing.*

These two ideas represent *feedforward*.

4. Listen attentively to the suggestions. Take notes if you like. Your only ground rule: You are not allowed to judge, rate, or critique the suggestions in any way. You can't even say something positive, such as, *"That's a good idea."* The only response you're permitted is, *Thank you.*

That's it. Ask for two ideas. Listen. Say thank you. Then repeat the process with someone else. In seeking feedforward ideas, you're not limited to one person. That would be like restricting your initial feedback (the one that told you where you needed to improve) to talking to one person; it would dramatically lessen the chances of getting an accurate picture of what you're doing wrong. You can do feedforward with as many people as you like. As long as people are providing you with good ideas that you can use or discard (but which don't confuse you), feed-forward is a process that never needs to stop.

All I've outlined here, really, are the ground rules for a conversation that *should* and *could* take place in the workplace all day long every day. These conversations rarely happen—precisely because in most workplace conversations we *aren't* working with these restrictions: Ask for two ideas; listen; say thank you. Even if we behave within the normal parameters of politeness and etiquette in the workplace, we think we have an obligation to be totally honest in every discussion. For some reason, when we're "engaged" in frank talk with another person, we interpret this to mean that we are locked in a debate. Because we like to succeed, we assume we have to win the debate. We think we have a license to use every debating trick to win, including bringing up the past to bolster our side of the "argument."

Is it any wonder that even in the least toxic environments, honest well-intentioned dialogues devolve into hurt feelings, misunderstandings, and counterproductive resentments?

Feedforward solves this dilemma.

In my scheme of things, feedforward is a dramatic improvement on what we traditionally think of as feedback. It grew out of a discussion I had with Jon Katzenbach in the early 1990s. We were frustrated with the limitations of the usual corporate feedback mechanisms to find out areas of improvement in an organization, such as the questionnaires that forced people to relive the past over and over again—the discussions among colleagues that descended into nightmarish arguments about who did what to whom way back when. As I hope I made clear in my brief history of feedback in Chapter 6, feedback has its virtues. It's a great tool for determining what happened in the past and what's going on in an organization. It's no different than reading history, which teaches us how we all arrived here right now in this moment. Like reading history, it provides us with facts about the past but not necessarily ideas for the future.

Feedforward, on the other hand, is feedback going in the opposite direction. That is, if feedback, both positive and negative, reports on how you functioned in the past, then feedforward comes in the form of ideas that you can put into practice in the future. If feedback is past tense, then feedforward is future perfect.

The best thing about feedforward is that it overcomes the two biggest obstacles we face with negative feedback—the fact that successful people in dominant positions don't want to hear it (no matter what they say, bosses prefer praise to criticism) and that their subordinates rarely want to give it (criticizing the boss, no matter how ardently he or she tells you to "bring it on," is rarely a great career move).

Feedforward shrinks the discussion down to the intimate parameters of two human beings. If it isn't obvious yet (and if it isn't then one of us has not been paying attention), this book and its process for getting better hinges on one inalterable concept.

I don't establish what you need to do to change for the better.

You don't establish it either.

They do.

Who are they?

Everyone around you. Everyone who knows you, cares about you, thinks about you, has you pegged.

Let's say you want to do a better job of listening. It's possible that a coach can explain to you how to be a better listener. The advice will be true, supportable, and impossible to dispute. But it will be generic. It's much better to ask the people around you, "What are some ways I can do a better job of listening to you?" They'll give you specific, concrete ideas that relate to them—how they perceive you as a listener—not the vague ideas a coach would give. They may not be experts on the topic of listening, but at that moment in time, they actually know more about how you listen, or don't, than anyone else in the world.

Until you get everyone who is affected by your behavior on your side and working to help you change, you haven't really begun to get better.

This is why the concept of feedforward is so important.

Feedforward eliminates many of the obstacles that traditional feedback has created.

It works because, while they don't particularly like hearing criticism (i.e., negative feedback), *successful people love getting ideas for the future.* If changing a certain type of behavior is important to them, they will gobble up any ideas that are aimed at changing that behavior. And they will be grateful to anyone who steps forward with an idea, not resentful. There's no arguing with this. Successful people have a high need for self-determination and will tend to accept ideas about concerns that they "own" while rejecting ideas that feel "forced" upon them.

It works because *we can change the future but not the past.* It doesn't deal in wishes, dreams, and conquering the impossible.

It works because *helping people be "right" is more productive than proving them "wrong."* Unlike feedback, which often introduces a discussion of mistakes and shortfalls, feedforward focuses on solutions, not problems.

On the most elemental level, it works because *people do not take feedforward as personally as feedback.* Feedforward is not seen as an insult or a putdown. It is hard to get offended about a suggestion aimed at helping us get better at what we want to improve (especially if we are not forced to implement the suggestion).

On a purely technical level, it works because when we receive feedforward, all we have to do is function as a listener. We can *focus on hearing without having to worry about responding.* When all you're allowed to say is "Thank you," you don't have to worry about composing a clever response. You also are not permitted to interrupt, which makes you a more patient listener. Practicing feedforward makes us "shut up and listen" while others are speaking.

However, feedforward is a two-way street—and it is designed to protect as well as bring out the best in the people who are providing it.

After all, who among us doesn't enjoy giving helpful suggestions when asked? The key is when asked. Feedforward *forces us to ask*—and in doing so, we enlarge our universe of people with useful ideas. Asking, of course, *gives the other person a license to answer.* I cannot overestimate how valuable this license can be. I'm sure that all of us are surrounded by smart well-meaning friends who "understand" us better than we "understand" ourselves. I suspect they would love to help us; most people like to help others. But they hold back because they think it is rude or intrusive to try to help someone who has not asked for our assistance. Asking solves this.

Also, there's no threat of pain in the process. If you're giving me two ideas that I've asked for, you will only receive my gratitude. Not resentment. Not an argument. Not punishment. On top of that, you don't even have to be right. You don't have to prove that your suggestions are good ideas—because I'm not judging them. All I can do is accept them or ignore them. A clever scheme that eliminates fear and defensiveness, don't you think?

More than anything, feedforward creates the two-way traffic I love to see in the workplace, the spirit of two colleagues helping each other rather than a superior being providing a critique. It's the feeling that when we help another person, we help ourselves.

Leave It at the Stream

If feedforward sounds like some eating technique you'd see advertised on late-night TV, guaranteeing weight loss with a faster metabolism, I apologize. Feedforward won't make you thinner.

But it may make you happier. The concept really is as simple as it sounds. Instead of rehashing a past that cannot be changed, feedforward encourages you to spend time creating a future by (a) asking for suggestions for the future, (b) listening to ideas, and (c) just saying thank you. Its strongest element, by far, is that it doesn't permit you to bring up the past—ever. It forces you to let go of the past.

That's important when you consider how many hours of organizational time and productivity are lost in the endless re-telling of our coworkers' blunders, or how much internal stress we generate reliving real or imagined slights, or how often team-building sessions degenerate into, "Let me tell you what you did wrong" slugfests rather than, "Let me ask you what we can do better" love-ins.

An old Buddhist parable illustrates the challenge—and the value—of letting go of the past.

Two monks were strolling by a stream on their way home to the monastery. They were startled by the sound of a young woman in a bridal gown, sitting by the stream, crying softly. Tears rolled down her cheeks as she gazed across the water. She needed to cross to get to her wedding, but she was fearful that doing so might ruin her beautiful handmade gown.

In this particular sect, monks were prohibited from touching women. But one monk was filled with compassion for the bride. Ignoring the sanction, he hoisted the woman on his shoulders and carried her across the stream—assisting her journey and saving her gown. She smiled and bowed with gratitude as the monk splashed his way back across the stream to rejoin his companion.

The second monk was livid. "How could you do that?" he scolded. "You know we are forbidden to touch a woman, much less pick one up and carry her around!"

The offending monk listened in silence to a stern lecture that lasted all the way back to the monastery. His mind wandered as he felt the warm sunshine and listened to the singing birds. After returning to the monastery, he fell asleep for a few hours. He was jostled and awakened in the middle of the night by his fellow monk.

"How could you carry that woman?" his agitated friend cried out. "Someone else could have helped her across the stream. You were a bad monk."

"What woman?" the sleepy monk inquired.

"Don't you even remember? That woman you carried across the stream," his colleague snapped.

"Oh, her," laughed the sleepy monk. "I only carried her across the stream. You carried her all the way back to the monastery."

The learning point is simple: When it comes to our flawed past, *leave it at the stream*.

I am not suggesting that we should *always* let go of the past. You need feedback to scour the past and identify room for improvement. But you can't change the past. To change you need to be sharing ideas for the future.

Race car drivers are taught, "Look at the road, not the wall."

That's what feedforward does. Who knows? Not only may it help you win the race, but you'll definitely have a better trip around the track.

Pulling Out the Stops

In which leaders learn how to apply the rules of
change and what to stop doing now

CHAPTER 13

Changing: The Rules

IF I HAD TO rank my best client, in terms of magnitude of improvement in the shortest amount of time, it would have to be the division chief at a major manufacturing company. Let's call him Harlan.

Harlan had 40,000 employees under his command and he was doing a great job within this enormous division. Harlan was considered a great leader by his direct reports. Harlan's boss, the CEO, desperately wanted him to focus more on reaching out across the organization and providing leadership for the *entire* company.

I went through the drill with Harlan—commit to changing, apologize to all the people who gave you feedback, tell them you're trying to change, and follow up with them regularly to find out how you're doing in their eyes. When I say Harlan's my best client, one of the things I remember is how quickly he "got it." He bought my methods lock, stock, and barrel—and put them into action immediately. I was thinking this would be the standard 18-month assignment, but after 12 months Harlan's feedback was already posting the biggest improvement scores I'd ever seen in the shortest amount of time.

I flew to Harlan's headquarters, strolled into his office, and said, "We're done. You have the biggest improvement scores I've ever seen!"

"Whaddayamean? We barely got started."

"Well, I spent a lot of time with your colleagues assembling the feedback. Let's not forget that. And, yes, our time together was brief. But these scores prove that any issues you had with your colleagues last year have evaporated. They see you as being incredibly inclusive and working to benefit the entire company.

"Don't forget, you're earning several million dollars a year. Your time is valuable, more valuable than mine. Where do you think your CEO would rather have you spending your valuable time? Making money for the company or shooting the breeze with me? I think we know the answer to that one. I'm not in the time-spending business. I'm in the getting-better business. And you're better."

Harlan conceded the point. I was feeling pleased with myself (about two ticks short of smug if you want the truth) so I opted to waste some of his valuable time to ask, "What do you think you've learned from this whole process?"

He surprised me with his answer.

"I've learned that the key to your job, Marshall, is client selection. You 'qualify' your clients to the point where you almost can't fail. The deck is totally stacked in your favor."

It surprised me because he wasn't talking about himself. He was turning the tables on me. Then he said something more profound.

"I admire that kind of selectivity because that's what I do here. If I have the right people around me, I'm fine. But if I have the wrong people, not even God can win with that hand."

I guess that's another reason Harlan is a great client. He saw through all the bells and whistles of my admittedly simple methodology and honed in on my little secret: I make it easy on myself. I don't place sucker bets. I only work with clients who have an extremely high potential of succeeding. Why would anyone want to operate any other way?

Jack Welch once told *Esquire* magazine what he had learned playing sandlot baseball as a kid. He said, "When you were small, you were always the last one picked for the team and put out in right field. The years passed, and then *you* were putting guys out in right field. You learned one thing as you got older: You picked the best players and you won."

As you go through life, contemplating the mechanics of success and wondering why some people are successful and others are not, you'll find that this is one of the defining traits of habitual winners: They stack the deck in their favor. And they're unabashed about it.

They do this when they hire the best candidates for a job rather than settle for an almost-the-best type.

They do this when they pay whatever it takes to retain a valuable employee rather than lose him or her to the competition.

They do this when they're fully prepared for a negotiation rather than winging it.

If you study successful people, you'll discover that their stories are not so much about overcoming enormous obstacles and handicaps but rather about avoiding high-risk, low-reward situations and doing everything in their power to increase the odds in their favor.

For example, have you ever wondered why the most successful people at the top of your organization tend to have the best personal assistants? Simple answer: Successful executives know that a great assistant can shield them from dozens of daily annoyances that would otherwise distract them from doing their real job. If you think all the top executives have top assistants because of luck rather than design, you need a few more lessons in stacking the deck in your favor.

This winning strategy is so obvious to successful people, I feel almost sheepish mentioning it—as if it will elicit a chorus of "duhs!" from readers. But it's amazing how some people go out of their way to unstack the deck against themselves.

When you're talking about interpersonal behavior, people's common sense gets fuzzy and opaque. They lose sight of their true mission in life. They have trouble identifying or accepting the behavior that's holding them back. They don't know how to choose a strategy to fix the problem. And they often pick the wrong thing to fix. In other words, they stack the deck against themselves.

The following seven rules will help you get a better handle on the process of change. If you obey them, you'll be stacking the deck in your favor.

Rule 1. You Might Not Have a Disease That Behavioral Change Can Cure

I was asked to coach the CEO of a top medical company some years ago. His feedback report was quite a remarkable document. His peers and direct reports genuinely loved this fellow. No one who came in contact with him had anything negative to say about him. I had never seen such perfect marks in interpersonal relations.

"What's going on?" I asked. "Why am I here?" The CEO said he felt completely at sea about the technological innovations that were changing the company, and as a result had trouble communicating with some subordinates.

"You're a great guy," I said. "I'd love to work with you. But you don't have a disease that I can cure. What you need is a technology wizard to sit by your side and mentor you. You don't need me." He was a little like a hypochondriac with a pain in his rib cage. He thinks he has lung cancer when all he has is a little muscle pull.

Sometimes we confuse interpersonal problems with something else. In the medical company case, it was obvious. But the line between a behavioral flaw and a technical shortcoming can get blurry.

I was called in to work with the CFO of a major investment bank. Let's call him David. This fellow was an interesting case—a young, ambitious, hard-working, motivated, hit-the-numbers type who was *not* an arrogant, know-it-all jerk. In fact, David was admired and beloved. In the poker game of life, David had drawn four aces and a nine (he wasn't perfect, but damn close). You could see this in the way people in the office related to him. The females swooned around him. The direct reports snapped to attention. His colleagues from other divisions felt comfortable enough around him to engage in the friendly towel-snapping banter you see among ex-jocks who genuinely like and would kill for each other. David seemed to work in a perfect world where everything fell into place the moment he walked into the room.

I thought, "Why am I here?"

When I studied David's feedback, a disorienting picture emerged. No significant problems on any of the usual interpersonal flaws. Except the consensus opinion was that David could be a better listener. He wasn't hearing them out and he didn't seem to understand their true accomplishments.

This didn't jibe with all of David's positives. Executives who share, inspire loyalty, and are well liked don't score low on listening. It's an integral part of their interpersonal portfolio.

When I dug deeper, though, a more complicated picture emerged. It turned out that David, as CFO, was the firm's frontman with the media. Every quarter he had to talk with analysts and the financial press to highlight the firm's achievements. The firm had fallen prey to the same ethical lapses that many financial services companies were guilty of in the early part of the new millennium. But whereas other firms were getting decent press treatment under the circumstances, David's firm was getting mauled. Every day was a new headline that damaged the firm's reputation. And David took the heat for it.

David's people wondered why he wasn't getting the message out properly. "We're great," they thought. "We're not getting recognized for our greatness. David's in charge of delivering that message to the public and failing at it. Therefore, David's not hearing us."

A logical train of thought, if you're the direct reports.

But not if you're David.

David's problem wasn't that he ignored what people told him. As CFO, he knew the results better than anyone. David's problem was that he wasn't very good at "spinning" the media.

That's not a behavioral problem. It's a skill problem. David needed a coach all right—a media coach. But he didn't need me.

You have to be careful with feedback. Conducted properly, feedback is not deceptive. It reveals what's on people's minds. But it can be misinterpeted (you see only what you want to see) or misread (you see something that isn't there).

Keep this in mind. Sometimes feedback reveals a symptom, not a disease. A symptom is a headache; give it time and it goes away. A brain tumor, on the other hand, can't be ignored. It needs treatment. I see this in organizations that have endured a temporary downturn; the feedback reveals angry employees lashing out at scapegoats. Angry employees need to be heard and dealt with.

Sometimes, as in David's case, feedback reveals a problem that's one or two steps removed from anything that the individual is doing wrong. Be careful, then. You may be trying to fix something that isn't broken, doesn't need fixing, or can't be fixed by you.

Rule 2. Pick the Right Thing to Change

One of the first things I have to face with clients is the difference between miswanting and mischoosing. It's subtle, but real. Wanting, after all, is different from choosing. So are those moments when we get either process wrong, when we miswant or mischoose.

The distinction comes from psychologists studying the science of shopping. We want a sweater, for example. Then we choose a certain sweater based on the thought matrix that went into wanting it. For example, there are all sorts of reasons people want a certain type of sweater. They might want it for warmth. They might want it for its feel. They might want one that looks great, or is reputedly the best in the world, or the most expensive (or cheapest), or the most au courant in style, or that complements the color or their eyes. The reasons for wanting a sweater are almost infinite. Basically, we want a sweater because we think it will make us happier. Miswanting occurs when we discover that what we wanted *did not make us happy*.

Choosing is slightly different. Once we decide what sweater we want, we must choose among a vast array of options that fit the bill. Will it be the blue cashmere sweater with the Armani label and $1000 price tag? Or the blue wool from Land's End for $49? Both will keep us warm and accent our eye color (if that's what we wanted), but if we're on a limited budget, the latter is a wiser choice than the former.

The same distinction arises with people deciding to change for the better. One of my first tasks is helping them distinguish between what they want in life and how they choose to reach that goal. Again, the difference is one of wanting and choosing. And I don't get involved in the wanting part. It's none of my business. To weigh in with an opinion on some individual's goal in life would mean passing a value judgment on his or her reason for living. I won't do that. (And in turn I wouldn't want them passing judgment on my goals.) That's what I mean by being mission neutral.

However, I do have strong opinions about how people *choose* to reach their goals. There I'm not neutral. After all, if they make the wrong choice, they'll fail—which means I'm a failure too, and that is decidedly not my mission in life. (See above.)

So I spend serious time with people helping them decide what they need to change.

The first thing we do is review what they're doing right and what they may need to change. Successful people, by definition, are doing a lot of things right. Nothing to fix there.

Then we narrow it down. Not every challenge needs to be addressed. Assuming that I have gotten an individual to commit to changing for the better and changing *something,* I often have a hard time convincing successful people that not everything needs improving. Successful people have a glaring tendency to overcommit. If you outline seven flaws, they'll want to tackle all of them. It's one reason they're successful—and the impetus behind the cliché, "If you want something done right, give it to a busy person." So, my first task is to tell them, "Don't overcommit," and get them to believe it.

I also know that giving people unlimited choices only confuses them. Faced with too many options, they go back and forth among the options, trying to maximize their choice. Successful people hate being wrong even more than they like being right. This can easily turn into paralysis; in their never-ending quest for the best option, they end up deciding nothing.

So I turn their attention to the one vital flaw that needs fixing. In most instances I treat it as a pure numbers game.

Let's say you come to me for coaching. We go through your

menu of five documented areas for improvement: 10 percent of your coworkers say you don't listen; 10 percent say you don't share information; 20 percent say you're bad at meeting deadlines; 40 percent say you gossip too much; and 80 percent say you get angry.

Which single issue should we focus on changing? Objectively speaking, it's a no-brainer. You have a serious issue with anger. Four out of five coworkers think you have a hot temper. We need to change that first.

You'd think that would be obvious. What's interesting, though, is how often the people I work with try to ignore that in-your-face problem and instead tackle one of the other flaws. I'm not sure why. Maybe it's denial (although at this point in the process, where you're committed to changing, denial should be long behind us). Maybe it's our natural urge to take the path of least resistance, to start with an easy fix first. Maybe it's just contrariness.

Whatever the reasons, my job as a coach is to make you see that you have to improve at controlling your emotions. The other issues are moot, off the radar. More than half your colleagues didn't even mention them as an issue. That's how you pick the right thing to change.

In a way, I can see why people have problems choosing what needs fixing. In golf, for example, it is common wisdom that 70 percent of all shots take place within 100 yards of the pin. It's called the short game, and it involves pitching, chipping, hitting out of sand traps, and putting. If you want to lower your score, focus on fixing your short game; it represents at least 70 percent of your score. Yet if you go to a golf course you'll see very few people practicing their short game. They're all at the driving range trying to hit their oversized drivers as far as they can. Statistically, it doesn't make sense because over the course of 18 holes, they'll only need their drivers fourteen times (at most) whereas they'll pull out their short irons and putters at least 50 times. Athletically it doesn't make sense either. The short game demands compact delicate small-muscle movements; it is much easier to master than the violent big-muscle movements of driving off the tee. Nor does it make sense competitively. If you improve your short game, you *will* shoot lower scores—and beat the competition.

The numbers don't lie, and yet even the most avid golfers hide from the truth and refuse to fix what really needs fixing. (My hunch is that hitting balls out of sand traps all day is simply not as much fun as taking big swipes at the ball off the tee. But who am I to judge?) If golfers really wanted to stack the deck in their favor, they'd spend three hours on their short game for every hour they spend trying to hit the ball a mile. Still few do. It would take a stern golf teacher standing over them every day to enforce the practice routines they know they should be pursuing.

If you think it's hard to get people to fix their flaws in golf, which (let's not forget) is a highly pleasurable game totally within our control, imagine how tough it is getting people to change at work, where the stakes are higher but the results are not completely under your control. That's one reason I take this stuff so seriously. When people commit to getting better, they are doing something difficult and heroic. In truth, I applaud my clients when they *begin* the process of fixing their flaws, not at the *end*. If they commit and follow my advice, their success is a foregone conclusion. I don't need to applaud a fait accompli.

Rule 3. Don't Delude Yourself About What You *Really* Must Change

I was called in to work with a Chief Financial Officer

named Matt. The problem, as usual, revolved around Matt's interpersonal skills. Nothing wrong with his CFO skills. Matt could read a balance sheet, outmuscle bankers, and keep his company financially viable with the best of them. In fact, as the fellow guarding the company's cash flow, Matt had accumulated more power than any CFO in the company's history. If you wanted to pursue any idea that cost money, you had to run it up the flagpole in Matt's office. Matt, almost as much as the CEO, could bless or kill any initiative.

That was the problem. Matt had developed an overweening sense of self-importance. It came out in brusque comments, dismissive opinions, and an increased inaccessibility to his direct reports.

That's when I showed up.

"Matt, we need to make changes," I said.

Matt cut me off.

"What I'd really like to do is lose twenty pounds and firm up my body."

"Are you serious?" I asked, thinking I'd get some resistance to changing his executive style but not expecting a discussion about physical fitness.

"Yes," he said. "Dead serious."

"You'd rather get a six-pack than get better at work?" I asked.

"That's what makes me unhappy," he said. "And that's why I'm so grouchy. If I can fix that, maybe everything else will improve, too."

I had to admire his honesty, if not his logic. It fit with his feedback, which said he was self-involved to the point of vanity. He thought he knew all the answers. That's what he needed to change.

At the same time, I knew the old saw, that if you don't have your health, nothing else matters. So maybe Matt was right.

Maybe if he felt better about his looks, his health, and his vigor, everything else would fall into place.

So I went with it.

I said, "Look, it says here you need to be more sensitive to other people, less abrupt, less self-absorbed. On the other hand, you're so into yourself, you want to fix your stomach muscles. Which do you think is easier to accomplish? A six-pack or one less interpersonal flaw at work?"

"A six-pack," he said. "It's just a matter of discipline, following a routine, and sticking with it."

"Hmmm . . ." I thought. "Can't argue with that. If you follow a routine and stick with it, you'll get results. You'll achieve your goals."

Only problem: It's very tough to do. Even tougher to maintain. But Matt wasn't seeing that.

I've spent 3000 nights in the last two decades in hotel rooms, jet lagged and wide awake with only the television to keep me company. In other words, I have seen my share of late-night infomercials hawking the latest fitness gadgets. I know all the hard sell promises.

"How much would you pay to have a body like this?"

"In one week you could be feeling great."

"It feels terrific. Let us show you how easy it is."

"In eight minutes a day, tighten your flabby abs into the sexy six-pack you always wanted."

I knew why Matt thought acquiring a bodybuilder's abs was easier to achieve than being a little more civil to his colleagues. His mind had been warped by the constant media promises that anyone can get in world-class physical shape with a little effort and willpower.

I wasn't questioning Matt's goal.

I was worried about his understanding of how we set and achieve goals. And why.

I've studied the research on goal-setting and goal achievement. A lot of it centers on diet and fitness because (a) there's a huge population of people interested in such goals, (b) it's easy to measure, and (c) with record numbers of Americans either obese or out of shape, there's a huge (and compelling) history of failure in this area. I've learned that there are five reasons people do not succeed with their diet and fitness goals. They mistakenly estimate:

- *Time:* It takes a lot longer than they expected. They don't have time to do it.
- *Effort:* It's harder than they expected. It's not worth all the effort.
- *Distractions:* They do not expect a "crisis" to emerge that will prevent them from staying with the program.
- *Rewards:* After they see some improvement, they don't get the response from others that they expected. People don't immediately love the new improved person they've become.
- *Maintenance:* Once they hit their goal, people forget how hard it is to stay in shape. Not expecting that they'll have to stick with the program for life, they slowly backslide or give up completely.

This is what I explained to Matt in his office. I wasn't trying to talk him out of his six-pack. (If it makes him happy, I'm cool with it.) I was trying to make him see that he was a little delusional about his goal.

Getting in shape was eminently doable. Lots of people have done it. But it would not be easy. For one thing, it would take *time* away from his job. It would probably take more *effort* than all those infomercials, exercise books, and personal trainers at the gym suggested. There was a good chance that some *distractions* at his superbusy CFO job or at home might sidetrack him. More important, even if he achieved his goal, there was no guaranteed *payoff* that it would make him less grouchy. On the contrary, it might make him even more vain, self-satisfied, and insufferable. And there was certainly no guarantee that his colleagues would suddenly admire him for his newfound physique (they might even resent it).

I could see this last point got to Matt. He was already in a hole with his colleagues. It never occurred to him that some private effort to look and feel better could somehow backfire and put him in a *deeper* hole with those same colleagues. But it could—because it loudly and specifically excluded them. It was just another example of Matt being self-involved.

Even though I didn't walk into Matt's office expecting to talk about abs and crunches, the meeting had a serendipitous benefit—because the reasons we miscalculate our diet and health goals apply to any goal achievement. If you want to succeed at goal setting, you have to face the reality of the effort and the payoff before you begin. Realize that the "quick fix" and the "easy solution" may not provide the "lasting fix" and the "meaningful solution." Lasting goal achievement requires lots of time, hard work, personal sacrifice, ongoing effort, and dedication to a process that is maintained over years. And even if you can pull that off, the rewards may not be all that you expect.

This may not be the best support for a late-night infomercial, but it is great material for achieving any real change.

"Now," I asked Matt, "are we ready to talk about what your colleagues think of you?"

Rule 4. Don't Hide from the Truth You Need to Hear

I am in my late 50s. At my age, the most important feedback I need is called an annual physical examination. As feedback, it's literally life-or-death information. I managed to avoid this feedback for seven years. It's not easy to avoid a doctor's visit for seven years, but I did it by telling myself, "I will get a physical after I go on my 'healthy foods' diet. I will get the exam after I begin my exercise program. I will get that exam after I get in shape."

Who was I kidding? The doctor? My family? Myself?

Have you ever avoided a physical exam and told yourself the same thing? Almost half the executives I've worked with have.

How about the trip to the dentist? After putting off the appointment as long as possible, do you orchestrate a frenzy of dental flossing two days before visiting the dentist's office?

Admittedly, a little bit of the impulse behind this behavior is our need to achieve. We want to score well in the doctor's or dentist's "test," so we prepare for it.

However, a much bigger reason for this behavior is our need to hide from the truth—often from what we already know. We know we need to visit a doctor or dentist, but we don't because we might not want to hear what he has to say. We figure if we don't seek out bad news about our health or teeth, there can't be any bad news.

We do the same in our personal life. For example, when I'm working in a large sales organization, I always throw a spot quiz at the sales force.

"Does your company teach you to ask customers for feedback?"

A chorus of yeses.

"Does it work? Does it teach you where you need to improve?"

Another yes chorus.

Then I focus on the men: "How many times do you do this at home? That is, ask your wife, 'What can I do to be a better partner?' "

No yes chorus. Just silence.

"Do you men believe this stuff?" I ask.

Back to the yes chorus. "Of course!" they say in unison.

"Well, I presume your wife is more important to you than your customers, right?"

They nod.

"So why don't you do it at home?"

I can see their collective wheels turning as the truth dawns on them: They're afraid of the answer. It might hit too close to home. And, worse, then they'd have to do something about it.

We do the same with the truth about our interpersonal flaws. We figure if we don't ask for critiques of our behavior, then no one has anything critical to say.

This thinking defies logic. It has to stop. You are better off finding out the truth than being in denial.

Rule 5. There Is No Ideal Behavior

Benchmarking—the notion that there is a performance ideal exemplified by people and organizations—is one of the biggest hazards in getting people to change for the better. It's not that there isn't something to be gained from modeling ourselves against the best in their category. But it can do more harm than good if applied poorly. Sometimes the desire for "perfect" can drive away "better."

In my line of work, there are a lot of benchmarks for

successful behavior, but they are composites. They are usually made from multiple people and multiple examples. The perfect benchmark human being, like the perfect benchmark organization, does not exist. That colors how people think. They believe that there is an ideal executive out there—and that they should be like him or her.

You can't be and don't have to be all things to all people. If there were a list of 39 successful attributes for the model executive, I would never argue that you have to be the perfect expression of all 39 of them. All you need are a few of them. No matter how many of the 39 attributes you *don't* embody, the real question is, how bad is the problem? Is it bad enough that it merits fixing? If not, don't worry about it. You're doing fine.

I take great comfort in the fact that Michael Jordan, to many the best basketball player to ever play the game, was a mediocre baseball player in the minor leagues and, as a golfer, would have a tough time keeping up with at least twenty golfers who live within an 800 yard radius of my home in San Diego. If Michael Jordan, a preternaturally superb athlete and competitor—in fact, *the* benchmark for other basketball players—could only excel at one sport, what makes you think you can do better?

It's not just sports. I work with a lot of clients in the financial services sector. When I check the annual rankings of how the firms are doing against their rivals, one firm is ranked #1 at investment banking, a different firm is #1 at mergers and acquisitions, yet another is #1 at fixed income securities, and so on through a dozen categories. No firm is #1 at everything, and very few firms are even tops in two categories. In an environment where all the big firms are loaded with the best and brightest out of the top business schools, the competition is too stiff for one firm to dominate all categories.

It's no different in the workplace. Take a look around your

office. Someone's the best salesman. Someone else is the best accountant. Someone else is the best manager. No one is the best at everything.

This isn't a license for mediocrity. It's a reality check. It's your permission to deal in trade-offs and pick one thing to improve upon rather than everything.

Even in my narrow profession of executive coaching, I've further narrowed my ambition to one thing: Helping people achieve long-term positive behavioral change. I don't do strategy. I don't do innovation. I don't coach information technology or media relations or industrial psychology. The list of what I don't do could fill several dozen books. I can live with that, because I've chosen to try to be the best I can be in my admittedly narrow corner of the coaching fiefdom. If I'm shooting for the gold at this, I have to come to terms with the fact that I ain't even stepping up to the starting blocks in everything else.

The same applies to your task of changing your behavior. Pick one issue that matters and "attack" it until it doesn't matter anymore. If you're a bad listener, choose to become a better listener—not the best listener in the world (whatever that means!). If you don't share information, get better at sharing until it's not an issue anymore (but realize that you will never be perfect in everyone's eyes, and you don't need to be).

Benchmarking is great because it teaches us to aim high. But when we apply it to ourselves, we often overreach. This is the "ready, fire, aim" school of self-improvement. We don't discriminate among benchmarks. We want to be the best at everything.

When it comes to creating long-term positive change in ourselves, we have one gun, one bullet. You can't hit more than one target with that ammunition.

P.S. There's a bonus to ignoring benchmarks. People commonly fear that if they get better at X they'll get worse at Y—as if improvement is a zero-sum game. Not true. Statistically, if you get better at X, it helps everything else get better, too. I have 20,000 feedback reports confirming this. If you're a bad listener who learns to listen more, then you are perceived as treating people with more respect. In deferring to their views, you probably hear their ideas better. Good ideas don't fall through the cracks because of your benign neglect. This is turn makes you appear as a more involved, concerned leader, which improves morale—and surely has an effect on delivering better numbers. Everything gets better with one change. That's a statistical fact.

Rule 6. If You Can Measure It, You Can Achieve It

Most of us in business spend a great deal of time measuring. We measure sales, profits, rate of growth, return on investment, income versus outgo, same-store sales from quarter to quarter, etc. In many ways, part of being an effective manager and leader is setting up systems to measure *everything*. It's the only way we can know for sure *how we're doing*. Given our addiction to measurement—and its documented value—you'd think we'd be more attuned to measuring the "soft-side values" in the workplace: How often we're rude to people, how often we're polite, how often we ask for input in a meeting rather than shut people out, how often we bite our tongue rather than spit out a needlessly inflammatory remark. These are the "soft" values that are hard to quantify but, in the area of interpersonal performance, are as vital as any hard number we can come up with. They demand our attention if we want to alter our behavior—and get credit for it.

About ten years ago, I decided I wanted to be a more attentive father. So I asked my daughter, "What can I do to be a better parent?"

She said, "Daddy, you travel a lot, but I don't mind that you're away from home so much. What really bothers me is the way you act when you *are* home. You talk on the telephone, you watch sports on TV, and you don't spend much time with me. One weekend, when you'd been traveling for two weeks, my friends were having a party. I wanted to go, but Mom wouldn't let me. She said I had to spend time with you. So I stayed home, but you didn't spend any time with me. That wasn't right."

I was hurt and stunned, because (a) she nailed me and (b) I was an oafish dad who had needlessly caused his daughter pain. There's no worse feeling in the world, I can assure you. You never want to see your children in any pain. And you certainly don't want to be the source of it.

I recovered quickly—and reverted to a simple response that I teach all my clients.

I said, "Thank you. Daddy will do better."

From that moment I started keeping track of how many days I spent at least four hours interacting with my family without TV, movies, football, or the telephone as a distraction. I'm proud to say I got better. The first year I logged in 92 days of unencumbered interaction with my family. The second year, 110 days. The third year, 131 days. The fourth year, 135 days.

Five years after that first conversation with my daughter, I was spending more time with my family and my business was more successful than it had been when I was ignoring them. I was beaming with pride—not only with the results but also with the fact that, like a skilled soft-side accountant, I documented them. I was so proud, in fact, that I went to my kids, both teenagers by this time, and said, "Look kids, 135 days. What's the target this year? How about 150 days?"

Both of them said, "No, Daddy, you have overachieved."

My son Bryan suggested paring down to 50 days. My

daughter Kelly agreed. In the end both voted for a massive cutback in time with Daddy.

I wasn't discouraged by their response. It was as eye-opening as that first conversation with my daughter five years earlier. I was so focused on the numbers, on improving my at-home performance each year that I forgot that my kids had changed, too. An objective that made sense when they were nine years old didn't make sense when they evolved into teenagers.

Everything is measurable if we're clever enough to see that it needs measuring—and can devise a way to track it. For example, no matter how busy you are or how much you travel for your job, it's easy to measure how many days a year you spend at home. All you have to do is look at the calendar—and count. Yet how many of us, especially the spouses and parents among us who feel guilty about our frequent absences from our loved ones, ever think about tracking our days at home?

The strange thing is we do this habitually in so many other parts of our lives outside the workplace. Runners training for a race constantly measure how fast they are running and keep a log of the miles they cover each week. Even a casual athlete trying to get in shape will go to the gym and maintain a rough memory that he lifted x amount of weight yesterday, so that three weeks later he would want to lift x weight plus 20 percent. So why don't we apply the same metrics to goals that really matter?

Once you see the beauty of measuring the soft values in your life, other variables kick in, such as the fact that setting numerical targets makes you more likely to achieve them. For example, another measurement I injected into my home life was seeing if I could spend 10 minutes each day engaging my wife and each of my kids in a one-on-one conversation. Ten minutes is not a long time, but it's a significant improvement on zero. I found that if I measured the activity I was much more likely to do it. If I faltered, I always told myself, "Well, I get a credit towards the goal and it only takes me ten minutes. Maybe I'm tired, but what the hell. I can just go ahead and do it." Without that measurable goal, I was much more likely to blow it off.

Rule 7. Monetize the Result, Create a Solution

The same metrics you apply to yourself to change behavior can be applied to other people, especially if money is part of the equation.

For example, when he noticed all the trash talk and vulgarity his children brought home from school, a friend of mine established a "swear jar" for the family. Every time anyone uttered a profanity, they had to donate a dollar to the jar. The first thing the father noticed, after depositing several dollars a day for the first week, was how foul-mouthed he was around the children. He learned where they were picking up the bad habit: from him. Monetizing the punishment does that. When you actually have to pay for your mistakes, you notice them more acutely. Unless you like losing money for no reason, you eventually change your ways. Within a month, the vulgarity had vanished.

There are all sorts of ways to incentivize people to change their behavior—and I approve of anything that works from bonuses to fines to gifts to vacations. It's a simple idea, but it's amazing how few people think of attaching a financial reward to ending a problem. I've been coaching executives for two decades now, but it was only in 2005 that one of my clients introduced a financial incentive into the process. He was one of the top officers at a West Coast industrial company, a real hard charger whose big issue was not sharing information. The company CEO assured me that, no matter how harsh the feedback and how severe the resistance from employees, I would collect my fee. "This guy will get better," said the CEO. "He would rather die than fail—at anything."

The CEO was right. This guy was a pleasure to work with because he was so determined to get better. He quickly picked up that neither he nor I was the important constituency in the process. The people who worked with and for him were. So he did something I'd never seen before. He concluded that the most vital person in the process was his executive assistant. She was the one who saw him day in and day out. She knew his faults best and she would have the strongest opinions about what he needed to do to get better. She was also in the best position to see if he was mending his ways as well as remind him when he was backsliding. So he made *his* improvement become as important to her as to him. He told her, "If Marshall gets paid, you get a $2,000 bonus."

Within 12 months she collected her bonus.

I'd never thought of this or seen it done before, but you can be sure that I'm mentioning it to all future clients.

You can monetize the punishment and end the problem. Or you can monetize the result and create a solution. Either way, it works.

Rule 8. The Best Time to Change Is Now

As I've written, of the tens of thousands of business people who have come to my lectures and classes, only 70 percent ever followed through on what they learned and actually did something about it. I am not ashamed of this fact—which means a 30 percent noncompliance rate. Actually, I'm proud of my noncompliance rate and amazed it isn't much higher.

If you've gotten this far in this book, I am sure you believe that you will do at least something (if only one simple thing) that is advised herein. (For example, how tough can it be to stop punishing the messenger?) But I'm resigned to the fact that while many readers will do this, many will not.

We have interviewed hundreds of people who have participated in our training programs one year later. We asked the people who did nothing why they did not live up to the commitments that they made after they attended leadership training. As far as we can tell, most people who do nothing are no worse as human beings than the people who change. They are no less intelligent. They have about the same values.

Then, why don't they do what they committed to do?

The answer can be found in a dream. It's a dream I have often—and you may, too. It goes something like this:

You know, I am incredibly busy right now. In fact, I feel about as busy today as I have ever felt. Some days I feel over-committed. In fact, every now and then my life feels out of control.

But we are working on some unique and special challenges right now. I feel like the worst of this is going to be over in a couple or three months. After that, I am going to take a couple of weeks, take a little time off, get organized, spend some time with the family, and start working out. Everything is going to change. This time will be here soon. After that, it won't be crazy anymore!

Have you ever had a dream that sounds vaguely like this? How long have you been having this dream? How's that working for you?

Perhaps it's time to stop dreaming of a time when you won't be busy. Because the time will never come. It's your dream—but it's also a mirage.

I have learned a hard lesson trying to help *real* people,

change *real* behavior in the *real* world. There is no "couple of weeks." Look at the trend line! Sanity does not prevail. There is a good chance that tomorrow is going to be just as crazy as today.

If you want to change anything about yourself, the best time to start is *now*. Ask yourself, "What am I willing to change now?" Just do that. That's more than enough. For now.

CHAPTER 14

Special Challenges for People in Charge

Memo to Staff: How to Handle Me

For years one of the most popular talk radio programs in the U.S. has been *Imus in the Morning* with Don Imus. The daily program is a curious mix of current events, satirical songs, rants by Imus, interruptions by his staff, and interviews with call-in guests who range from powerful politicians to network anchors to authors promoting their books to ordinary citizens. Imus's only rule for guests is, You cannot be boring.

Imus's on-air persona (which may or may not be real) is that of a curmudgeon. He's always mad about something—whether it's government hypocrisy or the air quality in the studio. You can't tell if Imus is liberal or conservative, Democrat or Republican, hard-line on moral issues or soft. Nor can you predict how he will treat his guests. He's an equal opportunity offender. Sometimes he's polite and deferential, other times rude, calling people "morons" and "weasels" and "liars" while they're on the air. The one thing you can be sure of listening to Imus is that at some point *you* will get upset. Imus gets away with this antisocial behavior because every once in a while he explains to the audience what he's up to. "The only thing you have to understand about this show," he says, "is that everything I say is jive. You cannot take it seriously. You'll know I'm serious only when I say the following six words: 'You have to stop that now.' Everything else is jive."

It's a little like the Surgeon General's warning on a cigarette pack—and brilliant. In effect, he's instructing the audience on how to deal with him. Perhaps as a result, *Imus in the Morning* is consistently one of the highest rated shows in its highly competitive time slot.

It's a technique every boss should learn.

Wouldn't it be great if all bosses came with similar product warnings? Wouldn't it be even better if, like Imus, they were sufficiently self-possessed that they could write the warnings themselves?

Imagine a workplace where the boss tells you, "Listen, I like to punish the messenger, so be very careful when you're bringing me bad news. I'll probably bite your head off, even though I know it's not your fault."

Or, "No matter how terrific your idea and how thoroughly you've thought it out, I'm going to add my two cents to it in order to improve it. Your first impulse will be to listen to me and act on my suggestion. Please don't. Just nod your head and pretend you're listening. If you're as smart as I thought you were when I hired you, you'll ignore me and do it your way."

A lot of bosses are already doing some variation on this with their employees. I know one self-made man who has a volcanic temper. He doesn't fly off the handle too often. But he leads a very busy schedule, starting at 4 A.M. with dictation to his secretary, phone calls to distant time zones, and not one but two breakfast meetings. By the time the rest of us begin our workday, he's already worked a full day—and begun another one. As a result, he's chronically tired, which means he's chronically testy. The slightest annoyance can set him off. The good news is that he knows this about himself. He's not putting on a show—like a baseball manager throwing a fake hissy fit over an umpire's bad call. He's genuinely mad. But the rage dies down as quickly as it erupted. To him, the tantrum acts as a release valve. I've seen him when he's lost it, and it's not a pretty picture. Employees have been to known to burst into tears during one of his tirades. To his credit, he regains his composure instantly and always tells his staff, "I'm not mad at you. I'm just mad. And now it's over and forgotten. I'm sorry you had to be here to witness it." A little bit of this is phony (he probably is angry at something a staffer has done) but he's smart enough to let them know that he's behaving like a jerk and they ought to ignore it.

This sort of candor is admirable—because it features a boss trying to get better by admitting to a managerial shortcoming, telling his colleagues, and helping them deal with it. (If I were his coach, I'd also have him soliciting suggestions—i.e., feedforward—from his staff on how he could correct this shortcoming, but let's take it one step at a time.)

Some years ago I worked with a public relations executive who was having a hard time hanging on to personal assistants. He'd hire perfect candidates, but they'd quit after six or seven months on the job. I wasn't able to track down this bevy of former assistants to get their feedback on why they left, so I tried an experiment. I asked the executive to imagine the feedback I would have gotten from all his departed assistants. What would they say good and bad about him? Then I asked him to write it down as if it were a memo to his next prospective assistant titled "How to Handle Me." Here's what he wrote:

I'm good with people and even better with ideas. If clients have a problem, it's my job to come up with a creative solution. I'm bad at everything else. I hate paperwork. I find it hard to perform the usual courtesies that clients expect of a personal services business. I don't follow up with thank you notes. I don't remember birthdays. I dread picking up the phone, because it's always someone with a problem, never someone calling to say that a huge check is on its way to me or that I've won the lottery. You need to know this about me. I have a pretty good idea how the business is doing, but I don't like budgets and expense reports and projections. People think I'm an unmade bed as a manager, and they're right. I'm not bragging or being self-deprecating. It's the truth.

On the personal side, I'm a decent, polite human being. I'll never yell at you. When things are going well and we've pulled off a few miracles in a row, I begin to think I'm one of the funniest, most charming people on earth. You may find my humor caustic at these times. Please don't take it personally. Better yet, tell me I'm out of line. I have a relaxed laissez-faire personality, and the more hectic things get, the calmer I get. That's my peculiar reflex to pressure. Don't misinterpret this cool demeanor to mean that I don't care. I care a lot. I only expect one thing of you: I want you to do as much of my job as you can handle. The less I have to do the better. Do that and we will succeed magnificently together.

He handed this document to his new assistant, a bubbly graduate fresh out of the University of Michigan named Michelle, on her first day at work. When I saw him again about 18 months later, I was dying to know if he was making progress with his so-called assistant-retention issues.

"Are things working out with Michelle?" I asked.

"Oh yes," he said.

"How can you tell?" I asked, ever the skeptic.

"Because last Christmas every client sent her—not me—a lavish fruit basket or bottle of champagne to thank her. When I told her that I wanted an assistant to do my job for me, she took it to heart. Apparently, she's been shielding me from almost every problem that comes across her desk—and solving it herself. That wouldn't have happened if I hadn't told her how to handle me."

What's interesting (and reassuring) about this story is that it's an example of a boss accurately assessing his shortcomings *and* his employee agreeing with him. That isn't always the case. Sometimes the gap between what a boss says about himself and what the staff believes is wide, very wide.

The most obvious disconnect is when the staff concludes that the boss's opinion of how he wants to be handled is either fantasy or wishful thinking. I saw this some years ago with a division chief who prided himself on his fairness and the fact that he didn't play favorites. He never wrote it down in a "How to Handle Me" memo to staff, but he was always warning employees that he didn't like yes men and suck-ups, that you earned your way on to his first team purely on performance. Unfortunately, his staff considered this self-assessment to be about 180 degrees removed from the truth. The man was a sucker for sycophants. He hated to be challenged and he habitually rewarded those who agreed with him at the expense of those who did not. What should have been an opportunity to bring boss and employees in sync actually became a toxic joke that divided both sides further.

The other disconnect is more subtle. It occurs when the boss's self-assessment is accurate but irrelevant.

I saw this with the CEO of an energy company who was famous for being a stickler for details, even to the point of correcting people's grammar and punctuation in memos and letters. He had been an English teacher who had switched to corporate law, where his attention to detail made him a great success. The energy company had been a client, and when he skillfully guided the company out of bankruptcy, again in part because of his fanatic attention to detail, the board appointed him CEO. That's when the trouble began.

He never wrote a "How to Handle Me" memo. (The idea had yet to occur to me.) But then again, he didn't have to. Every time he took a red pencil to one of his senior staff's writings, he was sending an unmistakable signal that "this matters to me." Word spread quickly through the executive ranks that if you wanted to make a favorable impression on the new CEO, all you had to do was write memos with perfect grammar and punctuation. If he didn't change his ways, he would either have a mutiny on his hands or an executive suite filled with gifted grammarians.

That's when I was called in. You can imagine the problem. The boss was sending a signal on what he expected from his executives. And it had the added virtue of being true. But the executives thought it was silly, that this was no way to run a company or judge executive talent. I went over his staff's feedback. The first comment was, "Five million dollars a year is a lot to pay for an editor." Second comment: "Put away the red pencil." Third comment: "This is no longer the first grade." And so on. It took me months to make the CEO accept that correcting grammar in internal memoranda was a poor—and humiliating—use of his time. What mattered to him did not matter to the troops. That was a dangerous disconnect that neither he nor the company could afford.

I mention this because writing a memo to staff on "How to Handle Me" is not only an admirable exercise in self-examination, but a surefire method for stimulating dialogue with the troops. But be careful. Your memo has to be brutally honest. Your employees have to believe it is accurate. And most important, they must believe it matters. Anything less on all three counts and you may as well keep your instructions to yourself.

Stop Letting Your Staff Overwhelm You

One of the great pleasures of being the boss (any kind of boss, whether you're running a three-person staff or a division of 30,000 employees) is that you get to call the shots—all the shots. Meetings begin when you say they begin. They take place where you want them to take place. They end when you say they're over. Whether you're a great boss or a bad one, you answer to no one who's under your charge. They all answer to you.

There's a dangerous underside to this, which eludes many bosses once they get inside their comfortable cocoon of all-powerfulness.

As a boss, you alone know how much you depend on your people. Without their loyalty and support, you are nothing. (You know this, and if you're a wise leader, you remind your people repeatedly that you know how much you need them.) But you should never forget that it's a two-way street. Just as you are dependent on your staffers, they're dependent on you— in ways that may have nothing to do with on-the-job performance. They crave your attention, your approval, your affection. If you've got any sort of charisma as a leader, they literally gauge their status in the organization by how much face time they get with you.

There's nothing wrong with this. What better way for the troops to develop than by getting face time with their leaders so they can observe and then emulate their behavior? But this codependency can develop into trouble.

I know the editor-in-chief of one of the top women's magazines. An incredibly well-organized woman, she took pride in her ability to juggle her high-pressure job and still maintain a sane home life with her husband and two young kids. She was pretty close to being a perfect boss: fair, egalitarian, kept her door open to everyone. (She was even fair to people after she fired them, always helping them land new jobs.)

The payoff for perfection, however, was not what she expected. As a dedicated having-it-all mom, she tried to be home by 6:30 each night to be with her children. Over time she noticed that she was making more and more excuses for working late, to the point that within two years she was regularly at her desk until 9:30 or 10 P.M. At first she thought it was simply because she loved her job (running a glamorous money-making magazine can be a ton of fun). But as she analyzed the problem, she realized it had nothing to do with her. Her staff depended on her too much. A lot of it could be blamed on her openness and availability. She had created an environment where it was easy to get face time with the boss. So everyone naturally wanted face time. Of course, this put her in a never-ending upward spiral where she could never leave the office. People were always coming in to her at the end of the day, saying, "I need 10 minutes of your time." Being the perfect boss, she would give it to them. Paradoxically, she was losing control *because she was in control.*

To regain control, she gathered her staff and announced, "From now on my door is closed after 5:45. After that it's 'get-out-of-my-face time.' Only my kids get face time."

That only solved half the problem. She got home by 6:30 every night. But her staff felt lost and abandoned. That's when I got involved.

Making the staff less dependent on her, I said, was a good thing. But they still needed leadership. They still needed to be re-directed.

I had her arrange discussions with each of her direct reports—to discuss two things:

One, I wanted her to ask each of them, "Let's look at your responsibilities. Are there areas where you think I need to be more involved and less involved?" She was making them define the areas where they could legitimately ask for face time with her—and areas where it was not legitimate. In effect, she was delegating more responsibility to them, but in a generous and empowering way. She was allowing *them* to determine how much responsibility they could take.

Two, I wanted her to say, "Now let's look at my job. Do you ever see me doing things that a person at my level shouldn't be doing, such as getting involved in details that are too minor to worry about?" She was forcing them to come up with ideas for how she could become more disengaged. In effect, she was letting them help her get home by 6:30. What better gift can a leader present to his or her troops? And vice versa.

I didn't have to remind her to say, "Thank you."

Remember this the next time you find yourself trapped by a needy, demanding staff. If they need too much of your time, you can't just tell them to stop bothering you. You have to wean them away and make it seem like it's their idea. Let them figure out what they should be doing on their own. Let them tell you where you're not needed. There's a fine line between legitimate face time and get-out-of-my-face time. It's up to you as boss to make the troops face that.

Stop Acting as if You Are Managing You

Telling staff how to handle the boss is admirable, but it doesn't completely solve one of the great unappreciated ironies of the boss vs. bossed dynamic. It is this: A lot of managers assume that their staff should be exactly like them—in behavior, in enthusiasm, in intelligence, and most especially, in how they apply that brainpower. You can't blame them. If I were a super-successful boss, I'd be inclined to populate my organization with clones of . . . *me*. What better way to assure that everything gets done *my* way? This, by the way, is a perfectly natural inclination. Given the choice, we all favor hiring people who closely resemble the person we see in the mirror every day.

At the same time, we're also smart enough to know that an organization stocked with clones marching in lockstep doesn't create diversity in an organization. You need different voices, different mindsets, different personalities in the mix. In my experience, it's the odd out-of-left-field dissenting voices, the ones challenging groupthink and the status quo, that make an organization hum and thrive.

Also, a staff of clones does not guarantee fluid teamwork. For example, if I were Michael Jordan starting a basketball team from scratch, I'd be glad to have one player like me, but I'd still need two or three taller, stronger players to man the front line and a smaller, lightning-quick player to feed me the ball. A basketball squad of five Michael Jordans, intriguing as it sounds, is surely a recipe for dysfunction.

Most bosses are smart enough to know this and therefore resist the temptation to hire only mirror images of themselves. But that doesn't mean the message sinks in completely. Sometimes I have to remind even the most sensitive, tuned-in bosses, "You are not managing you."

This hit me when I began working with the CEO of a large service company. Let's call him Steve. Steve prided himself on being a great leader who lived the values he encouraged all his employees to follow. In fact, he considered himself the role model for his company's leadership values.

As with all of my clients, I let Steve know what all of his coworkers thought of him. While they were generally ecstatic that Steve was the CEO, they were in general agreement that he stifled the flow of open communication. In this one area, his behavior was inconsistent with his message. He was not practicing what he was preaching.

A simple problem, I thought, easily solved if Steve is willing to change. I would get him to listen more and ask people for input. I would tell him that he cannot end any meeting without asking everyone present if they felt like they had a fair hearing of *their* views. If he did that consistently over 12 months or so, the no-dialogue rap would fade away.

It wasn't that simple. As I studied the feedback from Steve's staff, something didn't add up. On the one hand, the feedback said he killed open discussion. On the other hand, it said he was always changing his mind. That was confusing, because people who kill open discussion are not usually people who are always changing their mind. The two flaws tend to be mutually exclusive.

To make the situation more perplexing, when I talked to Steve, he practically laughed at the feedback. "I may have a lot of issues," he said, "but killing dialogue is not one of them. I'm always talking things out with my people."

I recalled interviewing one of Steve's directors, who said, "You have to understand, this fellow is the world champion at arguing with himself. He was a star debater in college."

Now the feedback made sense.

Time and time again, an employee would come to Steve with an idea. Being a debate champion, Steve's first reaction was to go into debate mode and shoot holes in the idea. The employee's reaction, as a direct report, was to shut down in the face of the verbal onslaught from the boss. Two people, two different perspectives. Steve thought he was having an open debate. The employee thought that he had just been blown away.

Steve compounded the problem by debating with himself as well. Someone would say, "Why don't we try this?" and Steve would approve. He inspired his whole staff to get behind the suggestion. But a few days later, after he had enough time to debate his decision strenuously with himself, he'd change his mind, saying, "Maybe that wasn't such a good idea." In his head, he was being open-minded. In his staff's collective brain, he was confusing them.

Let's not get into the fact that you can't do that in a leadership position. You can't motivate 200 people to conquer a hill and, when they all start charging, say, "Wait a minute. Maybe this isn't such a smart plan." Do that a few times, and no one's going to be inspired to take hills for you. They will just sit there and wait.

Let's focus on making Steve see the problem, which I like to call The Golden Rule Fallacy. You see it in situations where the boss makes the logical inference that the people being bossed are just like him and, in strict obedience to the Golden Rule, like to be treated the same way that the boss likes to be treated. *I like it when people treat me this way, therefore I will treat everyone else this way.*

When I pointed out to Steve that he liked heated debate because it played to his strengths, he agreed. "I like it when people do that for me, mix it up and argue."

"That's nice, but they aren't you," I said.

"What's wrong with it?" he asked. "What's wrong with me expressing an opinion, and someone else expressing an opinion, and we have a healthy debate? I love that."

I said, "Well, yes, but you are the boss—and they aren't. You were the star debater at college—and they weren't. This isn't a fair fight! All you're doing to them is saying, 'You lose. I win.' Their odds of beating you at this game are zero. So they opt not to play."

"That's not true," he countered. "I have someone on staff who loves it as much as I do."

"That's the problem," I said. "Sometimes your debating

style works, particularly with people who enjoy arguing both sides of every issue and don't back down from the verbal jousting. If everybody on your staff was like this one person, you wouldn't have a problem. Unfortunately, 99 percent of your team is not like that guy. Your one success is not being replicated with anyone else. Why? Because that single exceptional employee is just like you. But you are not managing you."

True to form, Steve the debating champion had lured me into a heated debate. Luckily, the "you're not managing you" line hit home. Suddenly he got it. He saw that he was operating under a bogus assumption that what was good for him was good for everyone else.

From that moment on, Steve's improvement was a sure thing. He paid close attention to his debating urges, and stifled them when they put his staff at a huge disadvantage. He apologized to everyone for the mistakes in his past, and promised to do better in the future. He routinely invited people to voice their opinions in meetings, and thought once, twice, three times before challenging them. (Nothing wrong with challenging people. His goal was to open up the dialogue, not become a doormat for every silly opinion.) He followed up with people, reminding them that he was trying to improve in this area. Lastly, he asked them for suggestions that could help him get even better.

It didn't happen overnight. These transformations require time to take hold with the people assessing you. As I say, you have to change 100 percent to get 10 percent credit for it. So, after 18 months, Steve was perceived as a better boss. He was the same guy in most ways. He still loved to argue with himself and anyone else in the room. The only difference: He now accommodated the fact that his staffers didn't necessarily feel the same way as he did.

Since my session with Steve, I've been more alert to this it's-not-a-fair-fight dynamic between bosses and the bossed.

A friend once told me about her boss and his obsession with documentation. He had been trained as a lawyer, someone who was slavishly devoted to evidence and paperwork and perfectly maintained files. When he started his marketing consulting business, he did not abandon his fondness for paper. He still saved everything. This was fine except he expected everyone else to be as obsessed with retaining documents as he was. He would call meetings during which everyone knew he would haul out some ancient letters and memos as evidence to chastise someone for letting things fall through the cracks.

I interpreted this behavior as typically wrongheaded management, classic Golden Rule Fallacy at work. This great entrepreneur overlooked the fact that as owner of the company, he had access to any and all documents, whereas his subordinates did not. He did not appreciate that he was instigating a fight that only he could win. He loved documents and documentation, and wrongly assumed everyone else did too.

See it once and you begin to see it everywhere.

By all means, do unto others as you would have them do unto you. But realize that it doesn't apply in all instances in management. If you manage your people the way you'd want to be managed, you're forgetting one thing: You're not managing you.

Stop "Checking the Box"

I was meeting with a chief executive recently, listening to him express puzzlement that his employees did not understand the company's mission and overall direction.

"I don't get it," he said. "I've spelled it out for them in meetings. I've summarized it in a memo. See, here's the memo. It's very clear. What more do the employees want?"

For a moment there, I thought he was kidding—that he had a very refined sense of irony. Making people understand the company's mission and vision doesn't happen by fiat, or by memo. It also doesn't happen overnight. Surely this smart CEO knew that. By the pained expression on his face, I could tell he was dead serious and (if only in this one area of management) clueless.

"Let's review the situation," I said. "How was this memo distributed?"

"By e-mail," he said. "It went to everyone in the company."

"Okay," I said, "but my hunch is that the method of distribution is all you know about this. How many people actually opened the e-mail and *read* the memo?"

"I don't know," he said.

"Of those, how many do you think *understood* the memo?"

"I have no idea," he said.

"Of those who understood it, how many *believed* it?"

He shook his head.

"Of this dwindling group of believers, how many *remembered* it?"

Another sorry head shake.

"That's a lot of unknowns for something you regard as vital to your company's existence," I said. "But that's not the worst part. Once you eliminate all the people who either didn't receive, or read, or understand, or believe, or remember the memo—and it's quite possible there's no one left—how many people do you think will adopt the memo's contents? How many will begin living and breathing the company's mission because of your memo?"

I think I heard the CEO mutter a contrite "I dunno," but it was hard to tell because by now his voice was nearly inaudible.

It's not my mission in life to deflate or depress clients, so I tried to revive his spirits by changing the subject—by pointing out that the problem was *him*, not his memo.

"The only thing you're guilty of," I said, "was checking the box!"

"Huh?" he said.

"You thought your job was done when you articulated the mission and wrote the memo—as if it were one more item on your to-do list for the day. You checked the box, and you moved on. Next."

I could see the scales slowly lifting from his eyes, so I pressed on with my theory about what may be the most egregious source of corporate dysfunction: the failure of managers to see the enormous disconnect between understanding and doing. Most leadership development revolves around one huge false assumption—that if people understand then they will do. That's not true. Most of us understand, we just don't do. As I said in Chapter 11, we all understand that being grossly overweight is bad for our health, but not all of us actually do anything to change our condition.

This CEO is no different from most executives who believe their organizations operate with strict down-the-chain-of-command efficiency. The boss says, "Jump." The subordinates ask, "How high?" In a perfect world, every command is not only obeyed, but obeyed precisely and promptly, almost as if it were a fait accompli. The boss doesn't have to follow up *ever*—because he said it and it was done. After all, he checked the box.

I'm not sure why bosses persist in thinking this way. Maybe their ego can't fathom that their orders might not be strictly followed. Maybe they're too lazy to investigate whether people did their bidding. Maybe they're too disorganized to adhere to strict follow-up procedures. Maybe they think that following up is beneath them. Whatever the reason, they blindly assume that if people understand, they will do.

The good news here for every manager, including my CEO client, is that this false belief has a simple cure. It's called follow-up. Once you send out a message, you ask people the next day if they heard it. Then you ask if they understood it. Then a few days later, you ask if they did something about it. Believe me, if the first follow-up question doesn't get their attention, the next one will, and so will the final one.

Stop Being Prejudiced About Your Employees

I spend most of my professional life trying to change people's behavior in the workplace. I tell people that change is a simple equation: Stop the annoying behavior and you'll stop being perceived as an annoyance. It's so easy, I'm amazed I get paid to teach it.

I wish I could say the same about changing the way people *think*. But lately that's become a critical part of my practice, too. The big reason for it is that there's been a radical shift in the way employees regard their roles in and their relationship to an organization. The magazine *Fast Company* nailed it in 1998 when it ran a notorious cover story titled "Free Agent Nation." It posited the then-radical notion that the "organization man" was dead, that the best performers in a company were no longer interested in sacrificing their lives for the good of the organization. The smart ones believed that their corporation would "drop them in a flash" when they no longer met the company's needs, so they in turn were willing to "drop the company" when it no longer met *their* needs. Free agency meant that each employee was operating like a small self-contained business rather than a cog in the wheel of a large system.

It took a while for this free agent virus to spread. But trust me, it's an epidemic now, a sweeping pathology that demands a change in the way bosses think.

The first thing I do with managers who are overwhelmed or confused by this workplace shift is make them see that they are *prejudiced* about their employees. This always gets their attention. "Me. Prejudiced? Get outta here!" But if prejudice means harboring inflexible, intolerant beliefs about a group of people that do not coincide with reality or how that group sees itself, it's true. Managers who are blind to the changes in this new cohort of free agents are operating like dangerous, deluded executive bigots. (It's no different than a manager refusing to hire a young married woman because he believes she will leave her job eventually to have babies and, therefore, is not serious about her career. It's easy to forget that there was a time not too long ago when almost everyone thought this way.) The prejudice against free agents takes many forms, but here are four that any of us can easily fall into.

1. I know what they want.

This is the biggest prejudice. And the easiest to understand. Almost every economic model has historically assumed that money is the key motivator for any employee. And so bosses assume that if they pay their people top dollar, they will get top performance and loyalty in return. Sorry, it doesn't work that way anymore.

There's no denying that money matters in everyone's career calculus. But at some point, the top performers achieve a level of financial comfort, however tenuous, when other considerations begin to dominate. As economist Lester Thurow pointed out in *Building Wealth*, free agents must wrestle with the paradox that the economic value of their experience falls rather than rises in the course of a career. The shelf life of knowledge, especially technical knowledge, is continuously shrinking. And so free agents respond by moving on to new challenges that enhance their knowledge and let them outpace the shrinking value of their experience—and in turn reward them with more satisfaction and, quite possibly, more money.

If you've ever been puzzled by a talented employee who left you to work at another company in a different job for less money, blame it on this prejudice.

This prejudice, carelessly or ruthlessly applied, can actually drive good people away. I remember a multimillionaire entrepreneur telling me in amazement about a well-paid writer on his staff who could never meet a deadline. The entrepreneur liked the writer, but wanted to change his cavalier attitude toward deadlines. So he instituted a seemingly simple carrot-and-stick scheme: Every time the writer made his monthly deadline, he'd get a $500 bonus. To no effect. The writer still missed his deadlines. Apparently, he was making enough money so that an additional $500 a month didn't make that much difference to him. It was no different when the entrepreneur increased the bonus to $3000. Still no improvement. Only when the boss resorted to *deducting* $3000 from the writer's paycheck did he change his ways. Economists would call this "loss aversion"—the phenomenon that we hate losing something more than we enjoy gaining its equivalent. I would call this prejudice—a failure to understand what motivates an employee. The writer did indeed meet his deadlines for a few months, but he left the company within six months.

Apparently, although the writer didn't care about the rewards for good performance, he felt strongly about being punished for poor performance. The bonus didn't motivate him. The deduction, though, insulted him. The entrepreneur figured out how to change his employee's behavior, but he also drove him away. They're a complicated lot, these free agents. And if you think you know what makes them tick, you first need to check your prejudices at the door.

This I-know-what-they-want delusion extends far beyond money. As a general rule, people in their 20s want to *learn* on the job. In their 30s they want to *advance*. And in their 40s they want to *rule*. No matter what their age, though, understanding their desires is like trying to pin down mercury. You have to find out what they want at every step—by literally asking them—and you can't assume that one size fits all. The person who sees the noble goal of "work-life balance" as irrelevant at age 24 may find it critical at 34.

Consider the still-young career of shortstop Alex Rodriguez. At age 20 he won a batting title with the Seattle Mariners. Four years later he moved to the Texas Rangers for the staggering salary of $25 million a year, where he was the American League MVP and three-time home run champion. Four years later, at the tender age of 28, he moved to the New York Yankees. He was by general consensus the best player in the game, and yet two teams let him go! Actually, the organization didn't let him go. He left the organization—the first time for more money, the second time for a shot at the World Series with the perennial front-running Yankees. This is classic "free agent nation" in action (in large part because baseball "invented" free agency in 1975 after a legal battle that let players move freely among the teams). It's an example of (a) the employee calling the shots, (b) the employee using the organization to fulfill *his* needs, and (c) those needs changing over time.

As for the entrepreneur and the writer above, I don't know what I would have done—other than to assure the entrepreneur that the traditional carrot-and-stick approach doesn't work anymore. Clearly, dangling the carrot of more money for meeting deadlines didn't work. But that doesn't mean that beating the writer with the stick of a salary deduction would appeal to him either.

2. I know what they know.

The days when managers know how to do every job in the company better than anyone else are over. The reason Peter Drucker said that the manager of the future will know how to ask rather than how to tell is because Drucker understood that knowledge workers would know more than any manager does. Well, the future is here with a vengeance. And smart managers need to shed the overconfident bias that they know as much as their employees know in specific areas. It's a blind spot that diminishes their employees' abilities and enthusiasm, and ultimately shrinks the boss's stature.

3. I hate their selfishness.

How many times has an employee come to you complaining that he or she isn't happy or fulfilled in a job, and the initial thought balloon hanging over your head is, "Quit griping, you selfish oaf! I pay you a lot of money to do a job, not to be happy. Get back to work."

How many times has an employee come to you with an outside job offer, hoping that you will counter the offer because he or she doesn't want to leave you or the company, and your initial response is to question the employee's loyalty, to regard him or her as an ingrate and traitor?

I contend that these crude Neanderthal responses are instances of prejudice, too. And it's easy to see why managers feel this way. They have decades of bias training on their side. Historically, large U.S. companies have benefited from a one-sided proposition. While the *company* was supposed to maximize return for itself and shareholders, the *individual* was expected to discount his or her self-interests and focus on the good of the company. It was considered outrageous for employees to openly demand, "What's in it for me?"

I hope we can all agree that in the new world order—where

the organization man has been replaced by the highly mobile free agent—no manager should be taken aback by employees who are looking out for themselves. You certainly shouldn't resent them for it, or brand them as selfish. Actually, you should embrace it, because it's a relatively easy problem to handle if you can beat the employees to the punch.

A talent agent once told me about an eye-opening encounter he had with Jack Welch when he was chairman of General Electric. The agent's firm had just concluded a long-term contract renewal, with an eye-popping raise and stock options, for an on-air broadcaster at GE's NBC broadcasting unit.

Welch mentioned the broadcaster's name in the meeting and the agent half-proudly, half-sheepishly said, "Yes, I'm afraid we took you guys to the cleaners with that one."

Welch's eyes flared for a second, and the agent feared that he had needlessly insulted the legendary CEO. In solemn, serious tones, Welch said, "You don't understand. You didn't hose us. We *wanted* to give him the money. We would have done anything to keep him happy."

Let that be your model for dealing with needy, demanding, allegedly "selfish" employees. To ignore them and resent them is to misunderstand them—and eventually lose them. You're committing the corporate equivalent of a hate crime.

4. I can always get someone else.

In the past, the key to wealth may have been control of land, materials, plants, and tools. In that environment, the worker needed the company more than the company needed the worker. Today the key to wealth is *knowledge*. As a result, the company needs the knowledge worker far more than the knowledge worker needs them. To make matters worse, the workers know this! They see themselves as fungible assets—no longer at the mercy of company whim—rather than dispensable commodities. The difference is subtle but real: As a fungible asset, the free agent sees himself as always getting a better job somewhere else; if he were merely a commodity, anyone could replace him (which, we know, is not true anymore).

Managers at smart companies are catching on. They're beginning to see that their relationship with top talent resembles a strategic alliance rather than a traditional employment contract. They know free agents can leave anytime. When I polled the top 120 executives at one of the world's leading high-tech companies, "Can the highest potential leader who works for you leave the company and get another job *with a pay raise* in one week?" all 120 executives said yes!

I'm sure this was the managerial prejudice at play when the Orlando Magic let Shaquille O'Neal slip out of their hands in 1995 and go off to the Los Angeles Lakers. (This is like Microsoft letting Bill Gates go elsewhere, or Sony Music letting Bruce Springsteen slip away from their recording label. Some talent is not replaceable.) Sure, Shaq was expensive to keep, but Orlando must have thought he was replaceable, that they could spend the money to buy another player just like him. That's a costly prejudice. The facts are that Orlando turned into a second-tier team when O'Neal left, and the Lakers won three world championships soon after he arrived.

I cite sports examples here because the information is public and readily available, not because it's free agent behavior at its most extreme. Believe me, this same extreme "what's in it for me" attitude goes on thousands of times a day in companies across America. People unhappy. People running off resumes at Kinko's. People testing the job market. People leaving good jobs for better ones. All because their bosses were blind to the real reasons they came to work each day. If that blindness isn't prejudice, I don't know what else to call it. But it's happening. The only difference is we don't read about each individual case in the newspaper.

If none of these examples hits home yet, let me hit you where it can really hurt.

If you continue to harbor these prejudices and ignore the changing realities in your workplace, it can cost you your job. It can cost you your job even if you're the top dog and are putting up great numbers.

I'm not saying that managers have been completely stripped of their authority. In most places, the top-down chain of command structure is still intact. People still obey their bosses' commands. But there's been a subtle shift in power in the workplace, and some of it now resides in the free agents. More of it than managers imagine. That's one reason I have a job. When I work one-on-one with a manager, it's often because he or she has done something to tick off his direct reports. Some are so annoyed that they leave the company. In effect, the departing employees are voting with their feet. At some point, if enough of them cast similar votes, the free agent workers' response to the manager registers as a serious problem. That's when I get called in—to find out what's annoying the employees, share that with the boss, and get him to change his ways.

Casey Stengel liked to point out that on any baseball team, one third of the players loved the manager, one third hated him, and one third were undecided. "The secret to managing a ballclub," said Stengel, "was to keep the third who hated you from getting together with the third who were undecided."

That's the real peril today in free agent nation. One employee can't bring a good manager down. But a bunch of employees can gang up and topple even the most productive bosses.

Remember this as you gently or brutally navigate your way through the ever-shifting management landscape of free agent nation. Take a temperature reading on your prejudices from time to time. Are you responding to your employees with outdated biases? Or are you meeting the new free agent mindset on its own terms? In the context of this book, accepting the new terrain can make you a more successful boss—and quite possibly save your job.

Your people are changing constantly and it's right in front of your eyes. If you don't change accordingly, you may as well be managing with your eyes wide shut. That's the most unforgivable prejudice of all.

Stop Trying to Coach People Who Shouldn't Be Coached

In the same way that some of your problems do not need fixing because they are an issue to only a small minority of people, as a boss you should stop trying to change people who don't want to change.

This may sound harsh, but some people are unsalvageable. You're only banging your head against a wall if you think you can fix them.

Believe me, I know. It's taken me years to appreciate that some problems are so deep and systemic and strange that they are impervious to my particular ministrations. Through trial and error, I have shed all illusions about my methods, and concluded that some flaws can't be coached away by any boss, especially with the following employees.

Stop trying to change people who don't think they have a problem. Have you ever attempted to change the behavior of a successful adult at work who has no interest in changing? How much luck have you had with this conversion activity? The answer is always the same: No luck. Now bring it closer to home. Have you had any luck trying to change a spouse, partner, or significant other who has no interest in changing? Again, same answer. My mother went to college for two years and was a superb and much-admired first grade teacher. She was so dedicated that she saw no line of demarcation between how she behaved in the classroom and in the real world. She talked to everyone with the same slow patient cadence and simple vocabulary that she employed with her six-year-olds each day. Mom lived in a world entirely populated by first graders. I was always in the first grade. Her siblings were always in the first grade. All of our relatives were in the first grade. My father was in the first grade. Mom was always correcting everyone's grammar. One day she was correcting my father (for the ten thousandth time). He looked at her, sighed, and said, "Honey, I'm 70 years old. Let it go."

If your people don't care about changing, don't waste your time.

Stop trying to change people who are pursuing the wrong strategy for the organization. If they're going in the wrong direction, all you'll do is help them get there faster.

Stop trying to change people who should not be in their job. Some people feel they're in the wrong job at the wrong company. Perhaps they believe that they were meant to be doing something else. Or that their skills are being misused. Or that they they're missing something. If you have any sensitivity, you have a good idea who these people are. Even if you pick up only a tiny molecule of this vibe, ask them, "What if we shut down today? Would you be surprised, sad, or relieved?" More often than not, they will choose "relieved." Take that as your cue to send them packing. You can't change the behavior of unhappy people so that they become happy. You can only fix the behavior that's making the people around them unhappy.

Finally, stop trying to help people who think everyone else is the problem.

I once dealt with an entrepreneur who, after a few high

profile employee departures, was concerned about employee morale. He ran a dominant company in a fun business. People loved working there. But the feedback said the boss played favorites in the way he compensated people. Some employees were handsomely paid; others got whatever he thought he could get away with. The only way to get a big raise was to put a gun to his head—i.e., threaten to quit and mean it.

When I reported this back to the entrepreneur, he surprised me by agreeing with the charge and defending it. Like many self-made men, he regarded every nickel he paid an employee as a nickel that didn't go into his pocket. He paid people according to a Darwinian scale of what he thought they were worth in the marketplace. If they could get more elsewhere, they'd have to prove it to him first.

I'm not a compensation strategist. I wasn't equipped to solve this problem. But he had another surprise in store for me. It turned out the entrepreneur hadn't called me to help *him* change. He wanted me to fix the employees.

In moments like this I tend to run, not walk, away. It's hard to help people who don't think they have a problem. It's impossible to fix people who think someone else is the problem.

You should, too. People like this will never give up on their near-religious belief that any failure is someone else's fault. They hold this belief as firmly as if it were their religion. Trying to convert them would like trying to convert an ardent Democrat into a Republican—or vice versa. Not gonna happen. So save time and skip the heroic measures. This is an "argument" you will never win.

CODA

You Are Here Now

TAKE A BREATH. Take a deeper breath.

Imagine that you're 95 years old and ready to die. Before taking your last breath, you're given a great gift: The ability to travel back in time—the ability to talk to the person who is reading this page, the ability to help this person be a better professional and lead a better life.

The 95-year-old you understands what was really important and what wasn't, what mattered and what didn't. What advice would this wise "old you" have for the "you" who is reading this page?

Take your time and answer the question on two levels: personal advice and professional advice. Jot down a few words that capture what the old you would be saying to the younger you.

Once you've written these words down, the rest is simple: Just do whatever you wrote down. Make it your resolution for the rest of the current year, and the next. You have just defined your "there."

I cannot define "there" for you. I cannot dictate it and I'm certainly not going to judge it as being worthy or noble. To do so would not only be presumptuous, it's none of my business.

But I can make a rough prediction about what some features of your "there" will look like—because a friend of mine actually had the opportunity to interview people who were dying and ask them what advice they would have had for themselves. The answers he got were filled with wisdom.

One recurring theme was to "reflect upon life, to find happiness and meaning now," not next month or next year. The Great Western Disease lies in the phrase, *I will be happy when . . .* As in, *I will be happy when I get that promotion*, or *I will be happy when I buy that house*, or *I will be happy when I get that money*. The wise old you has finally realized that the next promotion, the next achievement, the next move to a larger house or a more attractive corner office won't really change your world that much. Many older people say they were so wrapped up in looking for what they didn't have that they seldom appreciated what they did have. They often wish they would have taken more time to enjoy it.

A second recurring theme was "friends and family." Consider this: You may work for a wonderful company, and you may think that your contribution to that organization is very important. When you are 95 years old and you look at the people around your deathbed, very few of your fellow employees will be there waving good-bye. Your friends and family will probably be the only people who care. Appreciate them now and share a large part of your life with them.

Yet another recurring theme was the reflection to "follow your dreams." Older people who have tried to achieve their dreams are always happier with their lives. Figure out your true purpose in life, and go for it! This doesn't apply just to big dreams; it is also true for little dreams. Buy the sports car you always wanted, go to that exotic locale that's always held your fascination, learn how to play the piano or speak Italian. If some people think your vision of a well-lived life is a bit goofy or offbeat, who cares? It isn't their life. It's yours. Few of us will achieve all of our dreams. Some dreams will always elude us. So the key question is not, "Did I make all my dreams come true?" The key question is, "Did I try?"

I conducted a research project for Accenture involving more than 200 high-potential leaders from 120 companies around the world. Each company could nominate only two future leaders, the very brightest of its young stars. These are the kinds of people who could jump at a moment's notice to better-paying positions elsewhere. We asked each of these young stars a simple question: "If you stay in this company, why are you going to stay?" The three top answers were:

1. "I am finding meaning and happiness now. The work is exciting and I love what I am doing."
2. "I like the people. They are my friends. This feels like a team. It feels like a family. I could make more money working with other people, but I don't want to leave the people here."
3. "I can follow my dreams. This organization is giving me a chance to do what I really want to do in life."

The answers were never about money. They were always about happiness, relationships, following dreams, and meaning. When my friend asked people on their deathbeds what was important to them, they gave exactly the same answers as the high-potential leaders I interviewed.

Use that wisdom now. Don't look ahead. Look behind. Look back from your old age at the life you hope to live. Know that you need to be happy now, to enjoy your friends and family, to follow your dreams.

You are here.

You can get there!

Let the journey begin.

Appendix

This leadership inventory was developed as part of a research project (sponsored by Accenture) involving 200 specially selected high-potential leaders from 120 companies around the world. Respondents are asked to rate leaders on a five-point scale, ranging from Highly Satisfied to Highly Dissatisfied.

Global Leadership Inventory

Consider your own (or this person's) effectiveness in the following areas. How satisfied are you with the way he or she (or you) . . .

Thinking Globally

1. Recognizes the impact of globalization on our business

2. Demonstrates the adaptability required to succeed in the global environment

3. Strives to gain the variety of experiences needed to conduct global business

4. Makes decisions that incorporate global considerations

5. Helps others understand the impact of globalization

Appreciating Diversity

6. Embraces the value of diversity in people (including culture, race, sex, or age)

7. Effectively motivates people from different cultures or backgrounds

8. Recognizes the value of diverse views and opinions

9. Helps others appreciate the value of diversity

10. Actively expands her/his knowledge of other cultures (through interactions, language study, travel, etc.)

Developing Technological Savvy

11. Strives to acquire the technological knowledge needed to succeed in tomorrow's world

12. Successfully recruits people with needed technological expertise

13. Effectively manages the issue of technology to increase productivity

Building Partnerships

14. Treats coworkers as partners, not competitors

15. Unites his/her organization into an effective team

16. Builds effective partnerships across the company

17. Discourages destructive comments about other people or groups

18. Builds effective alliances with other organizations

19. Creates a network of relationships that help to get things done

Sharing Leadership

20. Willingly shares leadership with business partners

21. Defers to others when they have more expertise

22. Strives to arrive at an outcome *with* others (as opposed to *for* others)

23. Creates an environment where people focus on the larger good (avoids sub-optimization or "turfism")

Creating a Shared Vision

24. Creates and communicates a clear vision for our organization

25. Effectively involves people in decision-making

26. Inspires people to commit to achieving the vision

27. Develops an effective strategy to achieve the vision

28. Clearly identifies priorities

Developing People

29. Consistently treats people with dignity

30. Asks people what they need to do their work better

31. Ensures that people receive the training they need to succeed

32. Provides effective coaching

33. Provides developmental feedback in a timely manner

34. Provides effective recognition for others' achievements

Empowering People

35. Builds people's confidence

36. Takes risks in letting others make decisions

37. Gives people the freedom they need to do their job well

38. Trusts people enough to let go (avoids micromanagement)

Achieving Personal Mastery

39. Deeply understands her/his own strengths and weaknesses

40. Invests in ongoing personal development

41. Involves people who do not have strengths that he/she does not possess

42. Demonstrates effective emotional responses in a variety of situations

43. Demonstrates self-confidence as a leader

Encouraging Constructive Dialogue

44. Asks people what he/she can do to improve

45. Genuinely listens to others

46. Accepts constructive feedback in a positive manner (avoids defensiveness)

47. Strives to understand the *other person's* frame of reference

48. Encourages people to challenge the status quo

Demonstrates Integrity

49. Demonstrates honest, ethical behavior in all interactions

50. Ensures that the highest standards for ethical behavior are practiced throughout the organization

51. Avoids political or self-serving behavior

52. Courageously "stands up" for what she/he believes in

53. Is a role model for living our organization's values (leads by example)

Leading Change

54. Sees change as an opportunity, not a problem

55. Challenges the system when change is needed

56. Thrives in ambiguous situations (demonstrates flexibility when needed)

57. Encourages creativity and innovation in others

58. Effectively translates creative ideas into business results

Anticipating Opportunities

59. Invests in learning about future trends

60. Effectively anticipates future opportunities

61. Inspires people to focus on future opportunities (not just present objectives)

62. Develops ideas to meet the needs of the new environment

Ensuring Customer Satisfaction

63. Inspires people to achieve high levels of customer satisfaction

64. Views business processes from the ultimate customer perspective (has an "end to end" perspective)

65. Regularly solicits input from customers

66. Consistently delivers on commitments to customers

67. Understands the competitive options available to her/his customers

Maintaining a Competitive Advantage

68. Communicates a positive, "can do" sense of urgency toward getting the job done

69. Holds people accountable for their results

70. Successfully eliminates waste and unneeded cost

71. Provides products/services that help our company have a clear competitive advantage

72. Achieves results that lead to long-term shareholder value

Written Comments

What are your strengths? Or if you are evaluating someone, what does this person do that you particularly appreciate? (Please list two or three *specific* items.)

What *specifically* might you do to be more effective? Or if evaluating someone, what suggestions would you have for this person on how she or he could become even more effective? (Please list two or three *specific* items).

Index